TEACHING RESOURCES FOR ANIMALS

HOLT, RINEHART AND WINSTON

A Harcourt Classroom Education Company

Austin • New York • Orlando • Atlanta • San Francisco • Boston • Dallas • Toronto • London

Cover Credits

Cover Photo by John Cancalosi/Peter Arnold, Inc.

Printed in the United States of America

ISBN 0-03-064931-5

1 2 3 4 5 6 082 04 03 02 01 00

▪ CONTENTS ▪

Teaching Transparencies

Concept Mapping Transparencies

Teaching Resources Directory

Directed Reading Worksheets

These worksheets help students develop and practice fundamental reading comprehension skills. Completed Directed Reading Worksheets provide a comprehensive review tool for students to use when studying for an exam.

Study Guide

The Study Guide includes **Vocabulary & Notes Worksheets** and **Chapter Review Worksheets,** which are reproductions of the Chapter Highlights and Chapter Review sections that follow each chapter in the textbook.

Science Puzzlers, Twisters & Teasers

Science Puzzlers, Twisters & Teasers use vocabulary and concepts from each chapter of the Pupil's Editions as elements of rebuses, anagrams, logic puzzles, daffy definitions, riddle poems, word jumbles, and other types of puzzles.

Reinforcement and Vocabulary Review Worksheets

Reinforcement Worksheets approach a chapter topic from a different angle with an emphasis on different learning modalities to help students that are frustrated by traditional methods. **Vocabulary Review Worksheets** use a variety of puzzle formats to help students study and review chapter vocabulary.

Critical Thinking & Problem Solving Worksheets

Critical Thinking Worksheets develop the following skills: distinguishing fact from opinion, predicting consequences, analyzing information, and drawing conclusions. Problem Solving Worksheets develop a step-by-step process of problem analysis including gathering information, asking critical questions, identifying alternatives, and making comparisons.

Math Skills for Science Worksheets

Each Math Skills activity gives a brief introduction to a relevant math skill, a step-by-step explanation of the math process, one or more example problems, and a variety of practice problems.

Science Skills Worksheets

These worksheets help your students focus specifically on skills such as measuring, graphing, using logic, understanding statistics, organizing research papers, and critical thinking options.

Datasheets for Labs

These worksheets are a reproduction of the labs found in the *Holt Science & Technology* textbook. Charts, tables, and graphs are included to make data collection and analysis easier, and space is provided to write observations and conclusions.

Whiz-Bang Demonstrations

In each demonstration students discover an answer or use a scientific model.

Calculator-Based Labs

These experiments give students the opportunity to use graphing-calculator probes and sensors to collect data. In addition to standard lab equipment, these experiments require a TI graphing calculator, Vernier sensors, and a TI CBL 2 or Vernier Lab Pro interface.

EcoLabs and Field Activities

EcoLabs are indoor activities with an environmental or ecological focus. Field Activities focus on educational outdoor projects, such as wildlife observation, nature surveys, or natural history.

Inquiry Labs

Inquiry labs use the structure of a scientific method to help students find their own path in solving a real-world problem. Many of these labs are open-ended.

Long-Term Projects and Research Ideas

Long-Term Projects provide students with the opportunity to go beyond library and Internet resources to explore science topics. Research ideas can be used to develop library and Internet research skills and as practice in writing research papers.

All Labs Are Classroom Tested and Approved

We are grateful to the many teachers around the country who helped ensure the safety and accuracy of these demonstrations and labs.

Chapter Tests

Each four-page chapter test evaluates student's understanding of the chapter objectives. Each test consists of a variety of item types including Multiple Choice, Using Vocabulary, Short Answer, Critical Thinking, Math in Science, Interpreting Graphics, and Concept Mapping.

Performance-Based Assessments

Performance-based assessment strategies evaluate students' abilities to solve problems using the tools, equipment, and techniques of science. Rubrics included for each assessment make it easy to evaluate student performance. Student pages include step-by-step instructions, safety precautions, and space for students to record their answers.

Lesson Plans

Section lesson plans provide detailed descriptions for how to integrate all of the great resources in the *Holt Science & Technology* program into your daily teaching. Each lesson plan includes a correlation of the lesson activities to the National Science Education Standards.

Teaching Transparencies

Each transparency in the Teaching Resources is correlated to a particular lesson in the Chapter Organizer of your Annotated Teacher's Edition.

Concept Mapping Transparencies, Worksheets, and Answer Key

Concept Mapping Transparencies provide models for students to study the concepts within each chapter and to form their own logical connections. Student worksheets contain a blank concept map. Completed concept maps are available as transparencies.

Answer Keys

Answers for most all worksheets are found in the Answer Key section located in front of the Teaching Transparencies.

Calculator-Based Labs Guidelines for Teachers

Incorporating technology into the laboratory allows students to explore basic scientific principles using modern techniques. The following information will be helpful to you in working with the Calculator-Based Labs in this program.

- Calculator-Based Labs are designed to give students a hands-on approach to science and technology. At first, the equipment may seem complex. However, as you become familiar with the equipment, you will find that the procedures follow a definite pattern. Encourage students to *carefully* read the lab procedure for a better understanding of the lab and the purpose behind each piece of equipment.
- To collect data, Vernier probes and sensors are connected to either a Vernier Lab Pro or Texas Instrument CBL 2 interface that is linked to a TI (Texas Instruments) Graphing Calculator. These data collection devices are portable and versatile. Both devices are battery powered and can be taken out of the lab to monitor data in the field.
- The TI-73, 83, 83 Plus, 86, 89, 92, and 92 Plus graphing calculators are fully compatible with the Vernier Lab Pro or TI CBL 2 interface. The DataMate program is stored on the LabPro or CBL 2 interface. The DataMate program can be transferred to a TI Graphing Calculator. DataMate is a data-collection program that controls the data gathering process, and makes data analysis easier after experiments are completed.
- The TI-Graph Link software and cable allows you to transfer data from experiments to a Macintosh or PC computer. Alternatively, you may elect to use the Vernier Graphical Analysis program (along with the TI-Graph Link cable) in place of the TI-Graph Link Software.
- Review with students proper procedures for preparation, care, and use of all equipment. Proper care should be taken when using delicate pieces of equipment such as the LabPro, CBL 2, pH sensor, and light sensor.
- Be sure students are aware of proper safety procedures. The safety information that follows is designed to be handed out to students. A safety contract is a good device for students to read, sign, and return to you to verify that they understand proper safety procedures. Additional safety information is available on the *One-Stop Planner CD-ROM.*

For additional information on Vernier products and technical support, log-on to their Web site at **www.vernier.com.**

EcoLabs & Field Activities Guidelines for Teachers

Studying environmental topics in the laboratory and venturing into the field is exciting and productive. In order to ensure safe learning experiences for you and your students, please keep the following precautions in mind:

- Be sure students are aware of proper lab-safety procedures. The safety information on pages ix–xi should be handed out to students. Page xi is a short safety contract that students should read, sign, and return to you to verify that they understand proper safety procedures. Additional safety information is available on the *One-Stop Planner CD-ROM.*
- The following is a list of additional information to keep in mind while conducting field activities:

Know your mission. Tell students the goal of the field activity in advance. Be sure they have the necessary supplies, permission slips, and other materials they need to participate.

Know the hazards. Determine whether there are likely to be poisonous plants or dangerous animals where you will be going. Make sure students know how to identify any such species. Also find out about other hazards, such as steep or slippery terrain.

Suit up! Tell students in advance what kind of clothing is appropriate. Encourage students to dress in a manner that will keep them warm, comfortable, and dry. Encourage students to wear sunglasses, a hat, gloves, rain gear, or other protective gear suitable for local conditions.

Don't feed the bears. Students should avoid all animals, especially those that may sting, bite, scratch, or otherwise cause injury.

Don't pick that! Tell students not to pick, touch, or taste any wild plant without first obtaining your permission. Many wild plants can be irritating to the skin or toxic.

Stick together. Encourage students to travel with a partner at all times and to stay within calling distance of the group.

Report accidents immediately. Even if an incident seems unimportant, tell students to let you know immediately. Keep a well-stocked first-aid kit handy when working in the field.

Take only pictures, leave only footprints. Students should not remove anything from a field site without your permission. Direct students to stay on trails when possible to avoid trampling delicate vegetation. Students should take any garbage they produce with them and leave natural areas as they were found.

Safety Guidelines and Symbols for Students

Performing scientific investigations and field activities is exciting and fun, but it can be dangerous if the proper precautions aren't followed. To make sure that your laboratory or field experience is both exciting and safe, follow the general guidelines listed below. Also follow your teacher's instructions, and don't take shortcuts! When you have read and understood all of the information in this section, including the Student Safety Contract, sign your name in the designated space on the contract, and return the contract to your teacher.

GENERAL

Always get your teacher's permission before attempting any lab investigation or field activity. Before beginning, read the procedures carefully, paying attention to safety information and cautionary statements. If you are unsure about what a safety symbol means, look it up below or ask your teacher. If an accident occurs, inform your teacher immediately.

IN THE LAB

General Know the location of all safety equipment, such as fire alarms, fire blankets, and eyewash stations, and the procedures for using them. Know your school's fire-evacuation routes. Don't work alone in the laboratory. Walk with care in the lab, and keep your work area free from unnecessary clutter. Dress appropriately on lab days. If your hair is long, tie it back. Certain products, such as hair spray, are flammable and should not be worn while working near an open flame. Remove dangling jewelry. Don't wear open-toed shoes or sandals in the laboratory.

EYE SAFETY Wear approved safety goggles when working around chemicals, any mechanical device, or any type of flame or heating device. If any substance gets in your eyes, notify your teacher.

HAND SAFETY Avoid chemical or heat injuries to your hands by wearing protective gloves or oven mitts. Check the materials list in the lab for the type of hand protection you should wear while performing the experiment.

CLOTHING PROTECTION Wear an apron to protect your clothing from staining, burning, or corrosion.

SHARP/POINTED OBJECTS Use knives and other sharp instruments with extreme care. Do not cut an object while holding it in your hands. Instead, place it on a suitable work surface for cutting.

HEAT Wear safety goggles when using a heating device or a flame. Wear oven mitts to avoid burns.

ELECTRICITY Avoid using equipment with damaged cords. Be careful around equipment and cords to avoid accidents. Ensure that your hands are dry and that electrical equipment is turned off before you plug it into an outlet.

CHEMICALS Wear safety goggles when handling chemicals. Read chemical labels. Wear an apron and latex gloves when working with acids or bases or when told to do so. If a chemical spills on your skin or clothing, notify your teacher and immediately rinse it off with water for at least 5 minutes. Never touch, taste, or smell a chemical or mix any chemicals unless your teacher instructs you to do so.

ANIMAL AND PLANT SAFETY Handle animals only as directed by your teacher. Always treat animals carefully and with respect. Wash your hands thoroughly after handling an animal or any part of a plant.

Glassware Examine all glassware for chips and cracks before using it. Report damaged glassware to your teacher. Glass containers used for heating should be made of heat-resistant glass.

Cleanup Before leaving the laboratory, clean your work area. Wash glass containers with soap and water. Put away all equipment and supplies. Dispose of all chemicals and other materials as directed by your teacher. Make sure all equipment is turned off and unplugged. Wash your hands with soap and water. Never take anything from the laboratory without permission from your teacher.

Safety Contract

Carefully read the Student Safety Contract below. Then write your name in the blank, and sign and date the contract.

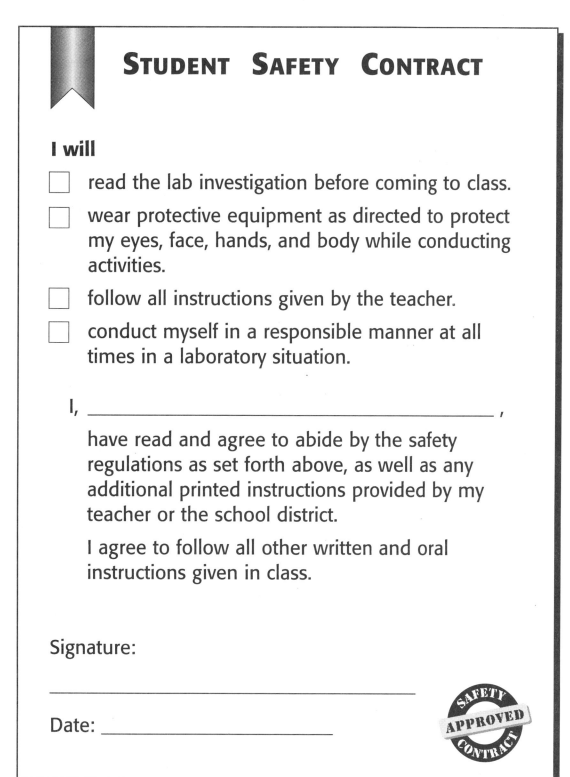

STUDENT SAFETY CONTRACT

I will

- [ ] read the lab investigation before coming to class.
- [ ] wear protective equipment as directed to protect my eyes, face, hands, and body while conducting activities.
- [ ] follow all instructions given by the teacher.
- [ ] conduct myself in a responsible manner at all times in a laboratory situation.

I, ______________________________,

have read and agree to abide by the safety regulations as set forth above, as well as any additional printed instructions provided by my teacher or the school district.

I agree to follow all other written and oral instructions given in class.

Signature:

____

Date: ____________________

SAFETY APPROVED CONTRACT

How To Do a Long-Term or Research Project

Whether you're getting ready to embark on a long-term project or preparing to do research, here are some tips to guide you along the way.

General Tips

- **Work on something you like.** You'll be working on this project for a while, so make sure you work on a subject you find interesting. Choose a topic that you want to know more about, or consider tackling a topic or question from your science class that puzzles you. Choosing a topic that's right for you can be difficult. If you're having trouble, be sure to talk to your teacher. Your teacher can offer strategies to help you find a good subject.

- **Start early!** If you start your research early, you'll have more time to find the information you need. If you're experimenting, you'll need plenty of time to thoroughly test your hypothesis. Starting early may give you time to redesign your experiment or change topics, just in case something doesn't work out as you planned. You'll also have more time to put together an informative and attractive presentation or paper.

- **Break it down.** For any type of project, it is a good idea to set small goals for yourself instead of conquering the project as a whole. For example, if you have 4 weeks to complete a project, break up the project into four smaller parts. Assign yourself one for each week. Small weekly goals are easier to accomplish than one big project, and they will also help you to monitor your progress.

Research Guidelines

- **Don't believe everything you read.** If a statement sounds fishy to you, question its source. Ask yourself if the source is reliable. Is it a government agency, professional association, museum, or well-known, scientifically accurate magazine? If not, you'll probably need to verify.

- **Keep track of your sources.** A bibliography is a list of sources used in writing a paper. Most teachers require research papers to include a bibliography. Find out what kind of information your teacher expects to see in your bibliography. Before you begin taking notes from a new source, record the source's bibliographical information. A detailed, well-organized bibliography makes your paper more credible. It shows how much work you've put into your research. It also provides a list of resources in case you, your teacher, or another scientist wants to study the topic further.

- **Keep track of your notes.** It is important to know which source your information comes from. One strategy is to keep notes on color-coded note cards. Use colored index cards or design your own system with plain cards and markers. Always keep your notes together so you don't lose them. You may want to use a pocket folder or a three-ring binder to keep your notes in one place.

Internet Research—Finding Reliable Sources

When you do research on the World Wide Web, avoid drawing conclusions before you've checked the information for reliability. Often you can tell when a Web page contains bias or is opinion-based. But in many cases, an author may present his or her ideas as facts while giving little scientific evidence to back them up. When you are uncertain of a source's reliability, consider the following criteria:

HELPFUL HINT

These criteria can be applied to library research as well.

Criteria for Reliable Web Pages

- The authors make their case based on adequate evidence.
- The authors interpret the data cautiously.
- The authors acknowledge and deal with opposing views or arguments.
- The authors list current sources that support their claims.

Some characteristics of unreliable Web pages require practice to identify. So put on your thinking cap and question what you read. The following list will clue you in to questionable Web pages:

Characteristics of Unreliable Web Pages

- The authors make extraordinary claims with little supporting evidence.
- The authors relate evidence based on personal experience instead of referencing controlled studies.
- The authors appeal to emotion rather than to logic.
- The authors misrepresent or ignore opposing views.
- The authors' arguments support a politically or financially rewarding viewpoint.

Deciding whether you can rely on information from a Web page may be difficult. But with practice, you'll become very good at spotting unreliable Web pages.

Experimenting Guidelines

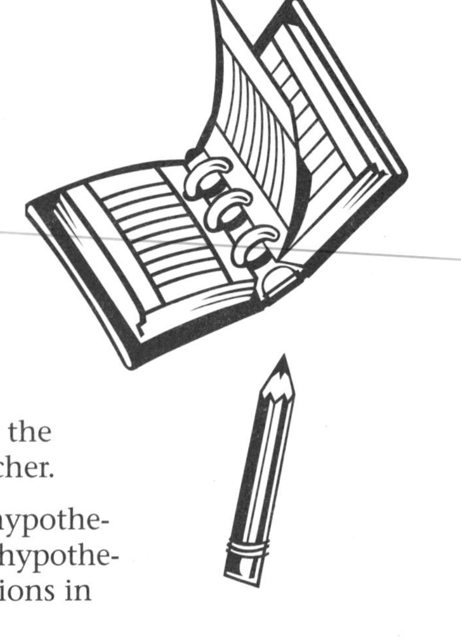

- Brainstorm ideas for topics, and write down those ideas in your ScienceLog or in a special lab journal.
- Keep all of your project notes in one place. This will make it easier for you to review the information later as you write a paper, make a presentation, or answer questions.
- Follow the steps of the scientific method.
- Take careful notes during your preliminary research and record your questions and your hypotheses. Keep all of your experimental designs and data in your journal.
- Don't do anything dangerous or unethical. Be sure to obey the safety and experimental guidelines established by your teacher.
- Remember, even if your experiment doesn't support your hypothesis, you will have learned something. Investigate why your hypothesis might have been wrong, and then explain your conclusions in your presentation.

Interviewing Guidelines

- Schedule interviews well in advance. Explain to the person you are interviewing who you are and why you want an interview. Before your interview, do some background research on the person you are interviewing.
- Go to the interview with a prepared list of questions, a notebook, and a pen to jot down your answers. If you want to make a video or audio recording of the interview, be sure to get permission from the person ahead of time.
- During the interview, remember that your prepared list of questions is just to help get you started. Be respectful, and don't be afraid to ask new or follow-up questions.

Presenting Your Results

At this stage, you will turn all your hard work into a product that you will use to share your research with others. Your worksheets offer one or more suggestions for how to present your research. Whether you decide to write a paper or an article, make an oral presentation, or present your results in a series of graphs and tables, be sure to follow the guidelines set by your teacher. Remember to get your teacher's permission before proceeding!

- **What medium should I use?** There are always a variety of options for sharing what you've learned, and you'll want to choose the best medium for highlighting your research. There are many issues to consider when choosing how to present your research. For example, if you are thinking about an audiovisual approach, do you have access to the appropriate equipment? Can you operate the equipment well enough to create a polished presentation? If you want to reflect your findings in the form of a play, story, or other creative work, will that medium allow you to adequately share what you learned? Or would a traditional method of presenting scientific research—such as a paper, poster, or oral presentation—be more suitable? Think carefully about which medium would be most appropriate for the research you have done.

- **What about length requirements?** Do enough research to allow you to explain the topic thoroughly. If your paper should be four pages long, rewrite and revise your paper until it is four pages long. If your oral presentation should take 10 minutes, practice your oral presentation and make sure that it is 10 minutes long. If you find that you don't have enough information to meet the length requirements of your project, you may have to do more research. A good way to avoid this problem is by starting with more research than you think you will need. Then cut out the extra or less important information.

- **How do I present my work scientifically?** Remember that scientific writing is different than creative writing. Be sure to state the facts, and be clear about what information is factual and what is your opinion. Show how the evidence you gathered supports your conclusions. If you are using graphs or tables, make sure they are easy to read. Give details about how and where you got your information. Even if you are presenting your findings in a creative manner, you must still document your sources and be able to explain the science behind your work.

Now you are ready to take part in a very important part of science—research. Good luck and have fun!

Module B
Chapter 1: Animals and Behavior
Lesson Plan
Section 1: What Is an Animal?

Pacing
1 Block = 45 minutes

Regular Schedule:	**with Lab(s):** N/A	**without Lab(s):** 1 Day
Block Schedule:	**with Lab(s):** N/A	**without Lab(s):** 1/2 Day

Objectives
1. Understand the differences between learned and innate behavior.
2. Explain the characteristics of animals.

Standards Covered
Unifying Concepts and Processes (UCP)
UCP 1. Systems, order, and organization

Science As Inquiry (SAI)
SAI 1. Abilities necessary to do scientific inquiry

History and Technology (HNS)
HNS 3. History of science

Life Science (LS)
Structure and Function in Living Systems (LS 1)
1a. Living systems at all levels of organization demonstrate the complementary nature of structure and function. Important levels of organization from structure and function include cells, tissues, organs, organ systems, whole organisms, and ecosystems.

1b. All organisms are composed of cells—the fundamental units of life. Most organisms are single cells; other organisms, including humans, are multicellular.

1d. Specialized cells perform specialized functions in multicellular organisms. Groups of specialized cells cooperate to form a tissue, such as a muscle. Different tissues are in turn grouped together to form larger functional units, called organs. Each type of cell, tissue, and organ has a distinct structure and set of functions that serve the organism as a whole.

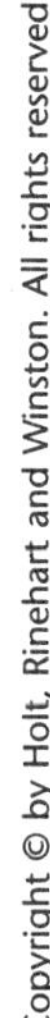

Reproduction and Heredity (LS 2)
2b. In many species, including humans, females produce eggs and males produce sperm. Plants also reproduce sexually—the egg and sperm are produced in the flowers of flowering plants. An egg and sperm unite to begin development of a new individual. That new individual receives genetic information from its mother (via the egg) and its father (via the sperm). Sexually produced offspring are never identical to either of their parents.

Name ______________________________ Date ____________ Class ____________

Populations and Ecosystems (LS 4)

4b. Populations of organisms can be categorized by the function they serve in an ecosystem. Plants and some microorganisms are producers—they make their own food. All animals, including humans, are consumers, which obtain food by eating other organisms. Decomposers, primarily bacteria and fungi, are consumers that use waste materials and dead organisms for food. Food webs identify the relationship among producers, consumers, and decomposers in an ecosystem.

Diversity and Adaptations of Organisms (LS 5)

5a. Millions of species of animals, plants, and microorganisms are alive today. Although different species might look dissimilar, the unity among organisms becomes apparent from an analysis of internal structures, the similarity of their chemical processes, and the evidence of common ancestry.

Key
PE = Pupil's Edition
ATE = Annotated Teacher's Edition
An asterisk indicates the item is part of the Unit Resource booklet for this unit.

Block 1

Focus *5 minutes*

_____ **Bellringer,** ATE p. 4. While you are taking attendance, ask students to ponder this question: What is the best material for washing a car—a cotton rag, a scratch pad, or an animal skeleton? Have them take a few moments to record their answers in their ScienceLog. Before you begin this section, call on individual students to give their answer and reasoning.

Motivate *10 minutes*

_____ **Group Activity,** ATE p. 5. To explore the diversity of the animal kingdom, have students work in groups of four. Each group will write down examples for each of the following: 2 Arctic animals, 2 Antarctic animals, 2 animals that fly, 2 animals with no bones, 2 African animals, 2 North American animals, 2 animals that live in the soil, 2 ocean animals, 2 animals with more than four legs. Answers should be as specific as possible. For example, they should answer "garter snake," not "snake," or "praying mantis" instead of "insect." Have each group share their answers while other groups cross out matches on their own page. How many animals did the class think of? That's diversity!

Teach *20 minutes*

_____ **Teaching Transparency 54,*** "The Animal Kingdom." This transparency illustrates the major phyla and subgroups of the animal kingdom in a pie chart.

_____ **Reinforcement Worksheet Chapter 1,*** "What Makes an Animal an Animal?" In this worksheet, students use a list of terms and phrases to complete a concept map that summarizes the main ideas in the section.

_____ **Self-Check,** PE p. 6. Students answer a question about vertebrates.

Close *10 minutes*

_____ **Review,** PE p. 7. Students answer three questions about animal characteristics.

Name ______________________ Date ____________ Class ____________

Homework

______ **Science Skills Worksheet 25,*** "Introduction to Graphs." This worksheet reviews bar graphs, pie graphs, and line graphs, and asks students to choose which type of graph would work best for three different sets of data.

______ **Alternative Assessment,** ATE p. 7. Have students write a summary of the characteristics shared by all animals. Tell them not to repeat the bold-faced paragraph headings in the text. Instead, students must explain each characteristic by first giving an example.

Additional Resource Options

______ **Science Puzzlers, Twisters & Teasers, Worksheet Chapter 1.*** These worksheets offer puzzles, games, and logic problems that use vocabulary and concepts from the chapter.

______ **Directed Reading Worksheet Chapter 1,* Section 1.** This worksheet reviews the main concepts in Section 1 while developing students' reading skills.

______ **Homework,** "Research/Presentation," ATE p. 6. Students research unusual animal characteristics that are exaggerated versions of ordinary characteristics and create a poster that illustrates their research results.

______ **Homework,** "Research Invertebrates," ATE p. 7. Students research any invertebrate and write one to two paragraphs about its range, habitat, food sources, and other related information.

______ **Quiz,** ATE p. 7. Students answer two questions that review the main content in the section.

______ **Module B Guided Reading Audio CD Program, Disc 14, Tracks 1-2.** The audio reading of the chapter provides essential chapter content for ESL students, auditory learners, and struggling readers.

______ **NSTA *sci*LINKS:** *Vertebrates and Invertebrates, sci*LINKS number HSTL330. Students research Internet resources related to vertebrate and invertebrate animals.

Name ______________________ Date ____________ Class __________

Module B
Chapter 1: Animals and Behavior
Lesson Plan
Section 2: Animal Behavior

Pacing

1 Block = 45 minutes

Regular Schedule:	**with Lab(s):** 3 Days	**without Lab(s):** 2 Days
Block Schedule:	**with Lab(s):** 1 1/2 Days	**without Lab(s):** 1 Day

Objectives

1. Explain the difference between learned and innate behavior.
2. Explain the difference between hibernation and estivation.
3. Give examples of how a biological clock influences behavior.
4. Describe circadian rhythms.
5. Explain how animals navigate.

Standards Covered

UCP 1. Systems, order, and organization
UCP 2. Evidence, models, and explanation
UCP 3. Change, constancy, and measurement
UCP 5. Form and formation

SAI 1. Abilities necessary to do scientific inquiry
SAI 2. Understandings about scientific inquiry

HNS 2. Nature of science

Regulation and Behavior (LS 3)

3a. All organisms must be able to obtain and use resources, grow, reproduce, and maintain stable internal conditions while living in a constantly changing external environment.

3b. Regulation of an organism's internal environment involves sensing its internal environment and changing physiological activity to keep conditions within the range required for the organism to survive.

3c. Behavior is one kind of response an organism can make to an internal or environmental stimulus. A behavioral response requires coordination and communication at many levels, including cells, organ systems, and whole organisms. A behavioral response is a set of actions determined partially by heredity and partially from experience.

3d. An organism's behavior evolves through adaptation to its environment. How a species moves, obtains food, reproduces, and responds to danger are all based on the species' evolutionary history.

Name ______________________ Date ____________ Class ____________

Populations and Ecosystems (LS 4)

4a. A population consists of all individuals of a species that occur together at a given place and time. All populations living together and the physical factors with which they interact make up an ecosystem.

4d. The number of organisms an ecosystem can support depends on the resources available and abiotic factors, such as the quantity of light and water, range of temperatures, and soil composition. Given adequate biotic and abiotic resources and no disease or predators, populations (including humans) increase at a rapid rate. Lack of resources and other factors, such as predation and climate, limit the growth of populations in specific niches in an ecosystem.

Diversity and Adaptations of Organisms (LS 5)

5b. Biological evolution accounts for the diversity of species developed through gradual processes over many generations. Species acquire many of their unique characteristics through biological adaptation, which involves the selection of naturally occurring variations in population. Biological adaptations include changes in structure, behavior, or physiology that enhance survival and reproductive success in a particular environment.

5c. Extinction of a species occurs when the environment changes and the adaptive characteristics of a species are insufficient to allow for its survival. Fossils indicate that many organisms that lived long ago are extinct. Extinction of a species is common; most of the species that have lived on Earth no longer exist.

Block 1

Focus *5 minutes*

_____ **Bellringer,** ATE p. 8. Ask students to write a sentence for each of the following terms: predator, prey. After each sentence have students list three animals that are predators and three that are prey.

Motivate *10 minutes*

_____ **Discussion,** "Yawning," ATE p. 9. Begin a discussion by yawning at the front of the classroom. Record how many students yawn as a result. Tell them yawning is one of the few specific behaviors shared by different animal groups. Reptiles, fish, amphibians, birds, and mammals all yawn. Ask students: Why do we yawn?

Teach *30 minutes*

_____ **Math and More,** ATE p. 9. Students solve a word problem to calculate how many species of beetles we know about, then convert the fraction of beetle species to a percentage.

_____ **Demonstration,** "Sign Language," ATE p. 10. Learn five basic signs in Sign Language, and demonstrate them for the class. Choose words such as hungry, sad, angry, tired, and happy. Tell students that because of our innate language ability, it's possible to learn another language, even a nonvocal one. But perhaps humans aren't the only species with this ability. Koko, a gorilla, learned more than 500 different signs while in captivity. She even created some of her own signs, such as "finger bracelet" for "ring." Once, her trainer became frustrated because Koko was not cooperating. The trainer signed "bad gorilla," and Koko corrected her by signing "funny gorilla." Koko fibbed at times to avoid getting in trouble and insulted trainers when she was angry. She even had her own kitten, a tiny tailless cat that she named All Ball.

Homework

_____ **Review,** PE p. 10. Students answer two questions about innate and learned behaviors.

_____ **Math Skills for Science Worksheet Chapter 1,*** "Percentages, Fractions, and Decimals." Students learn how to convert between percentages, fractions, and decimals through sample and practice problems.

Block 2

Teach *25 minutes*

_____ **Whiz-Bang Demonstration, Chapter 1,*** "Six-Legged Thermometer." Students observe the effect of temperature on the frequency of a cricket's chirping and learn how an animal's behavior may be affected by the environment.

_____ **QuickLab,** "How Long Is a Minute?" PE p. 12. Supply one stopwatch for each pair of students, and have them complete the QuickLab to evaluate the accuracy of their internal clocks.

Extend *10 minutes*

_____ **Going Further,** "Maritime Navigation," ATE p. 12. Have students write a report about maritime navigation. Tell students to include a comparison of the instruments that were used 100 years ago and their modern counterparts. Their report should also explain how ancient people navigated.

Close *10 minutes*

_____ **Quiz,** ATE p. 13. Students answer two questions about animal hibernation and navigation.

_____ **Alternative Assessment,** ATE p. 13. Have each student choose a species from each of the following categories: insects, birds, reptiles, and mammals. Have students write a brief report about the species describing all of the characteristics that make it an animal.

Homework

_____ **Review,** PE p. 13. Students answer four questions that review the lesson content.

_____ **Critical Thinking Worksheet 14, Chapter 1,*** "Masters of Navigation." Students read two paragraphs about bird migration, and then apply their knowledge of innate and learned behaviors to answer questions about the reading.

Name ______________________ Date ____________ Class ____________

Block 3

Lab Days *45 minutes*

_____ **Discovery Lab,** "Wet, Wiggly Worms!" PE p. 18. Students observe the behavior of a live earthworm and analyze their observations. This activity supports STANDARDS UCP 2, SAI 2, HNS 2, and LS4a.

_____ **Datasheets for LabBook,** Chapter 1,* "Wet, Wiggly Worms." This blackline master makes progressing through the lab easier for students and grading easier for you.

Additional Resource Options

_____ **Design Your Own,** "Aunt Flossie and the Bumblebee," p. 124. Students design an experiment to determine what characteristics attract bumblebees. This lab supports STANDARDS UCP 2, SAI 2, HNS 2, and LS4a.

_____ **Datasheets for LabBook,** Chapter 1,* "Aunt Flossie and the Bumblebee." This blackline master makes progressing through the lab easier for students and grading easier for you.

_____ **Inquiry Labs, Chapter 1,*** "Follow the Leader." Students observe ant behavior to form a theory about how ants navigate.

_____ **Directed Reading Worksheet Chapter 1,* Section 2.** This worksheet reinforces the main concepts in the section while developing students' reading skills.

_____ **Math Skills for Science Worksheet Chapter 1,*** "Average, Mode, and Median." Students learn the difference between average, mode, and median, and learn how to calculate the mode and median of a set of data through sample and practice problems.

_____ **Teaching Transparency 104,*** "Finding Direction on Earth." This transparency links to Earth Science, and illustrates the directions on Earth.

_____ **Reinforcement Worksheet Chapter 1,*** "Animal Interviews." Students read fictional interviews with different species of animals, then decide which behavior or characteristic is described by each.

_____ **Math and More,** ATE p. 11. Students calculate the average number of hours a sloth sleeps each day and convert their answer to a percentage.

_____ **Apply,** PE p. 11. Students apply their knowledge of circadian rhythms to explain why jet lag occurs.

_____ **Eye on the Environment,** "Do Not Disturb!" PE p. 24. Students read a feature about bats, and use the Internet or library to conduct further research on the subject.

_____ **Self-Check,** PE p. 12. Students answer a question about whether hibernation and circadian rhythms are related.

______ **Module B Guided Reading Audio CD Program, Disc 14, Track 3.** The audio reading of the chapter provides essential chapter content for ESL students, auditory learners, and struggling readers.

______ **NSTA *sci*LINKS:** *Animal Behavior, sci*LINKS number HSTL335. *The Rhythms of Life, sci*LINKS number HSTL340. Students research Internet resources related to animal behaviors and the rhythms of life.

Name ______________________ Date ______________ Class ______________

Module B
Chapter 1: Animals and Behavior
Lesson Plan
Section 3: Living Together

Pacing

1 Block = 45 minutes

Regular Schedule:	**with Lab(s):** N/A	**without Lab(s):** 2 Days
Block Schedule:	**with Lab(s):** N/A	**without Lab(s):** 1 Day

Objectives

1. Discuss ways that animals communicate.
2. List the advantages and disadvantages of living in groups.

Standards Covered

UCP 1. Systems, order, and organization

SAI 1. Abilities necessary to do scientific inquiry

Structure and Function in Living Systems (LS 1)

1a. Living systems at all levels of organization demonstrate the complementary nature of structure and function. Important levels of organization from structure and function include cells, tissues, organs, organ systems, whole organisms, and ecosystems.

Reproduction and Heredity (LS 2)

2a. Reproduction is a characteristic of all living systems; because no individual organism lives forever, reproduction is essential to the continuation of every species. Some organisms reproduce asexually. Others reproduce sexually.

Regulation and Behavior

3c. Behavior is one kind of response an organism can make to an internal or environmental stimulus. A behavioral response requires coordination and communication at many levels, including cells, organ systems, and whole organisms. Behavioral response is a set of actions determined partially by heredity and partially from experience.

3d. An organism's behavior evolves through adaptation to its environment. How a species moves, obtains food, reproduces, and responds to danger are all based on the species' evolutionary history.

4a. A population consists of all individuals of a species that occur together at a given place and time. All populations living together and the physical factors with which they interact make up an ecosystem.

4d. The number of organisms an ecosystem can support depends on the resources available and abiotic factors, such as quantity of light and water, range of temperatures, and soil composition. Given adequate biotic and abiotic resources and no disease or predators, populations (including humans) increase at rapid rates. Lack of resources and other factors, such as predation and climate, limit the growth of populations in specific niches within an ecosystem.

Name ______________________________ Date ______________ Class ____________

Block 1

Focus *5 minutes*

______ **Bellringer,** ATE p. 14. As you are taking attendance, play a tape of humpback-whale songs. Ask students to offer suggestions related to what information the whales might be communicating. Your library might be a good source for whale tapes. Sound bytes of whale songs can also be found on the Internet.

Motivate *15 minutes*

______ **Activity,** "Nonverbal Communication," ATE p. 14. Play a game of charades with students to demonstrate the importance of nonverbal communication among humans and other animals. Allow the class to provide feedback after a student guesses successfully.

Teach *25 minutes*

______ **Meeting Individual Needs,** "Learners Having Difficulty," ATE p. 15. Some students may not realize how often humans use nonverbal communication or the importance of such methods in negotiating even the mundane events of everyday life. Ask students how each of these nonverbal communication methods provides essential information: smell, facial expressions, sound.

______ **Activity,** "Investigate Grooming," ATE p. 16. Tell students that grooming, or cleaning behavior, represents another way that animals communicate with each other through touch. Encourage students to do research about animals that communicate in this fashion. Examples include birds (preening), many mammals (mutual grooming), and certain fish (cleaning symbiosis). Students can use their research to create illustrated booklets that they share with the class.

______ **Teaching Transparency 55,*** "The Dance of the Bees." This transparency shows how bees use special movements to communicate information about the location of nectar.

Homework

______ **Research Ant Behavior,** ATE p. 16. Have students research the behavior of ants. How do they organize the work of their colony? Several species of ants enslave other species. Have students investigate how one species of ant manages to capture and control another species.

Block 2

Teach *30 minutes*

______ **Guided Practice,** "Poster Project," ATE p. 16. Tell students that wolves use body language called posturing to communicate with members of the pack. Have small groups of students research wolf posturing and then create illustrated charts showing various postures and what they mean. After posting the charts on the bulletin board, lead a discussion about wolf communication. Encourage students who have a pet dog to talk about the similarities and the differences between the body language used by their pet and the body language used by wolves.

Close *15 minutes*

______ **Quiz,** ATE p. 17. Students answer two questions about animal communication.

______ **Review,** PE p. 17. Students answer three questions that review the lesson content.

Homework

______ **Alternative Assessment,** "Concept Mapping," ATE p. 17. Have students create a concept map, including all necessary linking words, using the following concepts: communication, identification of family members, pheromones, making noises, touch, courtship, defend a territory, warn about danger, body language.

Additional Resource Options

______ **Long-Term Projects & Research Ideas, Chapter 1,*** "Animal-Myth Behaviors." *Research ideas:* animal myths; animals in urban environments; *Project ideas:* the calming effect of animals on people; observing zoo animals

______ **Directed Reading Worksheet Chapter 1,* Section 3.** This worksheet reviews the main concepts in the section and reinforces students' reading skills.

______ **Cross-Disciplinary Focus,** "Geography," ATE p. 333. Students learn about the behaviors of river dolphins, and locate several major rivers where dolphins live on a globe or map.

______ **Weird Science,** "Animal Cannibals," PE p. 341. Students read about certain animal species that practice cannibalism, and conduct further research using the Internet or the library.

______ **Module B Guided Reading Audio CD Program, Disc 14, Track 4.** The audio reading of the chapter provides essential chapter content for ESL students, auditory learners, and struggling readers.

______ **NSTA *sci*LINKS:** *Communication in the Animal Kingdom, sci*LINKS number HSTL345. Students research Internet resources related to animal communication.

End of Chapter Review and Assessment

______ **Study Guide,*** Vocabulary, Notes, and Chapter Review

______ **Chapter Tests with Performance-Based Assessment, Chapter 1 Test***

______ **Chapter Tests with Performance-Based Assessment, Performance-Based Assessment 1***

______ **Concept Mapping Transparency 14***

Name ______________________ Date __________ Class __________

CHAPTER 1 **DIRECTED READING WORKSHEET**

Animals and Behavior

Chapter Introduction

As you begin this chapter, answer the following.

1. Read the title of the chapter. List three things that you already know about this subject.

____

____

____

____

2. Write two questions about this subject that you would like answered by the time you finish this chapter.

____

____

____

3. How does the title of the Start-Up Activity relate to the subject of the chapter?

____

____

____

Section 1: What Is an Animal? (p. 4)

4. Natural bath sponges used to be living plants. True or False? (Circle one.)

5. Describe the smallest animal you've ever seen.

____

____

____

The Animal Kingdom (p. 4)

6. Which of the following lists contains types of organisms that are NOT animals?
   - **a.** corals, birds, kangaroos
   - **b.** dolphins, cactuses, whales
   - **c.** spiders, humans, sponges
   - **d.** sea anemones, fish, slugs

Use Figure 3 to determine whether each of the following types of animals is an invertebrate or a vertebrate. In the space provided, write *I* if it is an invertebrate and *V* if it is a vertebrate.

7. _____ beetles
8. _____ mammals
9. _____ worms
10. _____ spiders

That's an Animal? (p. 5)

Mark each of the following statements *True* or *False*.

11. __________ All animals are multicellular.
12. __________ Animal cells are prokaryotic.
13. __________ Some animals can reproduce asexually.
14. In the ____________________ stage of its development, an organism is called an embryo.
15. Which of the following specialized parts are organs? (Circle all that apply.)
    - **a.** muscles
    - **b.** kidneys
    - **c.** heart
    - **d.** nerves
16. Animals are the only organisms that can move. True or False? (Circle one.)
17. Plants can make their own food, but animals cannot. How do animals survive?

    ____

    ____

    ____

Review (p. 7)

Now that you've finished Section 1, review what you learned by answering the Review questions in your ScienceLog.

Section 2: Animal Behavior (p. 8)

1. The activities that animals perform, such as building homes and stalking food, are called ________________ ________________.

Survival Behavior (p. 8)

2. Survival behaviors help animals find food, water, and a place to live, and help them avoid being eaten. True or False? (Circle one.)
3. Animals use different methods in order to obtain the most ________________ for the least amount of ________________.
4. Predators hunt and eat other ________________, called prey.
5. Use the text to give one example of an animal that uses camouflage.

____

____

____

6. How does the hooded pitohui bird defend itself from predators?
   a. Its bite injects a powerful acid into its attacker.
   b. It is covered in spines.
   c. It can spray a chemical that smells very bad.
   d. Its skin contains a toxin that can kill a predator.
7. Warning coloration is helpful to prey because it keeps prey from being eaten. Why is warning coloration sometimes helpful to predators?

____

____

____

Why Do They Behave That Way? (p. 10)

8. Animals always know instinctively what to do. True or False? (Circle one.)
9. Innate behaviors are influenced by ________________ and do not depend on experience or ________________.
10. Innate behavior cannot be changed. True or False? (Circle one.)

11. The tendency of humans to speak is a(n) ______________ behavior but the language we speak is a(n) ______________ behavior.

Review (p. 10)

Now that you've finished the first part of Section 2, review what you learned by answering the Review questions in your ScienceLog.

Seasonal Behavior (p. 11)

12. What are two ways animals deal with winter?

____

____

____

13. The only reason animals travel from one place to another and back again is to find food and water. True or False? (Circle one.)

14. Which of the following does NOT happen during hibernation?
    a. The animal's heart rate drops.
    b. The animal survives on stored body fat.
    c. The animal's temperature increases.
    d. The animal does not wake for weeks at a time.

15. Sometimes desert animals experience an internal slowdown during the summer. True or False? (Circle one.)

The Rhythms of Life (p. 12)

16. To set their biological clock, animals use clues such as the ______________ of the ______________ and the ______________.

17. Circadian rhythms are daily cycles. What is an example of a circadian rhythm?

____

____

How Do Animals Find Their Way? (p. 12)

18. Arctic terns have to ______________ to make their 38,000 km round trip.

19. All of the landmarks that animals use to navigate are things that they can see, such as mountains and rivers. True or False? (Circle one.)

20. Look at the Physical Science Connection on the right hand side of page 13. Migratory birds have crystals of a mineral called magnetite above their nostrils. How do scientists think this mineral helps them?

____

____

____

Review (p. 13)

Now that you've finished Section 2, review what you learned by answering the Review questions in your ScienceLog.

Section 3: Living Together (p. 14)

1. The ______________________ between animals of the same species requires communication.

Communication (p. 14)

2. What two things must happen for communication to occur between two animals?

____

____

____

____

3. Why are the cranes in Figure 15 dancing?
   - **a.** They are telling each other where to find food.
   - **b.** The dance leads to mating.
   - **c.** They are frightening away predators.
   - **d.** They are warning each other of danger.

4. The wolves in Figure 18 are howling to defend their living space from other wolves. True or False? (Circle one.)

How Do Animals Communicate? (p. 15)

5. Animals use their senses, such as sight and touch, to convey ______________________ information.

6. Which of the following messages do ants communicate using pheromones? (Circle all that apply.)
   a. Danger!
   b. I'm from your colony.
   c. Follow me!
   d. I'm your friend.

7. Insects use some of the same pheromones to attract mates that elephants use. True or False? (Circle one.)

Match the noise in Column B with the type of animal that uses that noise for communication in Column A, and write the corresponding letter in the space provided.

Column A	Column B
____ 8. elephants	a. songs
____ 9. male birds	b. low rumbles
____ 10. dolphins	c. howls
____ 11. wolves	d. complex clicks

12. Fireflies blinking and humans winking are both examples of communication. True or False? (Circle one.)

13. Look at the diagram "The Dance of the Bees" on page 16. If you were a honeybee, how would learning the waggle dance help you find food?

____

____

Part of the Family (p. 17)

14. Look at the ground squirrel in Figure 23. What is one benefit and one downside to living in a group?

____

____

____

____

Review (p. 17)

Now that you've finished Section 3, review what you learned by answering the Review questions in your ScienceLog.

Name ______________________ Date ______________ Class ______________

CHAPTER 1 VOCABULARY AND NOTES WORKSHEET

Animals and Behavior

By studying the Vocabulary and Notes listed for each section below, you can gain a better understanding of this chapter.

SECTION 1

Vocabulary

In your own words, write a definition for each of the following terms in the space provided.

1. vertebrate ______________________________

____

2. invertebrate ______________________________

____

3. embryo ______________________________

____

4. tissue ______________________________

____

5. organ ______________________________

____

6. consumer ______________________________

____

Notes

Read the following section highlights. Then, in your own words, write the highlights in your ScienceLog.

- Animals with a skull and a backbone are vertebrates. Animals without a backbone are invertebrates.
- Animals are multicellular. Their cells are eukaryotic and lack a cell wall.
- Most animals reproduce sexually and develop from embryos.
- Most animals have tissues and organs.
- Most animals move.
- Animals are consumers.

SECTION 2

Vocabulary

In your own words, write a definition for each of the following terms in the space provided.

1. predator ______________________________

2. prey ______________________________

3. innate behavior ______________________________

4. learned behavior ______________________________

5. hibernation ______________________________

6. estivation ______________________________

7. biological clock ______________________________

8. circadian rhythm ______________________________

Notes

Read the following section highlights. Then, in your own words, write the highlights in your ScienceLog.

- Many animals use camouflage, chemicals, or both to defend themselves against predators.
- Behavior may be classified as innate or learned. The potential for innate behavior is inherited. Learned behavior depends on experience.
- Some animals migrate to find food, water, or safe nesting grounds.
- Some animals hibernate in the winter, and some estivate in the summer.
- Animals have internal biological clocks to control natural cycles.
- Daily cycles are called circadian rhythms.
- Some biological clocks are regulated by cues from an animal's environment.
- Animals navigate close to home using landmarks and a mental image of their home area.
- Some animals use the positions of the sun and stars or Earth's magnetic field to navigate.

SECTION 3

Vocabulary

In your own words, write a definition for each of the following terms in the space provided.

1. social behavior ______________________

____

2. communication ______________________

____

3. territory ______________________

____

4. pheromone ______________________

____

Notes

Read the following section highlights. Then, in your own words, write the highlights in your ScienceLog.

- Communication must include both a signal and a response.
- Two important kinds of communication are courtship and territorial displays.
- Animals communicate through sight, sound, touch, and smell.
- Group living allows animals to spot both prey and predators more easily.
- Groups of animals are more visible to predators than are individuals, and animals in groups must compete with one another for food and mates.

Name ______________________ Date ______________ Class ______________

CHAPTER 1 CHAPTER REVIEW WORKSHEET

Animals and Behavior

USING VOCABULARY

To complete the following sentences, choose the correct term from each pair of terms listed below, and write the term on the space provided.

1. An animal with a skull and a backbone is ______________________. An animal with no backbone is ______________________. (an invertebrate or a vertebrate)
2. A behavior that does not depend on experience is ______________________. (innate or learned)
3. In the summer, an animal enters a state of reduced activity. The animal is ______________________. (estivating or hibernating)
4. Daily cycles are known as ______________________. (biological clocks or circadian rhythms)
5. When an egg and a sperm come together, they form ______________________. (an embryo or an organ)

UNDERSTANDING CONCEPTS

Multiple Choice

6. Which characteristic is NOT true of animals?
   - **a.** They are multicellular.
   - **b.** They usually reproduce sexually.
   - **c.** They make their own food.
   - **d.** They have tissues.
7. Living in groups
   - **a.** attracts predators.
   - **b.** helps prey spot predators.
   - **c.** helps animals find food.
   - **d.** All of the above
8. Warning coloration is
   - **a.** a kind of camouflage.
   - **b.** a way to warn predators away.
   - **c.** always black and white.
   - **d.** always a sign that an animal is poisonous to eat.
9. Some birds use Earth's magnetic field
   - **a.** to attract mates.
   - **b.** to navigate.
   - **c.** to set their biological clocks.
   - **d.** to defend their territory.
10. To defend against predators, an animal might use
    - **a.** camouflage.
    - **b.** warning coloration.
    - **c.** toxins.
    - **d.** All of the above

Short Answer

11. How are pheromones used in communication?

12. What is a territory? Give an example of a territory from your own environment.

13. What landmarks help you navigate your way home from school?

14. What do migration and hibernation have in common?

CONCEPT MAPPING

15. Use the following terms to create a concept map: *estivation, circadian rhythms, seasonal behaviors, hibernation, migration, biological clocks.*

CRITICAL THINKING AND PROBLEM SOLVING

Write one or two sentences to answer each of the following questions:

16. If you smell a skunk while riding in a car and you shut the car window, has the skunk communicated with you? Explain.

17. Flying is an innate behavior in birds. Is it an innate behavior or a learned behavior in humans? Why?

18. Ants depend on pheromones and touch for communication, but birds depend more on sight and sound. Why might these two types of animals communicate differently?

Name ______________________ Date ____________ Class __________

INTERPRETING GRAPHICS

The pie chart below shows the major phyla of the animal species on Earth. Use the chart to answer the questions that follow.

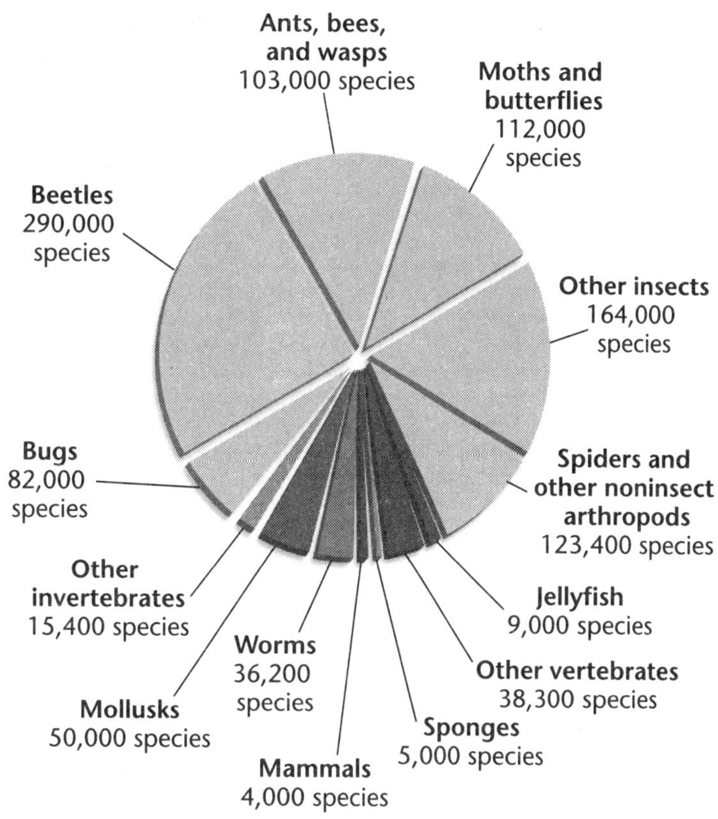

19. What group of animals has the most species?

____

____

____

20. How many species of beetles are on Earth? How does that compare with the number of mammal species?

____

____

21. How many species of vertebrates are known?

____

____

22. Scientists are still discovering new species. Which pie wedges are most likely to increase? Why do you think so?

____

____

____

____

____

____

MATH IN SCIENCE

Use the data from the pie chart to answer the following questions:

23. What is the total number of animal species on Earth?

____

____

24. How many different species of moths and butterflies are on Earth?

____

____

25. What percentage of all animal species are moths and butterflies?

____

____

26. What percentage of all animal species are vertebrates?

____

____

READING CHECK-UP

Take a minute to review your answers to the ScienceLog questions at the beginning of the chapter. Have your answers changed? If necessary, revise your answers based on what you have learned since you began this chapter. Record your revisions in your ScienceLog.

Name ______________________ Date ______________ Class ______________

CHAPTER 1

SCIENCE PUZZLERS, TWISTERS & TEASERS

Animals and Behavior

CHAPTER 1

Complements

1. Unscramble the words in the wheel below. Words opposite each other on the wheel are complementary terms.

a. ______________________ **b.** ______________________

h. ______________________ **c.** ______________________

g. ______________________ **d.** ______________________

f. ______________________ **e.** ______________________

Analogies

2. Give the animal-world equivalent to the human items below.

a. perfume ______________________

b. wearing a suit to the office or the team colors to a football game ______________________

c. house or bedroom ______________________

d. compass ______________________

e. the big red house on the corner or the oak tree across town ______________________

f. winking, frowning, or nodding your head ______________________

Name ______________________ Date __________ Class __________

Crazy 8's

3. Below are vocabulary words from the chapter that all end with the sound *eight*. Use the following clues to help you figure out each word.

a. "Country lodging" ______________________

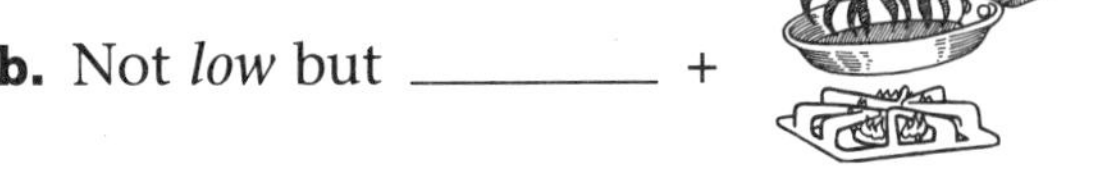

b. Not *low* but ________ + ______________________

c. French for *green* + ______________________

d. Not *yeah*, but ________ + ______________________

e. Not *your*, but ________ + tiger sound ______________________

Strange Birds

4. Almost all rules have exceptions. If the rule has any exceptions, list them in the blanks. If there are no exceptions, write "no exceptions."

a. All animals start life as an embryo. ______________________

b. No animals have cell walls. ______________________

c. No plants are consumers. ______________________

d. All animals are active. ______________________

e. All animals have nuclei. ______________________

Name ______________________ Date ____________ Class ____________

CHAPTER 1 REINFORCEMENT WORKSHEET

What Makes an Animal an Animal?

Complete this worksheet after reading Chapter 1, Section 1.

Whales, armadillos, hummingbirds, spiders… animals come in all shapes and sizes. Not all animals have backbones, and not all animals have hair. So what makes an animal an animal?

Complete the chart below by using the words and phrases at the bottom of the page.

Animal Characteristics

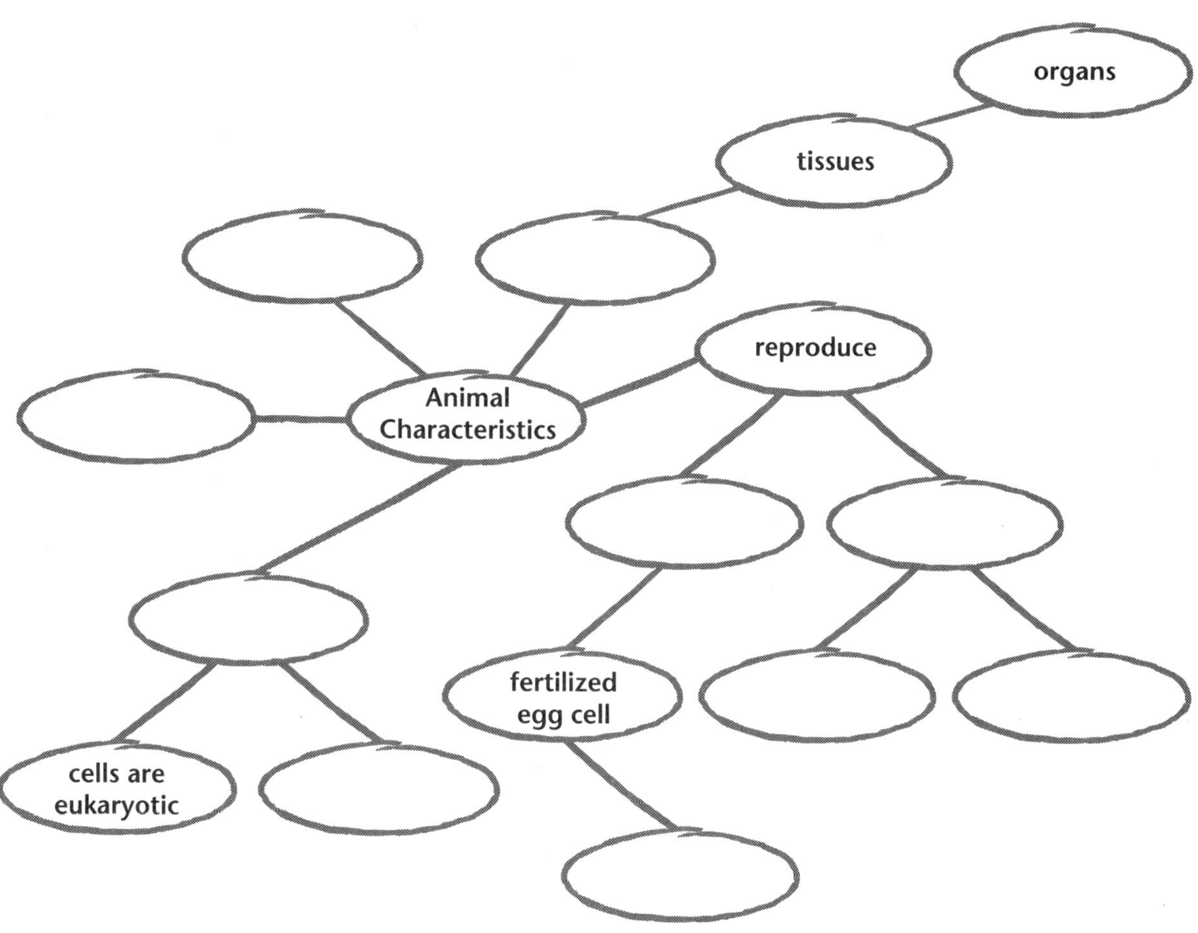

Words and Phrases

- move
- budding
- develop from embryos
- have specialized parts
- sexually
- asexually
- multicellular
- cells have no cell walls
- division
- are consumers

Name ______________________ Date ______________ Class ____________

CHAPTER 1 **REINFORCEMENT WORKSHEET**

Animal Interviews

Complete this worksheet after reading Chapter 1, Section 2.

Imagine that you work with Dr. Phishtof Finz, a researcher who can really talk to the animals. Below are some sections of his taped animal interviews. Your job is to decide what animal behavior or characteristic is being described and to write it in the space provided. Possible answers are *warning coloration, migration, hibernation, estivation,* and *camouflage.*

Interviewed animal		Behavior or characteristic
Canada goose:	During the summer, we stay up in Canada. It's really a nice place in summer, with lots of food and lots of sun. But before the snow starts to fly, we high-tail it south!	____________
Arctic ground squirrel:	What's the winter like in Alaska? Strange, I really don't know. I spend all summer eating and getting my nest ready, but then during the fall I get so sleepy! I go to bed and—*poof!*—when I wake up it's spring!	____________
Desert mouse:	Oh, living in the desert is wonderful! I love sunshine. During the really hot part of the summer, of course, I stay inside my nest, and I nap a lot. It's so much cooler inside.	____________
Ladybug:	Thank you! I am a lovely shade of red, aren't I? But just between you and me, did you know that this beautiful color tells birds that I am, well, rather nasty tasting?	____________
Chameleon:	Yoo-hoo! I'm over here! See? In the potted plant. Well, yes, I am rather proud of being able to turn that particular shade of green. Not all animals can do that, you know.	____________

Name ______________________ Date ______________ Class ____________

CHAPTER 1 VOCABULARY REVIEW WORKSHEET

Puzzling Animal Behavior

After you finish reading Chapter 1, give this crossword puzzle a try!
Solve the clues below, and write the answers in the appropriate spaces in the crossword puzzle.

ACROSS

3. to find one's way from one place to another

4. an organism that eats other organisms

6. this type of behavior can change item 17 down

7. an organism in the earliest stage of development

8. to travel from one place to another in response to the seasons or environmental conditions

10. an internal control of natural cycles

16. an area occupied by an animal or a group of animals from which other members of the species are excluded

18. this type of behavior is the interaction between animals of the same species

19. an animal that eats other animals

20. made of many cells

21. a period of inactivity that some animals experience in winter

DOWN

1. chemicals animals produce for communication

2. an animal without a backbone

5. coloration and/or texture that enables an animal to blend in with its surroundings

7. a period of reduced activity that some animals experience in summer

9. a collection of similar cells that work together to perform a specific job in the body

11. a combination of two or more of item 9 down

12. takes place when a signal travels from one animal to another and the receiver of the signal responds

13. fixed object an animal uses to find its way

14. ________ rhythms are daily cycles.

15. any animal with a skull and a backbone

17. behavior that is influenced by genes and does not depend on learning or experience

22. an animal that is eaten by another animal

Name ______________________ Date ______________ Class ____________

Puzzling Animal Behavior, continued

Name ______________________ Date ____________ Class ____________

CHAPTER 1 CRITICAL THINKING WORKSHEET

Masters of Navigation

FOR MANY PEOPLE, THE MOST INTRIGUING aspects of bird biology and behavior are associated with homing and migration. Several years ago, for example, a friend and I were nest-trapping Blue-winged Teal in Iowa. We captured a female that had been banded the previous year at a nest only thirty-five feet from the present one. I remember stroking her plumage and wondering if she spent the winter in Louisiana, Texas, or Mexico. It didn't make any difference as she certainly hit the bulls-eye on her return. While I found the accuracy of this hen teal to be remarkable, it is not extraordinary by avian standards. . . .

A very dramatic migration is seen in the New Zealand Bronzed Cuckoo. These birds are parasitic, laying their eggs in the nests of host species that hatch and rear the young cuckoos. In the fall, about a month after their parents migrate, the young cuckoos get together and begin migrating to their wintering ground. The birds fly almost 1,200 miles west to Australia and then nearly 1,000 miles north to the Solomon and Bismarck Islands where they join their parents.

USEFUL TERMS

intriguing
exciting interest or curiosity

homing
going home

nest-trapping
trapping birds in their nests for observation

plumage
feathers

avian
of or having to do with birds

parasitic
describes an organism that is dependent upon a host organism for survival, usually without killing its host

Observing for Detail

1. a. Do you think the migration of the Blue-winged Teal is more likely innate or learned behavior? Explain.

____

____

____

____

____

b. Do you think the migration of the New Zealand Bronzed Cuckoo is more likely innate or learned behavior? Explain.

____

____

____

____

____

Demonstrating Reasoned Judgment

2. In order to navigate, birds often use a combination of visual clues, their sense of smell, the Earth's magnetic field, and the sun. Which of these would be more useful in an unfamiliar area? Explain your answer.

____

____

____

____

____

Making Comparisons

3. a. How is the navigation of migratory birds similar to the navigation of an airplane pilot?

____

____

____

b. How is the navigation of migratory birds different from the navigation of an airplane pilot?

____

____

____

Making Inferences

4. Migration patterns vary among different species of birds. List three factors that might cause migration patterns to vary.

____

____

____

____

____

Name ______________________ Date ____________ Class ____________

CHAPTER 1 MATH SKILLS

Percentages, Fractions, and Decimals

Imagine that your science class is doing a school survey to determine which eye colors are most common. The report from the sixth-grade class says that $\frac{3}{5}$ of the students have black or brown eyes, while $\frac{2}{5}$ have blue or green eyes. The seventh-grade class reports that 45 percent have black or brown eyes, and 55 percent have blue or green eyes. The eighth-grade class reports that 0.8 have black or brown eyes, and 0.2 have blue or green eyes. Yikes! Each class has a different way of showing its data! So how do you compare the reports? Well, it's not as complicated as it might look. You see, percentages, fractions, and decimals are just different ways of expressing the same information. Each one tells you *how much* or *how many* of a certain amount. As you learned on the last page, a percentage can be changed to a decimal. For example, 45 percent is equal to 0.45. Percentages can also be changed into fractions. Likewise, every fraction can be expressed as a decimal or percentage, and so on. When comparing numbers or doing operations with numbers, it is often easier to have all of your numbers in the same form before doing calculations.

PROCEDURE 1: To change a fraction to a decimal or percentage, divide the numerator of the fraction by the denominator to make a decimal. To change the decimal number into a percentage, move the decimal point two places to the *right.*

SAMPLE PROBLEM: Change $\frac{3}{5}$ into a decimal number and a percentage.

Step 1: Divide the numerator by the denominator.

$$3 \div 5 = 0.6$$

Step 2: To change the decimal into a percentage, move the decimal point two places to the right.

$$0.6 \rightarrow 0.60 \rightarrow \mathbf{60\%}$$

PROCEDURE 2: To change a decimal number into a fraction or percentage, place the decimal over its place value and reduce. To change a decimal into a percentage, see Step 2 of Procedure 1.

SAMPLE PROBLEM: Express 0.56 as a fraction and a percentage.

Step 1: Because 0.56 is in the *hundredths* place, put the whole number over 100 and reduce.

$$\frac{56}{100} = \frac{14}{25}$$

Step 2: To change a decimal into a percentage, move the decimal point two places to the right, as in step 2 of procedure 1.

$$0.56 \rightarrow 0.56 \rightarrow 56\%$$

Practice What You've Learned

1. Express the following percentages as decimal numbers:

a. 52% ______________ **b.** 99% ______________

c. 7.8% ______________ **d.** 0.57% ______________

2. Express the following fractions as both a decimal number and a percentage.

a. $\frac{75}{100}$ = ______________ **b.** $\frac{1}{8}$ = ______________

c. $\frac{9}{20}$ = ______________ **d.** $\frac{12}{4}$ = ______________

e. $\frac{26}{13}$ = ______________ **f.** $\frac{8}{32}$ = ______________

3. Change the following decimal numbers into both a fraction and a percentage:

a. 0.3 = ______________ **b.** 0.12 = ______________

c. 0.99 = ______________ **d.** 1.5 = ______________

e. 0.505 = ______________ **f.** 0.01 = ______________

4. Write True or False next to each equation.

a. $2\frac{2}{5} = 2.4 = 24\%$ ______________

b. $0.03 = 3\% = \frac{3}{100}$ ______________

c. $0.45\% = \frac{90}{200} = 0.0045$ ______________

d. $5.25 = 5\frac{14}{28} = 525\%$ ______________

5. Convert the following equations into the same form and calculate. Hint: Do the calculation inside the parentheses before adding or subtracting.

a. $\frac{2}{5} + 0.12 =$ ______________

b. $(75\% \text{ of } 60) - 3\frac{3}{5} =$ ______________

c. $\frac{32}{8} - (15\% \text{ of } 20) =$ ______________

Name ______________________ Date ____________ Class ____________

CHAPTER 1 MATH SKILLS

Average, Mode, and Median

Although an average, or mean, is the most common way to simplify a list of numbers, there are other mathematical tools that can help you work with lists of numbers. **Mode** is the number or value that appears most often in a particular set of numbers. **Median** is the number that falls in the *numerical center* of a list of numbers. Read on to find out how to find mode and median.

PROCEDURE: *To find the mode,* list your numbers in numerical order. Then determine which number appears most often in the set. That number is the mode. **Note:** A list of numbers may have more than one mode. If no number appears more often than the others, that series of numbers does not have a mode.

SAMPLE PROBLEM: Find the mode of 4, 3, 6, 10, and 3.

Step 1: List the numbers in numerical order.

3, 3, 4, 6, 10

Step 2: Determine the number that appears most often in the set.

3, 3, 4, 6, 10

The mode of 4, 3, 6, 10, and 3 is **3.**

PROCEDURE: *To find the median,* list the numbers in numerical order. Next determine the number that appears in the middle of the set. **Note:** If more than one number falls in the middle, the median is the average of those numbers.

SAMPLE PROBLEM: Find the median of 25, 22, 24, 19, 25, 14, 26, and 15.

Step 1: List the numbers in numerical order.

14, 15, 19, 22, 24, 25, 25, 26

Step 2: Determine which number falls in the middle of the set.

14, 15, 19, 22, 24, 25, 25, 26

Because two numbers fall in the middle (22 and 24), the median is their average.

Median = (22 + 24) ÷ 2 = **23**

Get in the Mode!

1. Find the mode and median for the following sets of numbers:

a. 37, 30, 35, 37, 32, 40, 34

Mode ________ Median ________

b. 19, 29, 9, 12, 10

Mode ________ Median ________

c. 109, 84, 88, 107, 84, 94

Mode ________ Median ________

d. 26, 53, 39, 53, 49, 56, 35, 26

Mode ________ Median ________

e. 25 m, 24 m, 27 m, 27 m, 49 m, 47 m, 45 m

Mode ________ Median ________

f. 98 L, 99 L, 101 L, 111 L, 132 L, 103 L

Mode ________ Median ________

CHAPTER 1

Peregrine Falcons—How Fast Can They Fly?

The peregrine falcon is the fastest bird in the world. It can reach speeds of almost 300 km/h when hunting. An ornithologist, a scientist who studies birds, has gathered the data in the chart below to try to learn exactly how fast the falcons can fly. Use what you have learned about averages, modes, and medians to analyze some of the birds' top speeds.

Falcon Flight Speeds*

Day	Falcon A	Falcon B	Falcon C	Falcon D	Falcon E
1	189	199	211	253	199
2	275	261	241	235	279
3	262	225	271	190	271
4	203	199	223	185	265
5	241	227	209	199	253
6	222	240	265	253	232
7	203	203	240	260	279

*All flight speeds are in km/h.

2. What was the average top speed of Falcon B for the entire week?

____

____

3. What were the modes for Falcon D and Falcon E for the entire week?

____

____

4. Which had a faster median speed for the week, Falcon A or Falcon B?

____

____

____

5. What were the median speeds for Falcon B and Falcon D for days 1–6?

____

____

____

Name ______________________ Date ____________ Class ____________

CHAPTER 1 COMMUNICATING SKILLS

Introduction to Graphs

Examine the following table and graph:

Grade Distribution for Students Enrolled in Science Class

Grade	Number of students
A	22
B	79
C	50
D	9
F	2

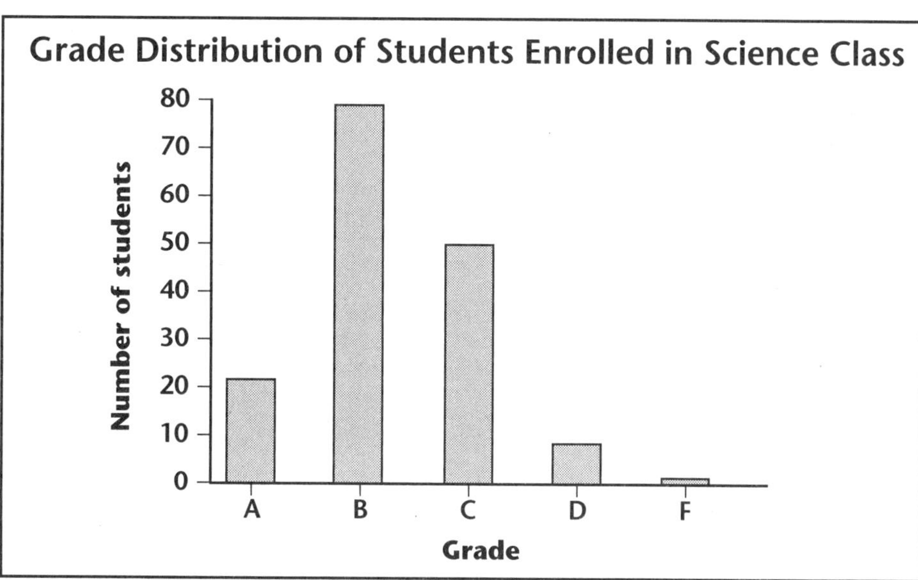

1. Both of these figures display the same information but in different ways. Which figure is easier to understand? Explain why you think so.

____

____

____

2. If you need to get specific data, such as the exact number of students who earned a B, which figure would you use? Explain your answer.

____

____

Choosing the Right Graph

Data tables provide an organized way of viewing information, and **graphs** are *pictures* of the information in a data table. Sometimes it is faster and easier to interpret data by looking at a graph. It is important to choose the type of graph that best illustrates your data. The following table summarizes the best uses for three of the most common graphs:

<table>
<tr><th>Type of graph</th><th>Best use for this graph</th></tr>
<tr><td>

Bar graph

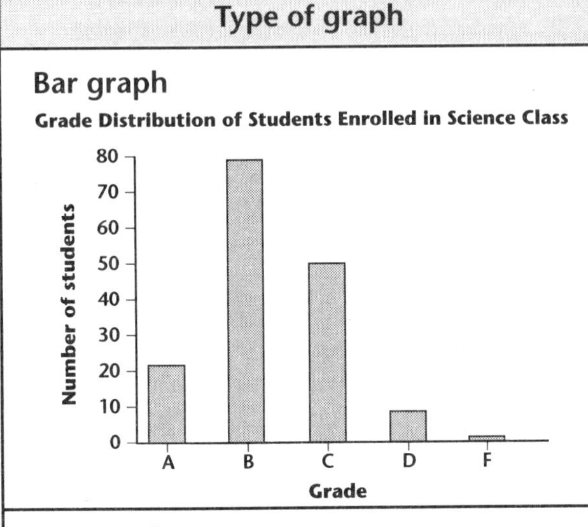

</td><td>A bar graph is best used for comparing data quickly and easily, such as the grade distribution of students enrolled in science class or the growth of plants in different pots.</td></tr>
<tr><td>

Pie graph

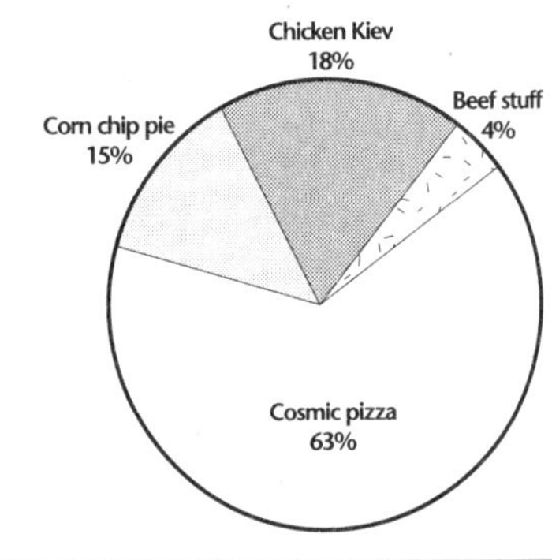

</td><td>A pie graph is best used for showing percentages, such as the percentage of the student body who picked certain entrees for lunch or the percentage of your allowance that will go toward purchasing various things.</td></tr>
<tr><td>

Line graph

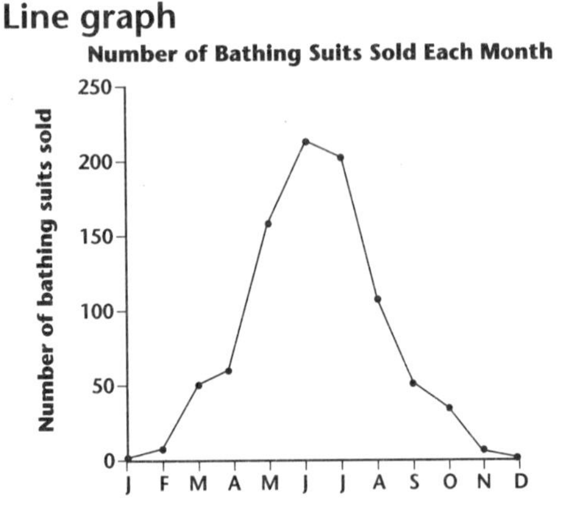

</td><td>A line graph is best used for looking at changes over time, such as the number of bathing suits sold each month during the year or the change in your sister's height throughout the year.</td></tr>
</table>

Name ______________________ Date ____________ Class ____________

Choose the Graph

What graph type do you think best presents each set of data? Explain.

1. The percentage of rabbits preferring various foods

Food	Percentage preferring that food
Skippy's Rabbit Chow	32
Homemade rabbit food	13
Happy Rabbit	10
Joe's Special Food for Rabbits	44
Premium Rabbit Nutrition Diet	1

____

____

2. Albert's grades for each month of the school year

Month	Grade in science class
September	98
October	94
November	88
December	78
January	82

Month	Grade in science class
February	83
March	86
April	81
May	97

____

____

3. The pH of solutions in experimental test tubes

Test-tube number	pH
1	6.7
2	7.1
3	7.4
4	7.1
5	7.0

____

____

Name ______________________ Date ____________ Class ____________

CHAPTER 1 LAB DATASHEET

Wet, Wiggly Worms!

Earthworms have been digging in the Earth for more than 100 million years! Earthworms fertilize the soil with their waste and loosen the soil when they tunnel through the moist dirt of a garden or lawn. Worms are food for many animals, such as birds, frogs, snakes, rodents, and fish. Some say they are good food for people, too!

In this activity, you will observe the behavior of a live earthworm. Remember that earthworms are living animals that deserve to be handled gently and with respect. Be sure to keep your earthworm moist during this activity. The skin of the earthworm must stay moist so that the worm can get oxygen. If the earthworm's skin dries out, the worm will suffocate and die. Use a spray bottle to moisten the earthworm with water.

MATERIALS

- spray bottle
- dissecting pan
- paper towels
- water
- live earthworm
- probe
- celery leaves
- flashlight
- shoe box with lid
- clock
- soil
- metric ruler

Procedure

1. Place a wet paper towel in the bottom of a dissecting pan. Put a live earthworm on the paper towel, and observe how the earthworm moves. Record your observations.

   ____

   ____

2. Use the probe to carefully touch the anterior end (head) of the worm. Gently touch other areas of the worm's body with the probe. Record the kinds of responses you observe.

   ____

   ____

3. Shine a flashlight on the anterior end of the earthworm. Record the earthworm's reaction to the light.

   ____

   ____

4. Place celery leaves at one end of the pan. Record how the earthworm responds to the presence of food.

   ____

   ____

5. Line the bottom of the shoe box with a damp paper towel. Cover half of the shoe box with the box top.

6. Place the worm on the uncovered side of the shoe box in the light. Record your observations of the worm's behavior for 3 minutes.

7. Place the worm on the covered side of the box. Record your observations of the worm's behavior for 3 minutes.

8. Repeat steps 6–7 three times.

9. Spread some loose soil evenly in the bottom of the shoe box so that it is about 4 cm deep. Place the earthworm on top of the soil. Observe and record the earthworm's behavior for 3 minutes.

10. Dampen the soil on one side of the box, and leave the other side dry. Place the earthworm in the center of the box between the wet and dry soil. Cover the box, and wait 3 minutes. Uncover the box, and record your observations. Repeat this procedure 3 times. (You may need to search for the worm!)

Analysis

11. How did the earthworm respond to being touched?

____

____

____

Were some areas more sensitive than others?

____

____

____

12. How is the earthworm's behavior influenced by light?

____

____

____

Based on your observations, describe how an animal's response to a stimulus might provide protection for the animal.

____

____

13. How did the earthworm respond to the presence of food?

____

____

14. When the worm was given a choice of wet or dry soil, which did it choose? Explain this result.

____

____

Name ______________________ Date ____________ Class ____________

CHAPTER 1 LAB DATASHEET

Aunt Flossie and the Bumblebee

Last week Aunt Flossie came to watch the soccer game, and she was chased by a big yellow-and-black bumblebee. Everyone tried not to laugh, but Aunt Flossie did look pretty funny. She was running and screaming, all perfumed and dressed in a bright floral dress, shiny jewelry, and a huge hat with a big purple bow. No one could understand why the bumblebee tormented Aunt Flossie and left everyone else alone. She said that she would not come to another game until you determine why the bee chased her.

Your job is to design an experiment that will determine why the bee was attracted to Aunt Flossie. You may simulate the situation by using objects that contain the same sensory clues that Aunt Flossie wore that day—bright, shiny colors and strong scents.

MATERIALS

- to be determined by each experimental design and approved by the teacher

SCIENTIFIC METHOD

Ask a Question

1. Use the information in the story above to help you form questions. Make a list of Aunt Flossie's characteristics on the day of the soccer game. What was Aunt Flossie wearing? What do you think she looked like to a bumblebee? What scent was she wearing? Which of those characteristics may have affected the bee's behavior? What was it about Aunt Flossie that affected the bee's behavior?

____

____

____

____

____

____

Form a Hypothesis

2. Write a hypothesis about insect behavior based on your observations of Aunt Flossie and the bumblebee at the soccer game. A possible hypothesis is, "Insects are attracted to strong floral scents." Write your own hypothesis.

____

____

____

____

Test the Hypothesis

3. Outline a procedure for your experiment. Be sure to follow the steps in the scientific method. Design your procedure to answer specific questions. For example, if you want to know if insects are attracted to different colors, you might want to display cutouts of several colors of paper.

4. Make a list of materials for your experiment. You may want to include colored paper, pictures in magazines, or strong perfumes as bait. **You may not** use living things as bait in your experiment. Your teacher must approve your experimental design before you begin.

5. Determine a place to conduct your experiment. For example, you may want to place your materials in a box on the ground, or you may want to hang items from a tree branch. **Caution:** Be sure to remain at a safe distance from your experimental setup containing the bait. Do not touch any insects. Have an adult help you release any insects that are trapped or collected.

Name ______________________________ Date ______________ Class ______________

Effects of Color

Color	Number of bees	Number of ants	Number of wasps
Red			
Blue			
Yellow			

6. Develop data tables for recording the results of your trials. For example, a data table similar to the one at left may be used to record the results of testing different colors to see which insects are attracted to them. Design your data tables to fit your investigation.

Analyze the Results

7. Describe your experimental procedure. Did your results support your hypothesis? Explain.

8. Compare your results with those of your classmates. Which hypotheses were supported?

What conclusions can you draw from the class results?

Communicate Results

9. On the back of this page or on a separate piece of paper, write a letter to Aunt Flossie telling her what you have learned. Tell her what caused the bee attack. Invite her to attend another soccer game, and advise her about what she should or should not wear!

CHAPTER 1 TEACHER-LED DEMONSTRATION

Six-Legged Thermometer

Purpose

Students observe the effect of temperature on the frequency of a cricket's chirping and learn how an animal's behavior may be affected by its environment.

Time Required

10–15 minutes

Lab Ratings

EASY → HARD

TEACHER PREP 3

CONCEPT LEVEL 2

CLEAN UP 1

MATERIALS

- 2 mature male crickets (available in many bait and pet stores)
- 2 glass jars
- 2 nylon stockings
- 2 rubber bands
- refrigerator
- watch or a clock that indicates seconds
- Fahrenheit thermometer

Advance Preparation

Only the mature male crickets will chirp. Keep each cricket in a separate container; male crickets are extremely territorial and have a tendency to kill other males.

You may wish to try this activity in advance. First put one cricket in each jar. Cover each jar with a nylon stocking, and secure the stocking with a rubber band. (Be sure the stocking is stretched enough to allow sufficient oxygen into the jars.) Leave one jar at room temperature. Leave the other in the refrigerator long enough to slow the chirping of the cricket significantly but not so long that the cricket is harmed. Note: Conduct this activity as soon as you remove the jar from the refrigerator. Record the temperature of the refrigerator in degrees Fahrenheit.

What to Do

1. Have students observe the cricket in the refrigerated jar. Ask them to count the number of chirps the cricket makes in 15 seconds and then to add 40 to that number. Record both numbers on the board.
2. Record the temperature of the refrigerator in degrees Fahrenheit on the board. Point out the similarity between this number and the data from step 1; they should be roughly equal.
3. Have students repeat step 1 with the other cricket.
4. Measure and record the temperature of the room in degrees Fahrenheit. Again, the temperature of the room and the data from step 3 should be almost equal.

Discussion

Use the following questions as a guide to encourage class discussion:

- What can you conclude from your observations? *(Sample answer: There is a relationship between temperature and chirping frequency. A cricket can serve as a kind of thermometer.)*
- If we refer to the number of chirps in 15 seconds as degrees cricket, what is the corresponding temperature in degrees cricket for 82° F? *(82 – 40 = 42 degrees cricket)*

Kevin A. Tierney
Rolling Hills Middle School
El Dorado, California

CHAPTER 1 TEACHER'S PREPARATORY GUIDE

DISCOVERY LAB

Follow the Leader

Purpose

Students observe ant behavior to form a theory about how ants navigate.

Time Required

One 45-minute class period

Lab Ratings

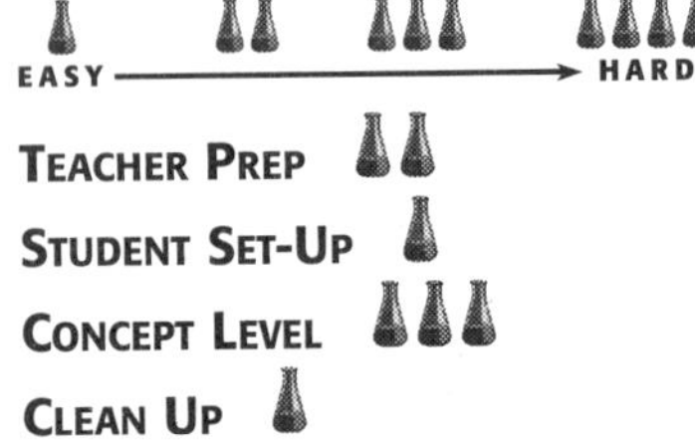

Advance Preparation

Obtain an ant colony from a biological supply house. Cans of compressed air are sold in photographic or computer supply stores. Dissolve 15 mL of sugar (1 tbsp) in 63 mL ($\frac{1}{4}$ cup) of tap water to make ant food.

Place a jar lid filled with ant food in one end of the aquarium. Place the ant colony in the other end. Place a plastic transparency sheet on the floor of the aquarium, between the ant colony and the jar lid. Seal the top of the aquarium to keep the ants from escaping. The ants should establish a trail from the nest to the food within a few hours. Perform this activity ahead of time to anticipate the ants' behavior.

Safety Information

Emphasize the importance of the humane treatment of lab animals. Do not permit students to touch the ants. If a student is bitten by an ant, a paste of baking soda and water will neutralize the formic acid in the bite. Be sure students keep the compressed air away from heat and their faces.

Teaching Strategies

This activity works best in groups of 4–6 students. Model for students the steps of the activity, including the rotation of the plastic sheet, the blowing of the air, and the wiping of the sheet. You may wish to conduct this activity as a teacher demonstration. After placing the aquarium on a stable surface, call up the groups individually to observe the ants' behavior.

While groups are waiting to observe the ant colony, ask students to draw and label the parts of an ant's anatomy. Encourage discussion about what part of the anatomy an ant might use to direct other ants. For example, do ants wave an arm? Do they shake their heads or transmit signals through their antennae? Do ants "follow the leader" with their eyes? Do they use their sense of smell? Do they "speak" to one another in some way?

After the activity, help students make sense of what they learned by discussing the role of ant pheromones—chemical signals used for communication. Explain that when ants travel, they leave behind a chemical trail for others to follow. A well-used trail has an abundance of pheromones that make it easy for other ants to follow. If the trail is disturbed, ants will stop to search for the continuation of the trail.

Ants are not the only animals that communicate with pheromones. Fish use pheromones to trigger spawning. Some mammals and reptiles release pheromones to mark their territories and to ward off potential intruders. They also use pheromones as a signal to initiate courtship.

Evaluation Strategies

For help evaluating this lab, see the Teacher Evaluation of Lesson in the *Assessment Checklists & Rubrics*. This checklist is also available in the *One-Stop Planner CD-ROM*.

Elizabeth Rustad
Crane Jr. High School
Yuma, Arizona

Name ______________________ Date ____________ Class ____________

CHAPTER 1 STUDENT WORKSHEET

DISCOVERY LAB

Follow the Leader

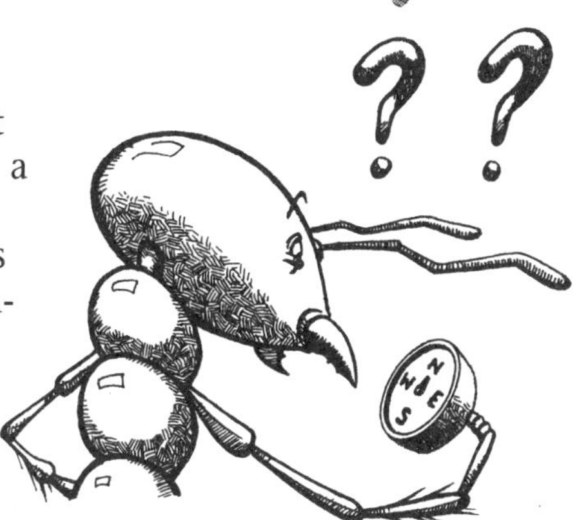

How do you find your way around in an unfamiliar place? You probably use a variety of tools; you might use a map, a compass, verbal directions, or even hire a guide. How do other animals navigate in unfamiliar territory? Birds respond to a variety of calls, dolphins and bats use sonar, and bees use visual cues and communicate directions in an elaborate, buzzing dance.

But how do ants find their way around? In this lab, you will discover that ants have an unusual way of finding their way to and from their anthill.

MATERIALS

- ant colony
- large, empty aquarium
- 15 mL of sugar
- jar lid
- tap water
- plastic transparency sheets
- sheet of paper
- 3–6 magnifying glasses
- can of compressed air
- damp sponge
- paper towels

SAFETY ALERT!

Do not touch the ants. Some ants bite.

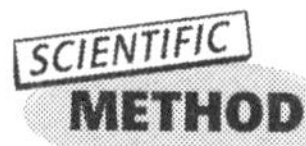

Ask a Question

How do ants navigate?

Make Observations

1. Observe the ants traveling to and from the food dish for 2–3 minutes. Record all of your observations.

____

____

____

____

Make a Prediction

2. How do you think ants find their way to and from food and water?

____

____

____

Conduct an Experiment

3. Slide a sheet of paper beneath the plastic that lines the bottom of the box. How does the paper affect the behavior of the ants? Record your observations.

____

____

____

4. While the ants are still on the plastic sheet, rotate the sheet 90° so that it is perpendicular to the original orientation. Record your observations.

____

____

____

5. Continue to observe the ants. Do the ants find their original destination?

____

____

____

6. Carefully rotate the plastic sheet back to its original position. How do the ants respond?

____

____

____

7. Describe the signal you think the ants are using to navigate.

____

____

____

SAFETY ALERT!

Keep the compressed can of air away from heat and away from people's faces.

Remember the importance of humane treatment of lab animals.

8. Use the can of compressed air to GENTLY blow the ants from a section of the plastic sheet. Practice using the can first to avoid harming the ants. Observe whether the ants reestablish their path.

9. Now blow the ants from the plastic and quickly wipe a section of the ant path clean with a damp sponge, and dry the area with a paper towel. Observe the ants' behavior, and record your observations below.

____

____

____

____

10. What do your observations tell you about the signal the ants follow?

11. Continue to observe the ants for several minutes. What change, if any, do you observe from their behavior in step 9?

Analyze the Results

12. Look over your answers in steps 3–11. List every method that ants might use to navigate. Which method do you think is the most important and why?

13. So, was your prediction in step 2 correct? Explain your answer.

Name ______________________ Date ______________ Class ______________

CHAPTER 1 STUDENT PROJECT WORKSHEET

Animal-Myth Behaviors

Have you heard about lemmings—small mammals that live in the Arctic and that gather by the thousands every few years to make suicide jumps into icy rivers? Do you think it's true? Well, not completely. When a population of lemmings gets too big, many of them migrate to find food, sometimes crossing large streams or lakes in their search. Countless lemmings die in this bold attempt to find food, which led some people to believe that the lemmings were throwing themselves into the water on purpose.

Fact or Fiction?

1. Do vampire bats drink human blood? Can salamanders walk through fire? Do Texas horned toads spit blood from their eyes? You may have heard a lot of amazing stories about animals—but are they true? Investigate some of the fantastic animal behaviors you've heard about and find out the facts. Write an article for your school paper describing the animals' unusual behaviors.

Another Research Idea

2. How have wild animals adapted to urban and suburban environments? Research animals that have suffered a loss of natural habitat, such as squirrels, coyotes, hawks, raccoons, deer, and pigeons. Which animals have adapted well to living among humans and which have not? Why are some animals more successful at city living than others? Create a poster display highlighting your findings.

Long-Term Project Ideas

3. Research shows that contact with a pet has a calming effect on people. Design and carry out an experiment to test how holding an animal affects the heart rate and blood pressure of people. You might want to test the human response to different animals, being sure to keep all of the other factors the same. Share your findings by using charts, graphs, and photos.

4. Do animals act differently in captivity than they do in the wild? Pick an active animal at a zoo, and observe and record its behaviors for an hour. Then research the animal's natural behavior. Do the behaviors in the zoo match the behaviors you'd expect to see in the wild? If not, can you think of reasons for the differences? Videotape your zoo animal, and share the tape with your class. If possible, also show video footage of your animal in the wild. Include a description of the animal's natural and captive behaviors.

HELPFUL HINT

Focus on specific behaviors, like how it eats, when and how long it sleeps, how often it moves around, and how it responds to people.

Name ______________________ Date ______________ Class ______________

CHAPTER 1 ANIMALS AND BEHAVIOR

Chapter 1 Test

USING VOCABULARY

To complete the following sentences, choose the correct term from each pair of terms listed, and write the term in the blank.

1. All animals are ______________________ and have eukaryotic cells. (vertebrates or multicellular)
2. A collection of similar cells is known as a(n) ______________________. (organ or tissue)
3. ______________________ is an animal's internal control of natural cycles. (Hibernation or The biological clock)
4. All animals are ______________________. (predators or consumers)
5. Some animals use the Earth's magnetic field to ______________________. (communicate or navigate)

UNDERSTANDING CONCEPTS

Multiple Choice

Circle the correct answer.

6. __________ is NOT an example of how animals might deal with a food shortage.
   a. Migration
   b. Estivation
   c. Social behavior
   d. Hibernation
7. Reading is an example of
   a. an innate behavior.
   b. a behavior controlled by genes.
   c. a learned behavior.
   d. an inherited behavior.
8. All __________ lack a skull and backbone.
   a. vertebrates
   b. eukaryotes
   c. multicellular organisms
   d. invertebrates
9. Which statement about communication between animals is false?
   a. Animals use it to find mates.
   b. It helps animals find their food.
   c. It helps animals avoid enemies.
   d. It occurs only between members of the same species.
10. The relationship between a worm and a robin can be expressed as
    a. vertebrate : invertebrate.
    b. prey : predator.
    c. producer : consumer.
    d. prokaryote : eukaryote.
11. The use of __________ is an example of chemical communication.
    a. camouflage
    b. pheromones
    c. hibernation
    d. estivation

12. Any animal with a skull and a backbone is classified as
   a. a vertebrate.
   b. a consumer.
   c. a mammal.
   d. multicellular.

Short Answer

13. Humans are able to navigate short distances in the dark if they are in a familiar area. Explain how this is done.

____

____

____

____

14. A male hanging fly will dangle a dead moth as a present for a future mate. The female hanging fly will choose as her mate the fly offering the largest dead moth. What form of communication is the male hanging fly using?

____

____

____

____

____

CRITICAL THINKING AND PROBLEM SOLVING

15. Describe four types of communication that dogs use.

____

____

____

____

____

____

____

____

MATH IN SCIENCE

16. There are approximately 21,000 known species of fish, 3,900 known species of amphibians, 7,000 known species of reptiles, 8,600 known species of birds, and 4,500 known species of mammals. What percentage of known vertebrate species are fish? Show your work.

____

____

____

____

CONCEPT MAPPING

17. Use the following terms to complete the concept map below: animals, multicellular, consumers, predators, prey.

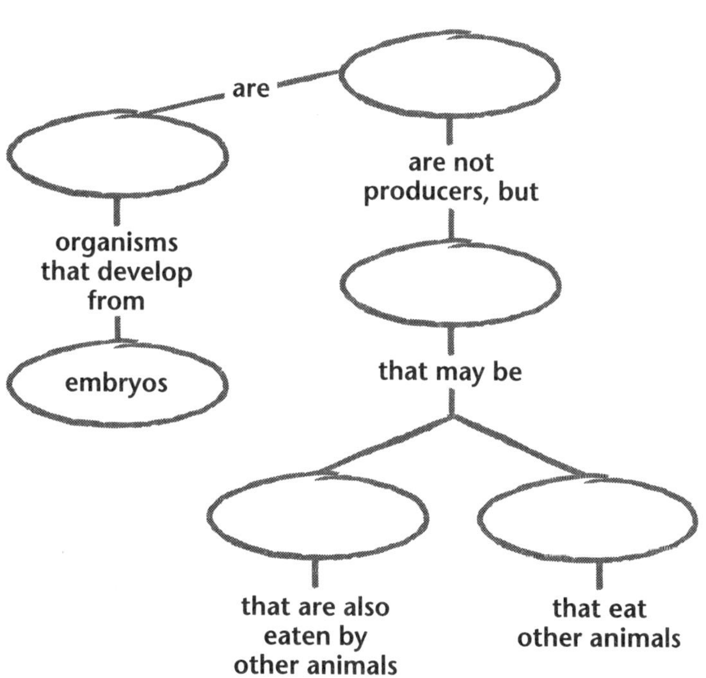

Name ______________________ Date __________ Class __________

INTERPRETING GRAPHICS

The graph below shows the relationship between the life span of primates and their dependence on parents and family. Examine the graph, and answer the questions that follow.

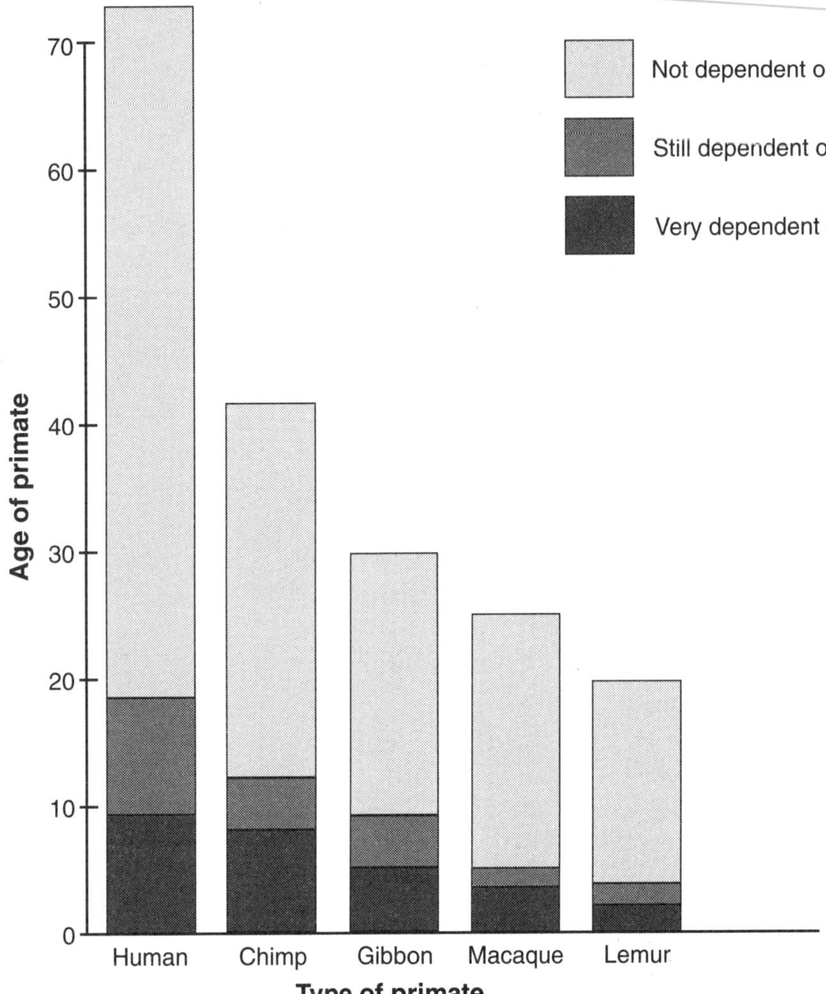

18. a. According to the graph, how does a primate's dependence on its parents and family relate to its life span?

____

____

____

b. Why do you think this relationship exists?

____

____

____

Name ______________________ Date ____________ Class ____________

CHAPTER

1 ANIMALS AND BEHAVIOR

Chapter 1 Performance-Based Assessment

TEACHER'S PREPARATORY GUIDE

Purpose

Students will use scents and sign language to communicate ideas.

Time Required

One 45-minute class period

P. B. A. Ratings

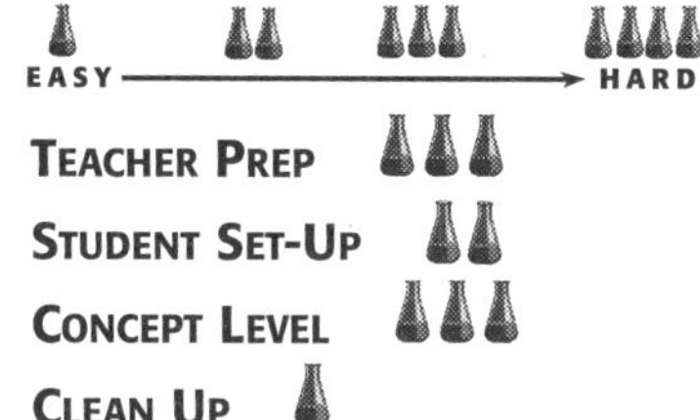

Advance Preparation

Equip each activity station with the necessary materials. Each station should have at least five distinct, recognizable scents. To prepare a scent sample, place a cotton ball in a film canister or some similar small sealable container. Saturate the cotton with vanilla extract, garlic oil, vinegar, lemon oil, peppermint oil, etc.

Safety Information

Ask students if anyone is allergic to any of the scented substances.

Teaching Strategies

This activity works best in pairs.

Susan Gorman
Northridge Middle School
North Richland Hills, Texas

Evaluation Strategies

Use the following rubric to help evaluate student performance.

Rubric for Chapter 1 Assessment

Possible points	Appropriate use of materials and equipment (30 points possible)
30–20	Successfully completes activity; safe and careful handling of materials and equipment; attention to detail; superior lab skills
19–10	Task is generally complete; successful use of materials and equipment; sound knowledge of lab techniques; somewhat unfocused performance
9–1	Tasks yield inadequate results; sloppy lab technique; apparent lack of effort
	Quality and clarity of procedure (50 points possible)
50–35	Superior observations stated clearly and accurately; high level of detail
34–20	Accurate observations; moderate level of detail
19–10	Observations are complete but expressed in unclear manner; may include minor inaccuracies
9–1	Erroneous, incomplete, or unclear observations; lack of accuracy or details
	Explanation of observations (20 points possible)
20–15	Clear, detailed explanation that shows superior knowledge of how pheromones work; use of examples to support explanations
14–10	Adequate understanding of the function of pheromones; minor difficulty in expression
9–1	Poor understanding of pheromones; explanation unclear or not relevant to animal communication; substantial factual errors

Name ______________________ Date ____________ Class ____________

CHAPTER 1 ANIMALS AND BEHAVIOR

Chapter 1 Performance-Based Assessment

Objective

Animals use pheromones and body language to communicate. In this activity, you will use scents (as pheromones) and body language to communicate something to your partner.

Know the Score!

As you work through the activity, keep in mind that you will be earning a grade for the following:

- how you work with the materials and equipment (30%)
- how you work out a code for communication (50%)
- how you analyze animal communication (20%)

MATERIALS

- various scents

Procedure

1. Examine the scents you have been given. With your partner, decide on a "code" for each scent. For example, vanilla could be used to show feelings of happiness. Describe the meaning of each scent below.

Scent	Meaning

2. Without discussing it with your partner, think of an idea you would like to communicate to him or her. You will be allowed to use only physical movements and the scents you were given. What will you communicate?

____

____

____

3. Communicate your idea to your partner using only movements and scents. Was the idea made clear? If not, why not?

4. Switch roles and repeat steps 2 and 3. Did you understand the idea your partner tried to communicate to you? If not, why not?

5. What senses do humans use to communicate with other humans?

6. How close did you need to be to your partner to smell each scent he or she used for his or her idea?

7. What kinds of movements do animals use to communicate with other animals? For example, a dog shows his teeth to show aggression.

Name ______________________ Date __________ Class __________

Module B
Chapter 2: Invertebrates
Lesson Plan
Section 1: Simple Invertebrates

Pacing

1 Block = 45 minutes

Regular Schedule:	**with Lab(s):** N/A	**without Lab(s):** 2 Days
Block Schedule:	**with Lab(s):** N/A	**without Lab(s):** 1 Day

Objectives

1. Describe the difference between radial and bilateral symmetry.
2. Describe the function of a coelom.
3. Explain how sponges are different from other animals.
4. Describe the differences in the simple nervous systems of cnidarians and flatworms.

Standards Covered

Unifying Concepts and Processes (UCP)

UCP 1. Systems, order, and organization
UCP 3. Change, constancy, and measurement
UCP 4. Evolution and equilibrium
UCP 5. Form and function

Science As Inquiry (SAI)

SAI 1. Abilities necessary to do scientific inquiry

Science in Personal and Social Perspectives (SPSP)

SPSP 3. Natural hazards
SPSP 4. Risks and Benefits

Life Science (LS)

Structure and Function in Living Systems (LS 1)

1a. Living systems at all levels of organization demonstrate the complementary nature of structure and function. Important levels of organization from structure and function include cells, tissues, organs, organs systems, whole organisms, and ecosystems.

1d. Specialized cells perform specialized functions in multicellular organisms. Groups of specialized cells cooperate to form a tissue, such as a muscle. Different tissues are in turn grouped together to form larger functional units, called organs. Each type of cell, tissue, and the organ has a distinct structure and set of functions that serve the organism as a whole.

1f. Disease is the breakdown in structures or functions of an organism. Some diseases are the result of intrinsic failures of a body system. Others are the result of damage by infection by other organisms.

Reproduction and Heredity (LS 2)

2a. Reproduction is a characteristic of all living systems; because no individual organism lives forever, reproduction is essential to the continuation of every species. Some organisms reproduce asexually. Others reproduce sexually.

Regulation and Behavior (LS 3)

3a. All organisms must be able to obtain and use resources, grow, reproduce, and maintain stable internal conditions while living in a constantly changing external environment.

3b. Regulation of an organism's internal environment involves sensing its environment and changing physiological activities to keep conditions within the range required for the organism to survive.

3c. Behavior is one kind of response an organism can make to an internal or environmental stimulus. A behavioral response requires coordination and communication at many levels, including cells, organ systems, and whole organisms. Behavioral response is a set of actions determined partially by heredity and partially from experience.

Populations and Ecosystems (LS 4)

4b. Populations of organisms can be categorized by the function they serve in an ecosystem. Plants and some microorganisms are producers—they make their own food. All animals, including humans, are consumers, which obtain food by eating other organisms. Decomposers, primarily bacteria and fungi, are consumers that use waste materials and dead organisms for food. Food webs identify the relationship among producers, consumers, and decomposers in an ecosystem.

Diversity and Adaptations of Organisms (LS 5)

5a. Millions of species of animals, plants, and microorganisms are alive today. Although different species might look dissimilar, the unity among organisms becomes apparent from analysis of internal structures, the similarity of their chemical processes, and the evidence of common ancestry.

Key
PE = Pupil's Edition
ATE = Annotated Teacher's Edition
An asterisk indicates the item is part of the Unit Resource booklet for this unit.

Name ______________________ Date ______________ Class ______________

Block 1

Focus *5 minutes*

______ **Bellringer,** ATE p. 28. Pose the following questions to your students: What is an invertebrate? What is your favorite invertebrate? What special features does this invertebrate have that help it survive in its environment? Have students write their answers in their ScienceLog.

Motivate *10 minutes*

______ **Activity,** "Determining Symmetry," ATE p. 28. Divide students into cooperative groups of three or four. Distribute to each group copies of simple, top-view drawings of a butterfly and a sea urchin and a small, rectangular hand mirror (mirrors without frames work best). Challenge students to use the mirror to demonstrate that the butterfly is bilaterally symmetrical and that the sea urchin is radially symmetrical. Encourage students to discuss their findings as a class.

Teach *30 minutes*

______ **Using the Figure,** ATE p. 29. Have students study the three invertebrates in the "Animal Body Plans" illustration and note their different habitats. Tell students that being bilaterally symmetrical is an advantage for animals that travel through their environment and that being radially symmetrical is an advantage for animals who live attached to a substrate and whose environment meets them on all sides. Ask students whether they think the organisms pictured in the figure support this statement. Point out to students that there is no way to divide the sponge to get two equal halves.

______ **Discussion,** "Digestion," ATE p. 29. Have students discuss the advantages of having a central gut specialized for digestion.

______ **Demonstration,** "Sponges," ATE p. 30. Place a thin, dry slice of a natural sponge under a microscope, and allow students to examine the sponge-fiber network. Next, add a few drops of water to the sponge, and have students examine the slice again. Students should be able to see clearly how the water is taken up by the fibers (the fibers will swell slightly) and the spaces between the fibers.

Homework

______ **Critical Thinking Worksheet Chapter 2,*** "A New Form of Danger in the Deep." Students read a selection from the magazine *Amazing Adaptations,* and use critical thinking skills to answer two conceptual questions about the reading.

______ **Review,** PE p. 31. Students answer three questions about sponges, the coelom, and symmetry.

Block 2

Teach *20 minutes*

______ **Activity,** "Observing Hydras," ATE p. 32. Obtain live hydras and water fleas *(Daphnia)* from a biological supply house. Distribute the hydras in water-filled specimen dishes, and have students work in pairs to study the hydras under a dissecting microscope. Then add several water fleas to the water in each specimen dish, and have students observe how hydras use their nematocyst-equipped tentacles to capture and subdue prey. Encourage students to make drawings of the hydras and to record their observations about how hydras move and manipulate captured prey into their mouths.

_____ **Self-Check,** PE p. 33. Students answer a question about the nervous system of medusas.

Extend *15 minutes*

_____ **Real-World Connection,** ATE p. 34. Schistosomiasis is an infectious disease caused by blood flukes of the genus *Schistosoma.* About 200 million people are afflicted by schistosomiasis worldwide, primarily in Africa, Latin America, tropical Asia, and the Middle East. Encourage students to research the *Schistosoma* blood fluke and, as a class, to create a bulletin-board display in which they describe the fluke's complex life cycle, the symptoms of the disease, and steps that can be taken to reduce the chance of an infection.

Close *10 minutes*

_____ **Quiz,** ATE p.35. Students answer three questions about simple invertebrates.

_____ **Review,** PE p. 35. Students answer three questions that review the lesson content.

Homework

_____ **Reinforcement Worksheet Chapter 2,*** "Life Without a Backbone." Students use a list of characteristics to answer questions about invertebrates.

Additional Resource Options

_____ **Science Puzzlers, Twisters & Teasers, Worksheet Chapter 2.*** These worksheets offer puzzles, games, and logic problems that use vocabulary and concepts from the chapter.

_____ **Skill Builder,** "Porifera's Porosity," PE p. 50. Students determine how much water sponges are capable of absorbing. This lab supports UCP3 and SAI1.

_____ **Datasheets for LabBook, Chapter 2,*** "Porifera's Porosity." This blackline master makes progressing through the lab easier for students and grading easier for you.

_____ **Directed Reading Worksheet Chapter 2,* Section 1.** This worksheet reinforces the main concepts in the section while developing students' reading skills.

_____ **Weird Science,** "Water Bears," PE p. 56. Students read a passage about an unusual phylum of invertebrate, the water bear, and give one reason why we should study these interesting creatures.

_____ **Homework,** ATE p. 34. Students research the life cycle of the roundworm parasite *Trichinella spiralis* and write a persuasive paragraph in their ScienceLog on the importance of cooking pork thoroughly to prevent contracting trichinosis.

_____ **Alternative Assessment,** ATE p. 35. Students create an illustrated book about the way sponges, cnidarians, and flatworms obtain food.

_____ **Module B Guided Reading Audio CD Program, Disc 15, Tracks 1-2.** The audio reading of the chapter provides essential chapter content for ESL students, auditory learners, and struggling readers.

_____ **NSTA *sci*LINKS:** Sponges, sciLINKS number HSTL355. Students research Internet resources related to sponges. *Roundworms, sci*LINKS number HSTL360. Students research Internet resources related to roundworms.

Name ______________________ Date ______________ Class ______________

Module B
Chapter 2: Invertebrates
Lesson Plan
Section 2: Mollusks and Annelid Worms

Pacing

1 Block = 45 minutes

Regular Schedule:	**with Lab(s):** 3 Days	**without Lab(s):** 2 Days
Block Schedule:	**with Lab(s):** 1 1/2 Days	**without Lab(s):** 1 Day

Objectives

1. Describe the body parts of a mollusk.
2. Explain the difference between an open circulatory system and a closed circulatory system.
3. Describe segmentation.

Standards Covered

UCP 1. Systems, order, and organization
UCP 2. Evidence, models, and explanation
UCP 3. Change, constancy, and measurement
UCP 5. Form and function

SAI 2. Understandings about scientific inquiry

SPSP 4. Risks and benefits

Structure and Function in Living Systems (LS 1)

1a. Living systems at all levels of organization demonstrate the complementary nature of structure and function. Important level of organization from structure and function include cells, tissues, organs, organ systems, whole organisms, and ecosystems.

Reproduction and Heredity (LS 2)

2a. Reproduction is a characteristic of all living systems; because no individual organism lives forever, reproduction is essential to the continuation of every species. Some organisms reproduce asexually. Others reproduce sexually.

Regulation and Behavior (LS 3)

3a. All organisms must be able to obtain and use resources, grow, reproduce, and maintain stable internal conditions while living in a constantly changing external environment.

Populations and Ecosystems

4b. Populations of organisms can be categorized by the function they serve in an ecosystem. Plants and some microorganisms are producers—they make their own food. All animals, including humans, are consumers, which obtain food by eating other organisms. Decomposers, primarily bacteria and fungi, are consumers that use waste materials and dead organisms for food. Food webs identify the relationship among producers, consumers, and decomposers in an ecosystem.

Diversity and Adaptations of Organisms (LS 5)

5a. Millions of species of animals, plants, and microorganisms are alive today. Although different species might look dissimilar, the unity among organisms becomes apparent from analysis of internal structures, the similarity of their chemical processes, and the evidence of common ancestry.

Block 1

Focus *5 minutes*

_____ **Bellringer,** ATE p. 36. Have students unscramble the following words, and write a sentence using them in their ScienceLog: gluss, isalns, sdusqi, klomssul.

Motivate *10 minutes*

_____ **Group Activity,** ATE p. 36. Divide students into cooperative groups of three or four. Distribute to each group copies of simple, top-view drawings of a butterfly and sea urchin and a small, rectangular hand mirror (mirrors without frames work best). Challenge students to use the mirror to demonstrate that the butterfly is bilaterally symmetrical and that the sea urchin is radially symmetrical. Encourage to discuss their findings as a class.

Teach *30 minutes*

Directed Reading Worksheet Chapter 2,* Section 2. This worksheet reinforces the main concept in the section while developing students' reading skills.

_____ **MathBreak,** "Speeding Squid,"p. 36. Students calculate how far a squid can swim at a given speed in one minute.

Homework

_____ **Review**, p.38. Students answer three questions about mollusks.

Block 2

Teach *10 minutes*

_____ **Apply,** p. 39. Students write a letter explaining whether it is a good idea for a friend to get rid of the earthworms in his garden.

Extend *20 minutes*

_____ **Using the Figure,** ATE p. 39. In their ScienceLog, have students compare and contrast the annelid worm shown in Figure 18 with the flatworms and roundworms pictured in Section 1. Students should note the segmentation is a distinctive characteristic of the phylum Annelida. Tell students that *annelida* comes from a Latin worm meaning "little ring".

_____ **Guided Practice,** ATE p. 39. To demonstrate earthworms' ability to mix soil, have that class work cooperatively to fill the bottom half of a large glass jar with sand and the top half with potting soil. Add enough water to moisten the soil and the sand, and add 5 to 10 and large earthworms (available from sporting goods or hardware stores). Punch air holes in the lid and place it securely on the jar. Put the jar in a cool, dimly lit location in the classroom. Add water periodically keep the soil moist. Encourage students to observe how the earthworms gradually mix the soil and sand during the next few weeks.

Name ______________________ Date ____________ Class ____________

Close *15 minutes*

______ **Quiz,** ATE p. 40. Students answer two questions about mollusks.

______ **Review,** PE p. 40. Students answer three questions that review the lesson content.

Homework

______ **Alternative Assessment,** ATE p. 40. Havc students select a mollusk or annelid worm that interests them and research its life cycle, habitat, food, and unique structural or behavioral adaptations. Then ask students to write a rhyming or free verse poem in their ScienceLog about invertebrates based on the information gathered in their research.

Block 3

Lab Days *45 minutes*

______ **Labs You Can Eat, Chapter 2,*** "Here's Looking at Your Squid. "Students dissect and identify the parts of a common ocean invertebrate in order to relate structure and function.

Additional Resource Options

______ **Inquiry Labs, Chapter 2,*** "At a Snail's Place. " Students investigate a snail's response to gravity, temperature, and light to learn about geotaxis, thermotaxis, and phototaxis of these invertebrates.

______ **Eye on the Environment,** "Sizable Squid, " PE p. 57. Students read a passage about giant squids, then write a fictional story about a giant squid.

______ **Module B Guided Reading Audio CD Program, Disk 15, Track 3.** The Audio reading of the chapter provides essential chapter content for ESL students, auditory learners, and struggling readers.

______ **NSTA *sci*LINKS:** *Mollusks and Annelid Worms, sci*LINKS number HSTL365. Students research Internet resources related to mollusks and annelid worms.

Name ______________________ Date ______________ Class ______________

Module B
Chapter 2: Invertebrates
Lesson Plan
Section 3: Arthropods

Pacing
1 Block = 45 minutes

Regular Schedule:	**with Lab(s):** N/A	**without Lab(s):** 2 Days
Block Schedule:	**with Lab(s):** N/A	**without Lab(s):** 1 Day

Objectives
1. List the four main characteristics of arthropods.
2. Describe the different body parts of the four kinds of arthropods.
3. Explain the two types of metamorphoses in insects.

Standards Covered
UCP 2. Evidence, models, and explanation
UCP 3. Change, constancy, and measurement
UCP 5. Form and formation

SAI 1. Abilities necessary to do scientific inquiry

SPSP 4. Risks and benefits

Structure and Function in Living Systems (LS 1)
1a. Living systems at all levels of organization demonstrate the complementary nature of structure and function. Important levels of organization from structure and function includes cells, tissues, organs, organs systems, whole organisms, and ecosystems.

1d. Specialized cells perform specialized functions in multicellular organisms. Groups of specialized cells cooperate to form a tissue, such as a muscle. Different tissues are in turn grouped together to form larger functional units, called organs. Each type of cell, tissue, and organ has a distinct structure and set of functions that serve the organism as a whole.

1f. Disease is the breakdown in structures or functions of an organism. Some diseases are the result of intrinsic failures of a system. Others are the result of damage by infection from other organisms.

Regulation and Behavior (LS 3)
3c. Behavior is one kind of response an organism can make to an internal or environmental stimulus. A behavioral response requires coordination and communication at many levels, including cells, organ systems, and whole organisms. Behavioral response is a set of actions determined partially by heredity and partially from experience.

Name ______________________ Date ____________ Class ____________

Populations and Ecosystems (LS 4)

4b. Populations of organisms can be categorized by the function they serve in an ecosystem. Plants and some microorganisms are producers—they make their own food. All animals, including humans, are consumers, which obtain food by eating other organisms. Decomposers, primarily bacteria and fungi, are consumers that use waste materials and dead organisms for food. Food webs identify the relationship among producers, consumers, and decomposers in an ecosystem.

Diversity and Adaptations of Organisms (LS 5)

5a. Millions of species of animals, plants, and microorganisms are alive today. Although different species might look dissimilar, the unity among organisms becomes apparent from analysis of internal structures, the similarity of the chemical processes, and the evidence of common ancestry.

Block 1

Focus *5 minutes*

_____ **Bellringer,** ATE p. 41. Have students pretend that, like a Caterpillar, they can undergo metamorphosis and emerge from a cocoon in a new form. Ask students the following questions about their metamorphosis: How long will you be inside a cocoon? What will you look like when you emerge? How will you find food, and what will you eat? What physical or behavioral adaptations will you have after metamorphosis that you do not have now?

Motivate *10 minutes*

_____ **Discussion,** "Characteristics of Arthropods, "ATE p. 41. After introducing the general characteristics of arthropods, have students discuss how these characteristics may have helped arthropods adapt to nearly all environments and to diversify to make up the largest group of animals on Earth.

Teach *30 minutes*

_____ **Activity:** "Making Models," ATE p. 43. It is a common misunderstanding that spiders are insects. Challenge students to disprove this misconception by using modeling clay and pipe cleaners to create models of a spider and an insect. Have students read this section before they begin. Students' models should reflect the fact that spiders have two main body parts, four pairs of legs, and no antennae, whereas insects have three main body parts, three pairs of legs, and one pair of antennae.

_____ **Reteaching,** ATE p. 43. In their ScienceLog, have students describe a lobster and list the characteristics it exhibits that make it a crustacean.

_____ **Math Skills for Science Worksheet Chapter 2,*** "Dividing Whole Numbers with Long Division." Students learn long division through sample and practice problems.

Homework

_____ **Directed Reading Worksheet Chapter 2,* Section 3.** This worksheet reviews the main concepts in the section and develops students' reading skills.

______ **Self-Check,** PE p. 43. Students answer a question about the difference between a segmented worm and a centipede.

Block 2

Teach *20 minutes*

______ **QuickLab,** "Sticky Webs," PE p. 44. Provide transparent tape and cooking oil for each student. Have students follow the steps of the QuickLab to learn why spiders don't stick to their own webs.

______ **Teaching Transparency 56,*** "Incomplete Metamorphosis." This transparency shows the three steps involved in incomplete metamorphosis.

______ **Teaching Transparency 57,*** "Changing Form—Complete Metamorphosis." This transparency illustrates the four states of complete metamorphosis.

Extend *15 minutes*

______ **Activity,** "Poster Project," ATE p. 45. Insecticides are routinely sprayed on lawns and gardens to kill insect pests. Unfortunately, these chemicals also kill many beneficial insects, persist in the environment, and accumulate in the bodies of animals (including people) higher up in the food chain. In recent years, a variety of biological controls for insect pests have been developed that are much more environmentally safe. Have students investigate different biological controls and create a poster on the topic that could be displayed at a local garden center.

Close *10 minutes*

______ **Review,** PE p. 46. Students answer three questions that review the lesson content.

Homework

______ **Alternative Assessment,** ATE p. 46. Have students write a narrative in which they describe a walk along a rocky ocean shore or through a tropical rain forest. Have them describe at least a dozen different arthropods that they are likely to encounter. Students should research the two different ecosystems before they begin writing. Some students may wish to create illustrations or collages to accompany their narratives.

Additional Resource Options

______ **Discovery Lab,** "The Cricket Caper," p. 126. Students observe a cricket's structure and the simple adaptive behaviors that help make it so successful. This lab supports STANDARDS SAI 1 and LS3c.

______ **Datasheets for LabBook,** Chapter 2,* "The Cricket Caper." This blackline master makes progressing through the lab easier for students and grading easier for you.

______ **Math Skills for Science Worksheet Chapter 2,*** "Checking Division with Multiplication." Students learn how to check long division with multiplication through sample and practice problems.

Name ______________________________ Date ______________ Class______________

______ **Math and More, ATE p. 42.** Students use long division to compare the number of ommatidia in dragonflies, butterflies, and houseflies, then speculate on the relationship between the number of ommatidia and the ways these three types of arthropods get food.

______ **Quiz,** ATE p. 46. Students answer four true-false questions about arthropods.

______ **Module B Guided Reading Audio CD Program, Disc 15, Track 4.** The audio reading of the chapter provides essential chapter content for ESL students, auditory learners, and struggling readers.

______ **NSTA *sci*LINKS:** Arthropods, *sci*LINKS number HSTL370. Students research Internet resources related to arthropods.

Name ______________________ Date ____________ Class ____________

Module B
Chapter 2: Invertebrates
Lesson Plan
Section 4: Echinoderms

Pacing

1 Block = 45 minutes

Regular Schedule:	**with Lab(s):** N/A	**without Lab(s):** 2 Days
Block Schedule:	**with Lab(s):** N/A	**without Lab(s):** 1 Day

Objectives

1. Describe three main characteristics of echinoderms.
2. Describe the water vascular system.

Standards Covered

UCP 5. Form and function

Regulation and Behavior (LS 3)

3a. All organisms must be able to obtain and use resources, grow, reproduce, and maintain stable internal conditions while living in a constantly changing external environment.

Populations and Ecosystems (LS 4)

4b. Populations of organisms can be categorized by the function they serve in an ecosystem. Plants and some microorganisms are producers—they make their own food. All animals, including humans, are consumers, which obtain food by eating other organisms. Decomposers, primarily bacteria and fungi, are consumers that use waste materials and dead organisms for food. Food webs identify the relationship among producers, consumers, and decomposers in an ecosystem.

Diversity and Adaptations of Organisms (LS 5)

5a. Millions of species of animals, plants, and microorganisms are alive today. Although different species might look dissimilar, the unity among organisms becomes apparent from analysis of internal structures, the similarity of their chemical processes, and the evidence of common ancestry.

Block 1

Focus *5 minutes*

_____ **Bellringer,** ATE p. 47. Pose the following question to your students: Echinoderms include marine animals such as sea stars, sea urchins, and sea cucumbers. All these organisms are slow-moving bottom dwellers. How do you think they protect themselves from predators? Have them write their thoughts in their ScienceLog.

Name ______________________________ Date ______________ Class ____________

Motivate *10 minutes*

_____ **Activity,** "Sea Star Hypotheses," ATE p. 47. Display an example of an echinoderm, such as a sea star. Have students draw it in their notebook and write a brief hypothesis describing (1) what it eats, (2) how it moves, (3) where it most likely lives. Discuss before beginning the section.

Teach *30 minutes*

_____ **Teaching Transparency 58,*** "Water Vascular System." This transparency depicts the water vascular system of a sea star.

_____ **Teaching Transparency 155,*** "The Three Groups of Marine Life." This transparency illustrates the three types of marine life: plankton, nekton, and benthos.

_____ **Independent Practice,** "Concept Mapping," ATE p. 48. Have students make a concept map in their ScienceLog using the terms that describe echinoderms' physical characteristics and nervous and water vascular systems. Students should connect at least 12 terms, and link them with meaningful phrases. Encourage students to share their concept maps with the class.

Homework

_____ **Directed Reading Worksheet Chapter 2,* Section 4.** This worksheet reinforces the main concepts in the section while developing students' reading skills, and supports STANDARDS 5 and 5a.

Block 2

Teach *15 minutes*

_____ **Reinforcement Worksheet Chapter 2,*** "Spineless Variety." Students identify words or phrases that are incorrectly used to describe echinoderms, mollusks, cnidarians, and arthropods and place them in the appropriate category of annelid worms.

Extend *20 minutes*

_____ **Going Further,** ATE p. 49. Encourage interested students to investigate a fifth class of echinoderms mentioned but not discussed in the text. The class Crinoidea includes sea lilies and feather stars. Crinoids are the most ancient of living echinoderms. Have students present their findings to the class, along with pictures of these echinoderms in their natural habitats.

Close *10 minutes*

_____ **Quiz,** ATE p. 49. Students answer two questions about echinoderms.

_____ **Review,** PE p. 49. Students answer three questions that review the lesson content.

Homework

_____ **Alternative Assessment,** ATE p. 49. Have students compare and contrast the members of the four main classes of echinoderms discussed in the text. Students may wish to create a chart to accompany their narrative that lists characteristics all echinoderms have in common and those that are unique to each class.

Additional Resource Options

_____ **Long-Term Projects and Research Ideas,*** Chapter 2 "Creepy, Crawly Food?". *Research ideas:* a mollusk's role in photography; the Great Barrier Reef; leeches and their uses; scorpions; *Project idea:* insects as food

_____ **Module B Guided Reading Audio CD Program, Disc 15, Track 5.** The audio reading of the chapter provides essential chapter content for ESL students, auditory learners, and struggling readers.

_____ **NSTA *sci*LINKS:** Echinoderms, *sci*LINKS number HSTL375. Students research Internet resources related to echinoderms.

End of Chapter Review and Assessment

_____ **Study Guide,*** Vocabulary, Notes, and Chapter Review

_____ **Chapter Tests with Performance-Based Assessment, Chapter 2* Test**

_____ **Chapter Tests with Performance-Based Assessment, Performance-Based Assessment 2***

_____ **Concept Mapping Transparency 15***

Name ________________ Date ________ Class ________

CHAPTER 2 DIRECTED READING WORKSHEET

Invertebrates

Chapter Introduction

As you begin this chapter, answer the following.

1. Read the title of the chapter. List three things that you already know about this subject.

____

____

____

____

2. Write two questions about this subject that you would like answered by the time you finish this chapter.

____

____

____

3. How does the title of the Start-Up Activity relate to the subject of the chapter?

____

____

____

Section 1: Simple Invertebrates (p. 28)

4. There are ________________ 1 million species of invertebrates on Earth. (more than or less than)

No Backbones Here! (p. 28)

5. List three features scientists use to compare different animals.

____

____

____

____

In the space provided, write *B* if the animal has bilateral symmetry, *R* if the animal has radial symmetry, or *A* if the animal is asymmetrical. To see an example of each body plan, look at page 29 in your text.

6. ______ sea anemone

7. ______ ant

8. ______ sponge

9. ______ butterfly

10. A ______________________ controls many nerves in different parts of the body, while a ______________________ controls only the functions near its location. (ganglion or brain, ganglion or brain)

11. The coelom and the gut are both digestive organs. True or False? (Circle one.)

12. In animals without a coelom, moving from one place to another can aid or hinder digestion. True or False? (Circle one.)

Sponges (p. 30)

13. Is a sponge considered an animal? Explain.

____

____

____

14. Sponge spicules are made of ______________________ or ______________________.

15. Can you kill a sponge by breaking it into pieces? Explain.

____

____

____

16. What physical characteristic of a sponge does the name Porifera suggest?

____

____

17. Why doesn't the sponge need to have a gut?

____

____

Review (p. 31)

Now that you've finished the first part of Section 1, review what you learned by answering the Review questions in your ScienceLog.

Cnidarians (p. 32)

18. Which of the following are true about cnidarians? (Circle all that apply.)
    a. They have stinging cells.
    b. They can regenerate lost body parts.
    c. They live only in fresh water.
    d. They include sponges, corals, and hydras.

19. Cnidarians are either in ______________ form or in ______________ form. Both body types have ______________ symmetry.

20. The sea anemone is a polyp. True or False? (Circle one.)

21. A cnidarian will always have the same body form for its entire life. True or False? (Circle one.)

22. All cnidarians have a nerve ______________, which controls movement of the body and tentacles.

23. Jellyfish have a nerve ______________, which coordinates swimming.

Flatworms (p. 34)

24. Which of the following does NOT describe flatworms?
    a. They have a head.
    b. They are radially symmetric.
    c. They have eyespots.
    d. They have sensory lobes.

25. Flukes and tapeworms can live inside or outside a host. True or False? (Circle one.)

26. Like all tapeworms, the tapeworm on page 35 has no

______________, ______________,

or ______________.

Roundworms (p. 35)

27. Name two roundworm parasites that infect humans.

____

____

28. Which of the following meats could give you trichinosis if it is infected and you don't cook it thoroughly?

a. chicken
b. pork
c. steak
d. fish

Review (p. 35)

Now that you've finished Section 1, review what you learned by answering the Review questions in your ScienceLog.

Section 2: Mollusks and Annelid Worms (p. 36)

1. What features of mollusks make them more sophisticated organisms than roundworms, flatworms, and corals?

____

____

____

Mollusks (p. 36)

2. Which of the three main classes of mollusks are you most likely to encounter on land?

____

____

3. Which of the following are true of the phylum Mollusca? (Circle all that apply.)

a. Some mollusks are 1 mm in length.
b. Some mollusks are 18 m in length.
c. Some land mollusks can move 40 km/h.
d. Some marine mollusks can swim 40 km/h.

Name ______________________ Date ____________ Class ____________

Choose the part of the mollusk in Column B that best matches the definition in Column A, and write the corresponding letter in the space provided.

Column A	Column B
____ **4.** a layer of tissue that protects mollusks that do not have a shell	**a.** shell
____ **5.** this contains the gills, gut, and other organs	**b.** mantle
____ **6.** this keeps land mollusks from drying out	**c.** foot
____ **7.** mollusks use this to move	**d.** visceral mass

8. Snails and slugs have a ______________________ to scrape food off rocks.

9. How are open and closed circulatory systems different?

a. Open circulatory systems have sinuses.
b. Closed circulatory systems have sinuses.
c. Only open circulatory systems have blood vessels.
d. Only closed circulatory systems have blood vessels.

10. Octopuses have advanced nervous systems. Name two examples of difficult tasks that some octopuses can do.

____

____

____

Review (p. 38)

Now that you've finished the first part of Section 2, review what you learned by answering the Review questions in your ScienceLog.

Annelid Worms (p. 39)

11. An earthworm has a brain. True or False? (Circle one.)

12. All the segments of an annelid worm are identical.

True or False? (Circle one.)

13. How do earthworms increase soil fertility? (Circle all that apply.)

a. They eat bugs that poison the soil.
b. Their excreted wastes provide nutrients to plants.
c. They burrow tunnels that allow water and air to reach deep into the soil.
d. They have bristles that protect plant roots.

14. What does the bristle worm in Figure 19 use its bristles to do?
   a. burrow
   b. filter food out of water
   c. deter predators
   d. protect itself from drying out

15. How can leeches help sick people?

____

____

____

Review (p. 40)

Now that you've finished Section 2, review what you learned by answering the Review questions in your ScienceLog.

Section 3: Arthropods (p. 41)

1. Which of the following invertebrates is NOT an arthropod?
   a. a crab
   b. a spider
   c. a centipede
   d. a sea urchin

Characteristics of Arthropods (p. 41)

2. Why are jointed limbs important to an arthropod?

____

____

3. The "suit of armor" that arthropods wear is called a(n) ______________________, which is made of ______________________.

Kinds of Arthropods (p. 42)

4. The difference between a centipede and a millipede is that a millipede has ______________________ pairs of legs per segment, while a centipede has ______________________ pair(s). (two or three, one or two)

5. All crustaceans have ______________________ and two pairs of ______________________. (legs or mandibles, antennae or eyes)

6. Ticks and mites are types of insects. True or False? (Circle one.)

7. Why are insects important to us?

____

____

____

Read pages 43–46 before answering questions 8–15. Match each type of arthropod in Column B to the correct statement in Column A, and write the corresponding letter in the appropriate space. Arthropod types can be used more than once.

Column A	Column B
____ **8.** has eight eyes	**a.** arachnid
____ **9.** has simple eyes	**b.** insect
____ **10.** has compound eyes	
____ **11.** has two main body parts	
____ **12.** has three main body parts	
____ **13.** has antennae	
____ **14.** has mandibles	
____ **15.** has chelicerae	

Look at the diagram on page 46. Place the following stages of complete metamorphosis in order by writing the appropriate number in the space provided.

16. _____ pupa

17. _____ larva

18. _____ egg

19. _____ adult

Review (p. 46)

Now that you've finished Section 3, review what you learned by answering the Review questions in your ScienceLog.

Section 4: Echinoderms (p. 47)

1. If you went snorkeling in a freshwater lake, would you see any echinoderms? Why or why not?

____

____

Spiny Skinned (p. 47)

2. How do echinoderms use their endoskeleton like an exoskeleton?

____

____

____

3. An endoskeleton is covered by an outer skin, while a true exoskeleton has no covering. True or False? (Circle one.)

Bilateral or Radial? (p. 47)

4. Most echinoderms begin their life with ______________ symmetry and later have ______________ symmetry.

The Nervous System (p. 48)

5. Which sense does a sea star have?
   a. smell
   b. sight
   c. hearing
   d. taste

6. A sea star has a circle of nerve fibers around its ______________ called a nerve ring. (mouth or arms)

Water Vascular System (p. 48)

7. Which of the following is NOT part of the water vascular system?
   a. ampulla
   b. radial canals
   c. sieve plate
   d. radial nerve

8. Tube feet help a starfish to capture food and hang onto rocks. True or False? (Circle one.)

Kinds of Echinoderms (p. 49)

9. Besides using their tube feet how else do some sea urchins get around?

____

____

Review (p. 49)

Now that you've finished Section 4, review what you learned by answering the Review questions in your ScienceLog.

Name ______________________ Date ____________ Class ____________

CHAPTER 2

VOCABULARY & NOTES WORKSHEET

Invertebrates

By studying the Vocabulary and Notes listed for each section below, you can gain a better understanding of this chapter.

SECTION 1

Vocabulary

In your own words, write a definition for each of the following terms in the space provided.

1. invertebrate ______________________________

____

____

____

2. bilateral symmetry ______________________________

____

____

____

3. radial symmetry ______________________________

____

____

____

4. asymmetrical ______________________________

____

____

5. ganglia ______________________________

____

____

6. gut ______________________________

____

____

7. coelom ____

____

____

Notes

Read the following section highlights. Then, in your own words, write the highlights in your ScienceLog.

- Invertebrates are animals without a backbone.
- Most animals have radial symmetry or bilateral symmetry.
- Unlike other animals, sponges have no symmetry.
- A coelom is a space inside the body. The gut hangs inside the coelom.
- Ganglia are clumps of nerves that help control the parts of the body.
- Sponges have special cells called collar cells to digest their food.
- Cnidarians have special stinging cells to catch their prey.
- Cnidarians have two body forms, the polyp and the medusa.
- Tapeworms and flukes are parasitic flatworms.

SECTION 2

Vocabulary

In your own words, write a definition for each of the following terms in the space provided.

1. open circulatory system ____

____

____

2. closed circulatory system ____

____

____

3. segment ____

____

____

Name ______________________________ Date ______________ Class ______________

Notes

Read the following section highlights. Then, in your own words, write the highlights in your ScienceLog.

- All mollusks have a foot, a visceral mass, and a mantle. Most mollusks also have a shell.
- Mollusks and annelid worms have both a coelom and a circulatory system.
- In an open circulatory system, the heart pumps blood through vessels into spaces called sinuses. In a closed circulatory system, the blood is pumped through a closed network of vessels.
- Segments are identical or nearly identical repeating body parts.

SECTION 3

Vocabulary

In your own words, write a definition for each of the following terms in the space provided.

1. exoskeleton ______________________________

____

____

____

2. compound eye ______________________________

____

____

____

3. antennae ______________________________

____

____

____

4. mandible ______________________________

____

5. metamorphosis ______________________________

____

____

Name ______________________ Date __________ Class __________

Notes

Read the following section highlights. Then, in your own words, write the highlights in your ScienceLog.

- Seventy-five percent of all animals are arthropods.
- The four main characteristics of arthropods are jointed limbs, an exoskeleton, segments, and a well-developed nervous system.
- Arthropods are classified by the type of body parts they have.
- The four kinds of arthropods are centipedes and millipedes, crustaceans, arachnids, and insects.
- Insects can undergo complete or simple metamorphosis.

SECTION 4

Vocabulary

In your own words, write a definition for each of the following terms in the space provided.

1. endoskeleton ______________________________

2. water vascular system ______________________________

Notes

Read the following section highlights. Then, in your own words, write the highlights in your ScienceLog.

- Echinoderms are marine animals that have an endoskeleton and a water vascular system.
- Most echinoderms have bilateral symmetry as larvae and radial symmetry as adults.
- The water vascular system allows echinoderms to move around by means of tube feet, which act like suction cups.
- Echinoderms have a simple nervous system consisting of a nerve ring and radial nerves.

Name ______________________ Date ____________ Class ____________

CHAPTER 2

CHAPTER REVIEW WORKSHEET

Invertebrates

USING VOCABULARY

To complete the following sentences, choose the correct term from each pair of terms listed below, and write the term in the space provided.

1. Animals without a backbone are called ______________________.
(invertebrates or vertebrates)
2. A sponge uses ______________________ to pull water in and releases water out through ______________________. (an osculum or pores)
3. Cnidarians have ______________________ symmetry and flatworms have ______________________ symmetry. (radial or bilateral)
4. The shell of a snail is secreted by the ______________________. (radula or mantle)
5. Annelid worms have ______________________. (jointed limbs or segments)
6. An ampulla regulates ______________________.
(water pressure in a tube foot or blood pressure in a closed circulatory system)

UNDERSTANDING CONCEPTS

Multiple Choice

7. Invertebrates make up what percentage of all animals?
   a. 4 percent
   b. 50 percent
   c. 85 percent
   d. 97 percent

8. Which of the following describes the body plan of a sponge:
   a. radial symmetry
   b. bilateral symmetry
   c. asymmetry
   d. partial symmetry

9. What cells do sponges have that no other animal has?
   a. blood cells
   b. nerve cells
   c. collar cells
   d. None of the above

10. Which of the following animals do not have ganglia?
   a. annelid worms
   b. cnidarians
   c. flatworms
   d. mollusks

11. Which of the following animals has a coelom?
   a. sponge
   b. cnidarian
   c. flatworm
   d. mollusk

12. Both tapeworms and leeches are
   a. annelid worms.
   b. parasites.
   c. flatworms.
   d. predators.

Name ______________________ Date __________ Class __________

13. Some arthropods do NOT have

a. jointed limbs.
b. an exoskeleton.
c. antennae.
d. segments.

14. Echinoderms live

a. on land.
b. in fresh water.
c. in salt water.
d. All of the above

15. *Echinoderm* means

a. "jointed limbs."
b. "spiny skinned."
c. "endoskeleton."
d. "shiny tube foot."

16. Echinoderm larvae have

a. radial symmetry.
b. bilateral symmetry.
c. no symmetry.
d. radial and bilateral symmetry.

Short Answer

17. What is a gut?

____

____

18. How are arachnids different from insects?

____

____

____

____

____

19. Which animal phylum contains the most species?

____

____

20. How does an echinoderm move?

____

____

CONCEPT MAPPING

21. Use the following terms to create a concept map: *insect, sponges, sea anemone, invertebrates, arachnid, sea cucumber, crustacean, centipede, cnidarians, arthropods, echinoderms.*

CRITICAL THINKING AND PROBLEM SOLVING

Write one or two sentences to answer each of the following questions:

22. You have discovered a strange new animal that has bilateral symmetry, a coelom, and nerves. Will this animal be classified in the Cnidaria phylum? Why or why not?

____

____

____

____

23. Unlike other mollusks, cephalopods can move rapidly. Based on what you know about the body parts of mollusks, why do you think cephalopods have this ability?

____

____

____

____

____

24. Roundworms, flatworms, and annelid worms belong to different phyla. Why aren't all the worms grouped in the same phyla?

____

____

____

____

____

____

____

____

____

____

____

Name ______________________ Date ____________ Class ____________

MATH IN SCIENCE

25. If 75 percent of all animals are arthropods and 40 percent of all arthropods are beetles, what percentage of all animals are beetles?

____

____

____

INTERPRETING GRAPHICS

Below is an evolutionary tree showing how the different phyla of animals may be related to one another. The "trunk" of the tree is on the left. Use the tree to answer the questions on the next page.

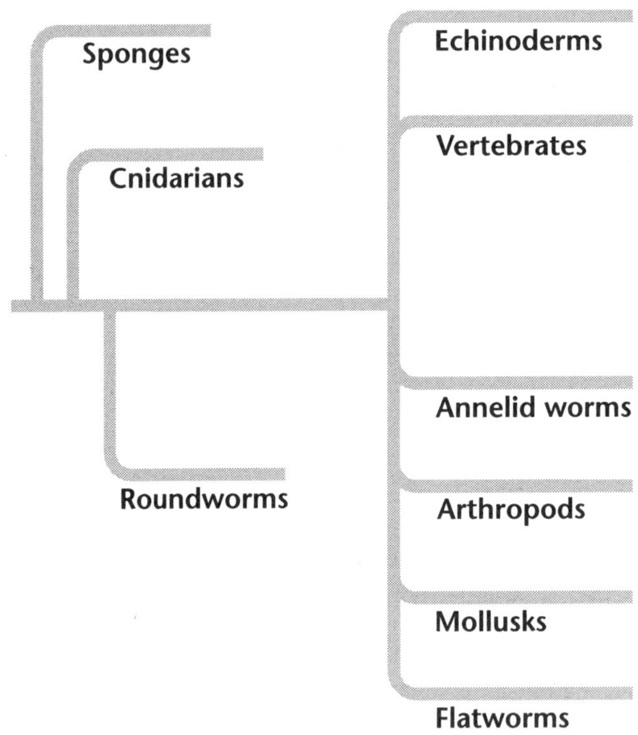

26. Which phylum is the oldest?

____

____

____

____

____

____

27. Are mollusks more closely related to roundworms or flatworms?

____

____

____

____

____

____

28. What phylum is most closely related to the vertebrates?

____

____

____

____

____

____

READING CHECK-UP

Take a minute to review your answers to the ScienceLog questions at the beginning of the chapter. Have your answers changed? If necessary, revise your answers based on what you have learned since you began this chapter. Record your revisions in your ScienceLog.

Name ______________________________ Date ______________ Class______________

CHAPTER 2 **SCIENCE PUZZLERS, TWISTERS & TEASERS**

Invertebrates

Odd One Out

1. For each group of terms, circle the one that doesn't belong and explain why not.

a. earthworm, bristle worm, roundworm, leech

____

____

b. dog, sponge, planarian, human

____

____

c. lobster, squid, crab, pillbug

____

____

d. hydra, clam, sea urchin, centipede

____

____

e. spineless, asymmetrical, invertebrate, without backbone

____

____

Analogies

2. In the analogies below, the first word is related to the second word in the same way that the third word is related to a fourth. For instance, the example below can be read, "Lemon is to yellow as lime is to green." Lemons are yellow in color, while limes are green. Fill in the blanks to complete the following analogies.

Example: lemon : yellow :: lime : ______green______

a. blood vessels : cats :: ______________________ : mollusks

b. skin : echinoderm :: ______________________ : arthropod

c. ladybug : 6 :: tarantula : ______________________

d. ganglia : nervous :: coelom : ______________________

Name ______________________ Date ______________ Class ______________

Crack the Code

3. Use the clues to help you decode the secret message. By substituting the correct word for the coded word in each clue, you will find what each code letter stands for in the secret message. Each letter represents a different letter in the code. Each coded letter represents the same letter throughout the message. You may want to write each word below the code to help you break the code.
   a. Sponges have no LNZZFCWN and no MFKI.
   b. Slugs and snails eat with a WKIYOK.
   c. Centipedes and millipedes have a single pair of KBCFBBKF, jaws called ZKBIAEOFL, and a hard MFKI RKVLYOF.
   d. Roundworms are also called BFZKCSIFL.
   e. Annelid worms and arthropods have LFJZFBCFI bodies.

Secret message: Don't be alarmed, but . . .

ABLFRCL KWF FTFWNHMFWF (KOZSLC)

Wordy Numbers

4. Vanity phone numbers are phone numbers that can be spelled out in easy-to-remember words. For example, a car dealer might choose the number 289-2277, which can be spelled as BUY CARS. What word from the chapter could each of these phone numbers represent? The words in parentheses are clues.

   a. 467-3287 (Creepy!) ______________________
   b. 665-5875 (Slimy!) ______________________
   c. 776-6437 (Bath buddies.) ______________________

Name ______________________ Date ____________ Class ____________

CHAPTER 2 REINFORCEMENT WORKSHEET

Life Without a Backbone

Complete this worksheet after you finish reading Chapter 2, Section 1.

What do a butterfly, a spider, a jellyfish, a worm, a snail, an octopus, and a lobster have in common? All of these animals are invertebrates. Clearly, there are many differences between these animals. Yet the most important characteristic these animals share is something none of them have—a backbone!

Despite their obvious differences, all invertebrates share some basic characteristics. Using the list of words provided, fill in the boxes with the correct answers. There will be some words that you will not use at all.

Characteristics

spicules
asymmetry
ganglia
gut
nerve cords
bilateral symmetry
collar cells
neutron
uniform
nerve networks
radial symmetry

All About Invertebrates

An invertebrate has a body plan that can have

____

____

____

An invertebrate might use these structures to digest its food.

____

____

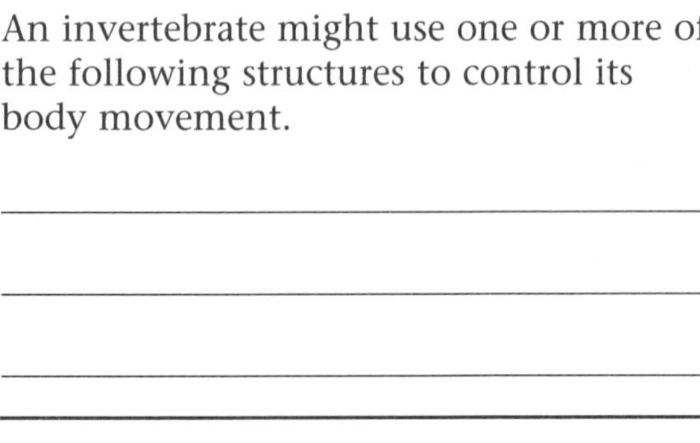

An invertebrate might use one or more of the following structures to control its body movement.

____

____

____

Name ______________________ Date ______________ Class ____________

CHAPTER 2 REINFORCEMENT WORKSHEET

Spineless Variety

Complete this worksheet after you finish reading Chapter 2, Section 4.

In each of the four completed lists, seven phrases were accidentally placed in the wrong list. Those seven phrases describe Annelid Worms. Circle the phrases that were placed incorrectly in the complete lists, and use those phrases to complete the list for Annelid Worms.

Echinoderms

live only in the ocean
have a brain
have an endoskeleton
have a nerve ring
are covered with spines or bumps
some have a radial nerve
have a water vascular system
sand dollar
sea urchin
a bristle worm

Annelid Worms

____

____

____

____

____

____

____

Arthropods

have a well-developed brain
have jointed limbs
have a head
have an exoskeleton
have a well-developed nervous system
a tick
an earthworm
a dragonfly

Mollusks

live in the ocean, fresh water, or land
have open or closed circulatory system
have a foot and a mantle
usually have a shell
have a visceral mass
have complex ganglia
a leech
a clam
a snail
have segments

Cnidarians

live in the ocean or fresh water
have a nerve cord
have a gut
have a nerve net
are in polyp or medusa form
have stinging cells
a jellyfish
a sea anemone
coral
have a closed circulatory system

Name ______________________ Date ______________ Class ______________

CHAPTER 2 VOCABULARY REVIEW WORKSHEET

Searching for a Backbone

After you finish Chapter 2, give this puzzle a try!

Identify the word described by each clue, and write the word in the space provided. Then circle the word in the puzzle on the next page.

1. external body-support structure made of protein and chitin ______________
2. combination of head and thorax ______________
3. type of circulatory system in which blood is pumped through a network of vessels that form a closed loop ______________
4. symmetry in which an organism's body has two halves that are mirror images of each other ______________
5. groups of nerve cells ______________
6. identical or almost identical repeating body parts ______________
7. form of cnidarian that looks like a mushroom with tentacles ______________
8. an animal without a backbone ______________
9. vase-shaped form of cnidarian ______________
10. type of circulatory system in which blood is pumped through spaces called sinuses ______________
11. the process through which an insect develops from an egg to an adult while changing form ______________
12. without symmetry ______________
13. three specialized parts of arthropods formed when two or three segments grow together
    a. ______________
    b. ______________
    c. ______________
14. symmetry in which an organism's body parts are arranged in a circle around a central point ______________
15. eye made of many identical light-sensitive cells ______________
16. pouch where almost all animals digest food ______________
17. jaws found on some arthropods ______________

Name ______________________ Date ____________ Class ____________

18. the space in the body where the gut is located ____________

19. an organism that feeds on another organism, usually without killing it ____________

20. feelers that respond to touch or taste ____________

21. internal body-support structure ____________

22. organism on which the organism in item 19 lives ____________

23. system that allows echinoderms to move, eat, and breathe ____________

M	K	D	J	P	F	B	I	L	A	T	E	R	A	L	T	A
X	E	N	D	O	S	K	E	L	E	T	O	N	P	S	K	N
F	B	T	C	O	E	L	O	M	Y	E	P	V	O	E	X	T
P	A	G	A	A	S	U	D	E	M	L	E	H	F	T	M	E
I	Q	S	H	M	Z	O	W	A	Q	V	N	X	E	I	R	N
N	V	E	Y	K	O	D	A	N	I	P	A	X	J	S	A	N
V	G	L	L	M	P	R	E	A	G	R	O	N	S	A	L	A
E	X	B	N	X	M	M	P	M	O	S	Q	L	O	R	U	E
R	D	I	A	V	O	E	D	H	K	A	W	R	Y	A	C	F
T	L	D	W	D	B	N	T	E	O	B	P	X	G	P	S	S
E	A	N	B	A	P	O	L	R	D	S	A	R	A	M	A	E
B	S	A	O	C	L	E	J	E	I	R	I	W	N	S	V	G
R	E	M	P	A	T	G	S	G	O	C	P	S	G	U	R	M
A	D	E	H	O	B	O	X	H	U	K	A	X	L	N	E	E
T	A	P	N	X	L	Q	T	N	Z	T	S	L	I	V	T	N
E	E	J	P	C	O	M	P	O	U	N	D	O	A	Z	A	T
C	H	Z	G	F	R	I	L	A	I	D	A	R	T	U	W	S

Name ______________________ Date ____________ Class ____________

CHAPTER

2 **CRITICAL THINKING WORKSHEET**

A New Form of Danger in the Deep

This selection is from the magazine *Amazing Adaptations:*

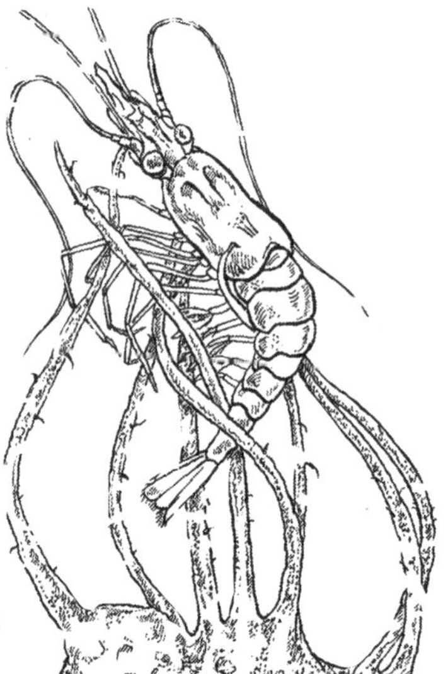

A shrimp swims through the cool, still waters of a dark cave. There are fewer nutrients in the cave than in the open sea, and the shrimp is extremely hungry.

In its search for food, the shrimp swims too close to the floor of the cave. Suddenly, it is caught by a tentacle with spiky, hook-shaped filaments. The shrimp struggles to free itself, but it is no use. Slowly, tentacles wrap around the shrimp until it can no longer move.

Within a day, the shrimp is buried alive by the tentacles. New filaments on the tentacles begin to grow directly over the shrimp's body. Then the shrimp is slowly digested. Once digestion is complete, the organism returns to its normal shape. Slowly moving along the sea cave floor, it awaits its next victim.

Scientists were shocked to discover that this organism is a type of sponge! This cave sponge was found in the Mediterranean Sea about 20 m below the surface of the water.

Making Comparisons

1. How is this sponge different from other sponges?

____

____

____

____

____

HELPFUL HINTS

Think about the conditions that exist in the cave.

Demonstrating Reasoned Judgment

2. Why do you think the cave sponge has developed a different method of feeding?

____

____

____

____

____

____

3. The closest relative to the cave sponge lives 8,840 m below the sea surface. How is the cave environment similar to an environment 8,840 m below the sea surface?

Evaluating Information

4. Biologists have disagreed about how to classify the cave sponge. Do you think this organism should be classified in the phylum Porifera? Explain your answer.

Thinking Logically

5. Why would this article appear in a magazine called *Amazing Adaptations*?

Name ______________________ Date ____________ Class ____________

CHAPTER

2 MATH SKILLS

Dividing Whole Numbers with Long Division

Long division, which is used to divide numbers of more than one digit, is really just a series of simple division, multiplication, and subtraction problems. The number that you divide is called the *dividend.* The number you divide the dividend by is the *divisor.* The answer to a division problem is called a *quotient.*

SAMPLE PROBLEM: Divide 564 by 12, or 12)564.

Step 1: Because you cannot divide 12 into 5, you must start by dividing 12 into 56. To do this, ask yourself, "What number multiplied by 12 comes closest to 56 without going over?" 4 × 12 = 48, so place a 4 in the quotient.

```
     4
12)564
```

Step 2: Multiply the 4 by the divisor and place the product under the 56. Then subtract that product from 56.

```
     4
12)564
  -48
    8
```

Step 3: Bring the next digit down from the dividend (4), and divide this new number (84) by the divisor, as you did in Step 1. Because 12 divides into 84 seven times, write 7 in the quotient.

```
    47
12)564
  -48↓
    84
   -84
     0
```

The quotient is **47.**

Divide It Up!

1. Fill in the blanks in the following long-division problems:

a.

```
    □1
13)663
   □5
    □3
    1□
     □
```

b.

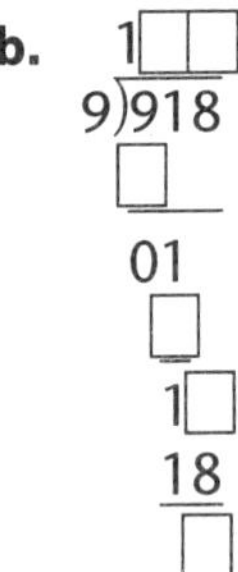

c.

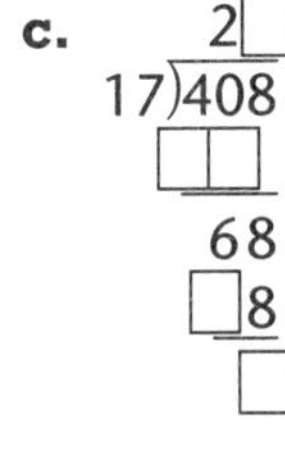

2. Complete the following long-division problems on a separate sheet of paper:

a. 3575 ÷ 11 = ______________

b. 52)1664 = ______________

c. 3)2940 = ______________

d. 4630 ÷ 5 = ______________

Name ______________________ Date __________ Class __________

CHAPTER 2 MATH SKILLS

Checking Division with Multiplication

Multiplication and division "undo" one another. This means that when you ask yourself, "What is 12 divided by 3?" it is the same as asking, "What number *multiplied* by 3 gives 12?" You can use this method to catch mistakes in your division.

PROCEDURE: To check your division with multiplication, multiply the quotient of your division problem by the divisor and compare the result with the dividend. If they are equal, your division was correct.

SAMPLE PROBLEM 1: Divide 564 by 47, and check your result with multiplication.

Step 1: Divide to find your quotient.	**Step 2:** Multiply the quotient by the divisor.	**Step 3:** Compare the product with your dividend.
47)564 = 12 −47 94 −94 0	12 × 47 84 48 564	**564** = **564** Correct!

Check It Out!

Complete the following divisions, and check your math by multiplying the quotient by your divisor. Are the product and the dividend equal?

1. 15)405

quotient × *divisor* ×

quotient = ________ product = ____________

2. 14)1694

quotient × *divisor* ×

quotient = ________ product = ____________

3. 12)252

quotient × *divisor* ×

quotient = ________ product = ____________

CHAPTER 2

Name ______________________________ Date ______________ Class ______________

CHAPTER 2 LAB DATASHEET

Porifera's Porosity

Early biologists thought that sponges were plants because sponges are like plants in some ways. In many species, the adults stick to a surface and stay there. They cannot chase their food. Sponges absorb and filter a lot of water to get food.

In this activity, you will observe the structure of a sponge. You will also think about how a sponge's structure affects its ability to hold water and collect food. You will think about how the size of the sponge's holes affects the amount of water the sponge can hold.

MATERIALS

- natural sponge
- kitchen sponge
- paper towel
- balance
- water
- bowl (large enough for sponge and water)
- graduated cylinder
- funnel
- calculator (optional)

Make Observations

1. Put on your safety goggles and lab apron. Observe the natural sponge. Identify the pores on the outside of the sponge. See if you can find the central cavity and oscula. Record your data.

____

____

____

____

2. Notice the size and shape of the sponge's holes. Look at the holes in the kitchen sponge and the holes in the paper towel. How do their holes compare with the sponge's holes?

____

____

____

Form a Hypothesis

3. Which item do you think can hold the most water per gram of dry mass? Formulate a testable hypothesis and record it below.

____

____

____

Test the Hypothesis

4. Read steps 5–9. Design a data table and draw it below. Remember, you will collect data for the natural sponge, the kitchen sponge, and the paper towel.

5. Use the balance to measure the mass of your sponge. Record the mass.

____

6. Place the sponge in the bowl. Use the graduated cylinder to add water to the sponge. Add 10 mL at a time, until the sponge is completely soaked. Record the amount of water added.

____

7. Gently remove the sponge from the bowl. Use the funnel and graduated cylinder to measure the amount of water left in the bowl. How much water did the sponge absorb? Record your data.

____

8. Calculate how many milliliters of water your sponge holds per gram of dry sponge. For example, let's say your sponge's dry mass is 12 g and your sponge holds 59.1 mL of water. Your sponge holds 4.9 mL of water per gram. (59.1 mL ÷ 12 g = 4.9 mL/g)

9. Repeat steps 5–8 using the kitchen sponge and the paper towel.

Analyze the Results

10. Which item held the most water per gram of dry mass?

11. Did your results support your hypothesis?

12. Do you see a connection between the size of an item's holes and the item's ability to hold water?

Draw Conclusions

13. What can you conclude about how the size and shape of a sponge's holes affects the feeding ability of a sponge?

Going Further

You have just studied how a sponge's body structure complements its feeding function. Now collect a few different types of insects. Observe how they eat, and examine the structure of their mouthparts. How does the structure of their mouthparts complement the mouthparts' function? Record your answers.

CHAPTER 2 LAB DATASHEET

The Cricket Caper

Insects are a special class of invertebrates with more than 750,000 known species. Insects may be the most successful group of animals on Earth. In this activity you will observe a cricket's structure and the simple adaptive behaviors that help make it so successful. Remember, you will be handling a living animal that deserves to be treated with care.

MATERIALS

- 2 crickets
- 600 mL beakers (2)
- plastic wrap
- apple
- hand lens (optional)
- masking tape
- aluminum foil
- lamp
- sealable plastic bags (2)
- crushed ice
- hot tap water

Procedure

1. Place a cricket in a clean 600 mL beaker, and quickly cover the beaker with plastic wrap. The supply of oxygen in the container is enough for the cricket to breathe while you complete your work.

2. Without much movement, observe the cricket's structure. Record your observations.

______

______

______

______

______

3. Place a small piece of apple in the beaker. Set the beaker on a table. Sit quietly still for several minutes and observe the cricket. (Any movement may cause the cricket to stop what it is doing.) Record your observations.

______

______

______

4. Remove the plastic wrap and the apple from the beaker, and quickly attach a second beaker. Join the two beakers together at the mouths with masking tape. Handle the beakers carefully. Remember a living thing is inside.

Name ______________________ Date ____________ Class ____________

5. Wrap one of the joined beakers with aluminum foil. Lay the joined beakers on their sides. If the cricket is not visible, gently tap the sides of the beaker until it is exposed.
6. Record the cricket's location. Shine a bright lamp on the uncovered side of the beaker. Record the cricket's location after 5 minutes.

____

____

7. Without disturbing the cricket, move the aluminum foil to the other beaker. Repeat step 6 to see if you get the same result.

____

____

8. Fill a sealable plastic bag halfway with crushed ice and seal it. Fill the other bag with hot tap water and seal it. Lay the bags side by side. Remove the aluminum foil from the beakers.
9. Gently rock the beakers until the cricket is in the center. Place the beakers on the plastic bags, so that one beaker is over the hot bag and the other beaker is over the cold one. Observe the cricket's behavior for 5 minutes. Record your observations.

____

____

____

____

____

Name ______________________ Date ____________ Class __________

Cricket (alone)

15 s	
30 s	
45 s	
60 s	
75 s	
90 s	
105 s	
120 s	
135 s	
150 s	
165 s	
180 s	

Cricket A and Cricket B

	A	B
15 s		
30 s		
45 s		
60 s		
75 s		
90 s		
105 s		
120 s		
135 s		
150 s		
165 s		
180 s		

10. Set the beakers on one end. Carefully remove the masking tape and separate the beakers. Quickly replace the plastic wrap over the beaker with the cricket.

11. Observe the cricket's movement in the beaker every 15 seconds for 3 minutes. Fill in the Cricket (alone) data table using the following codes: 0= no movement, 1= slight movement, and 2 = rapid movement.

12. Place a second cricket (Cricket B) into the beaker with the first cricket (Cricket A). Observe both crickets' behavior every 15 seconds. Record data using the codes given in step 12.

Analysis

13. Describe crickets' feeding behavior. Are they lappers, suckers, or chewers?

____

14. Do crickets prefer light or dark? Explain.

____

15. From your observations, what can you infer about a cricket's temperature preferences?

____

16. Based on your observations of Cricket A and Cricket B, what general statements can you make about the social behavior of crickets?

____

____

____

SKILL BUILDER

Here's Looking at You, Squid!

Cooperative Learning Activity

Group size: 2–3 students

Group goal: To dissect and identify the parts of a common ocean invertebrate in order to relate structure and function

Positive interdependence: Each group member should choose a role, such as dissection leader, discussion leader, or materials coordinator.

Individual accountability: After the activity, each group member should be able to identify the major parts of a squid and explain the function of each part.

Time Required

One 45-minute class period

Lab Ratings

EASY → HARD

TEACHER PREP: 3

STUDENT SET-UP: 2

CONCEPT LEVEL: 3

CLEAN UP: 2

Advance Preparation

You will need one whole, edible squid per student group. Such squids are available frozen, in bulk, from large grocery stores.

A dissection knife works best in this activity. However, very sharp scissors will also work if a dissection knife is not available.

You may wish to have an electric frying pan, oil or butter, flour, and salt handy to fry the squid mantles and arms for the class to enjoy after completing the activity. Do so only if the squid has been left unrefrigerated for no more than one hour.

Students may be interested to know that squid is also known as *calamari*. To make fried calamari, mix the cut pieces of squid with the flour and salt. Let them sit on wax paper for 10 minutes before placing them in the heated oil or butter. When cooking is complete, drain the calamari on paper towels, and serve with lemon wedges or a red cocktail sauce. Be sure you do not overcook the squid; it can become tough and rubbery.

ADDITIONAL MATERIALS

- the mantle and tentacles from 1 squid
- small bag of flour
- pinch of salt
- electric frying pan
- oil or butter, enough to coat the pan
- lemon wedges
- red cocktail sauce
- paper plates
- paper towels
- forks
- spatula

Safety Information

Instruct students to be very careful when using sharp tools. Students should also thoroughly wash their hands after dissecting the squid.

Before beginning this activity, ask students if they are allergic to any of the foods used in this lab. Students should avoid contact with any such foods. Instruct students to notify you as soon as possible if they have an allergic reaction.

Teaching Strategies

Students are asked to consider the possible functions of various structures in the squid body. If they are having difficulty, you may wish to help them by offering suggestions for possible functions.

continued...

Georgiann Delgadillo
Continuous Curriculum School
Spokane, Washington

Review with students the diagram of squid anatomy on page 33. You may wish to have students sketch their squids on a separate piece of paper.

Language Arts Connection

To get students excited about the lab, you may wish to read to them an excerpt from Chapter 18 of Jules Verne's classic science-fiction novel, *20,000 Leagues Under The Sea,* in which there is a fictional encounter with a giant squid. You will find a brief excerpt describing the squid below. As you read the excerpt to the class, you may wish to explain any unfamiliar terms, such as *cephalopod, mollusc, poulp,* or *cuttlefish.*

> *"I looked in my turn, and could not repress a gesture of disgust. Before my eyes was a horrible monster worthy to figure in the legends of the marvellous. It was an immense cuttlefish, being eight yards long. It swam crossways in the direction of the* Nautilus *with great speed, watching us with its enormous staring green eyes. Its eight arms, or rather feet, fixed to its head, that have given the name of cephalopod to these animals, were twice as long as its body, and were twisted like the furies' hair. One could see the 250 air-holes on the inner side of the tentacles. The monster's mouth, a horned beak like a parrot's, opened and shut vertically. Its tongue, a horned substance, furnished with several rows of pointed teeth, came out quivering from this veritable pair of shears. What a freak of nature, a bird's beak on a mollusc! Its spindle-like body formed a fleshy mass that might weigh 4,000 to 5,000 lb.; the varying colour changing with great rapidity, according to the irritation of the animal, passed successively from livid grey to reddish brown. What irritated this mollusc? No doubt the presence of the* Nautilus, *more formidable than itself, and on which its suckers or its jaws had no hold. Yet, what monsters these poulps are! what vitality the Creator has given them! what vigour in their movements! and they possess three hearts! Chance had brought us in presence of this cuttlefish, and I did not wish to lose the opportunity of carefully studying this specimen of cephalopods. I overcame the horror that inspired me, and, taking a pencil, began to draw it."*

After students complete the dissection, you may wish to revisit this excerpt and ask the class how the squids they dissected differ from Verne's portrayal of a giant squid in this passage.

Evaluation Strategies

For help evaluating this lab, see the Observation of Cooperative Group in the *Assessment Checklists & Rubrics.*

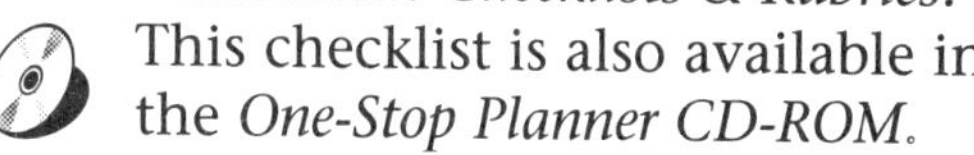

This checklist is also available in the *One-Stop Planner CD-ROM.*

Name ______________________ Date __________ Class __________

CHAPTER

2 STUDENT WORKSHEET

Here's Looking at You, Squid!

In Jules Verne's classic science-fiction novel, *20,000 Leagues Under the Sea,* the heroes battle a deadly giant squid that threatens to crush the hull of a submarine. Although giant squids do exist, most of us have only encountered their smaller, more timid relatives. Yet even the smaller squid looks like the stuff of science fiction. The top of the squid's head is actually a combined body-tail unit called a *mantle.* The head has two large eyes and is surrounded by two long tentacles and eight arms with rows of round suckers underneath. Underneath the head is a small opening to the funnel. The squid forces a jet of water through the funnel to propel itself backward or forward. Two fins are attached to the tail end of the squid to help it steer. Although the squid doesn't have a backbone, it does have a hard internal structure called a *pen.*

Now *you* can take a closer look at the unusual features of a squid.

MATERIALS

- squid
- paper plate
- magnifying glass
- dissection knife
- paper towels

Objective

To identify a number of structures and their functions in a squid, an aquatic invertebrate

Propel Yourself into Squid Dissection

1. Your teacher will provide you with a squid. Lay the squid flat on the plate, and examine it closely. Use the diagram below to help you identify the external parts of the squid.

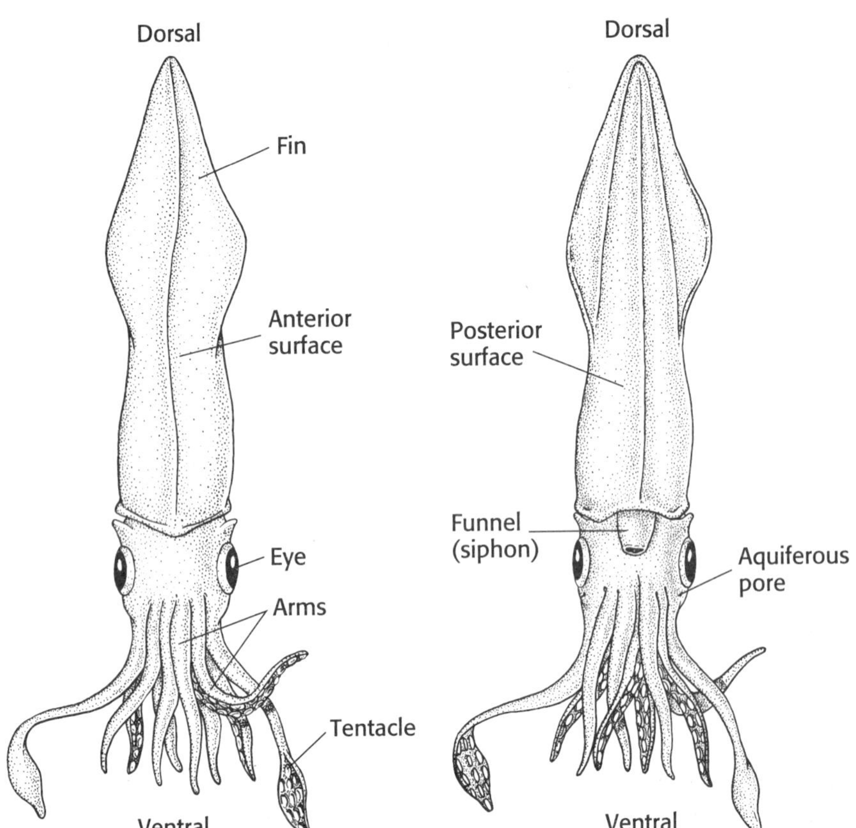

2. Use the magnifying glass to examine the suckers. How do you think the structure of the suckers helps the squid?

3. The squid's arms and tentacles both have suckers, but the suckers serve different functions. Describe what functions you think the different suckers might serve.

4. Spread apart the arms, and look in the center of the squid. You will see a small black structure. Rub your finger over it, and describe what you observe.

5. What do you think the function of this structure is?

6. Using the dissection knife, carefully remove the mantle from the head. Make a cut down the side of the mantle, and spread the mantle open on the plate. Use the diagram on page 116 to help you identify as many internal structures as you can.

Here's Looking at You, Squid! continued

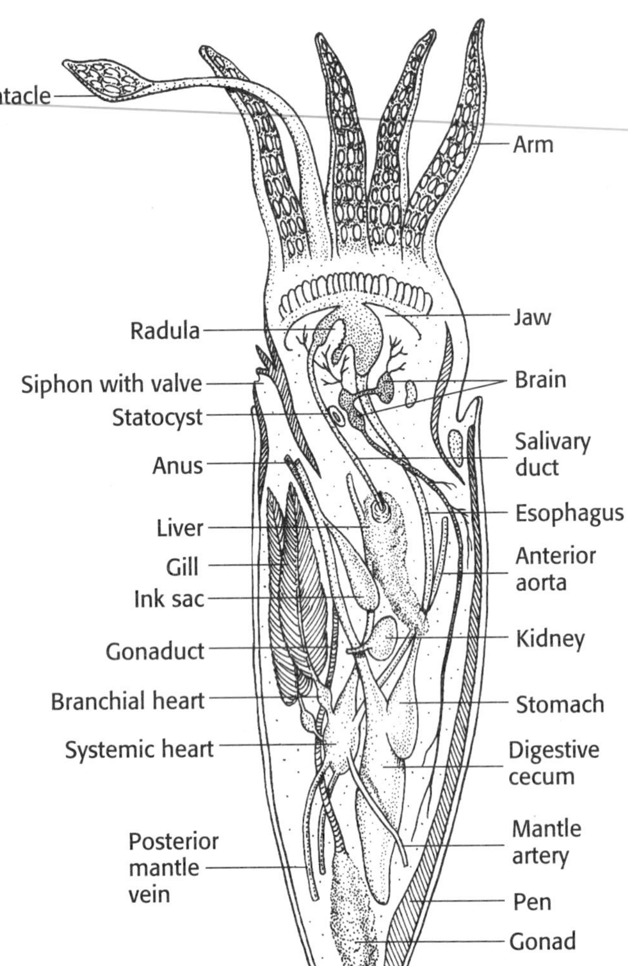

7. Remove the internal organs by pulling them from the mantle.

8. Locate a dark-silver baglike structure. This is known as the *ink sac.* Explain what you think this structure does. Why might this structure be important to the squid?

____

____

____

____

9. Locate the pen, and remove it by pulling it from the mantle. Describe the material and one possible function of the pen.

____

____

____

____

10. Did you have trouble identifying any structures that you saw in the illustrations on page 114 and at left? If so, why?

____

____

____

11. Explain two ways squid and human anatomies are similar and two ways they are different.

____

____

____

____

CHAPTER 2 TEACHER'S PREPARATORY GUIDE

DISCOVERY LAB

At a Snail's Pace

Purpose

Students investigate a snail's response to gravity, temperature, and light to learn about geotaxis, thermotaxis, and phototaxis of these invertebrates.

Time Required

One to two 45-minute class periods

Lab Ratings

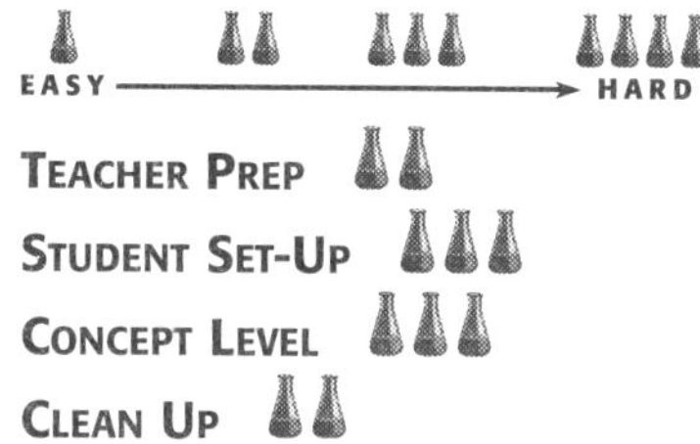

Advance Preparation

Either land or aquatic snails may be used, but the results are more dramatic with land snails. Have extra snails available because some snails might hide in their shells, making observations difficult. Prepare aquariums or tubs of water to keep the aquatic snails moist during the lab.

Safety Information

Emphasize the importance of humane treatment of lab animals. Students should wash their hands thoroughly after handling the snails.

Teaching Strategies

This activity works best in groups of 3–4 students. To help students make reasonable predictions, begin by asking them about their experiences with snails. For instance, you may ask them where they have seen snails.

The following snail facts might generate student interest:

- The giant African snail is one of the largest freshwater snails, growing to a length of up to 31 cm.
- Snails that have shells that coil counterclockwise are called left-handed snails.
- In France, a popular dish called *escargot* is made from steamed snails.

Before students begin the activity, you may wish to have them make some preliminary observations of snail movement and behavior. To clarify the procedure, model for students the setup for each portion of the lab, and review the use of a protractor. After the activity, combine the class results in a table on the chalkboard and discuss the results. Did the responses of the snails follow a general trend? You may wish to graph the data on the computer and compare results for the whole class.

Background Information

The snails in this activity demonstrate *geotaxis,* or gravity sensitivity. Geotaxis is controlled by special sensory organs called statocysts, which regulate equilibrium, or balance. Snails move against gravity (negative geotaxis), probably to right themselves. Snails also demonstrate *phototaxis,* or light sensitivity. Snails move away from the light (negative phototaxis), perhaps to keep from dehydrating. Snails also demonstrate *thermotaxis,* or heat sensitivity. Snails are more active in cool temperatures and tend to withdraw into their shells in warm temperatures.

Evaluation Strategies

For help evaluating this lab, see the Self-Evaluation of Cooperative Group Activity and the Teacher Evaluation of Lesson in the *Assessment Checklists & Rubrics*. These resources are also available in the *One-Stop Planner CD-ROM*.

CLASSROOM TESTED & APPROVED

Elizabeth Rustad
Crane Jr. High School
Yuma, Arizona

Name ______________________ Date ____________ Class ____________

CHAPTER 2 STUDENT WORKSHEET

DISCOVERY LAB

At a Snail's Pace

Dear Professor Sloe:

We would like to send a group of snails to outer space on the next shuttle mission. During a month-long study, these snails will be subject to fluctuations in gravity, light, and temperature. To ensure the safety of the snails while in space, we will need you to conduct a study in advance to learn about the snails' performance under various conditions. If the results conclude that a space mission with snails is possible, a representative will visit you to collect the most responsive of your snail candidates. Please report your results to me as soon as possible. Thank you for your cooperation.

Sincerely,

Dr. C. Stars
Director of Zoological Studies
AstroPet Project

MATERIALS

- 20 × 20 cm picture frame
- masking tape
- live snail
- watch or clock that indicates seconds
- washable marker
- metric ruler
- paper towels
- books
- protractor
- magnifying glass
- tub of warm water
- tub of ice water
- cardboard
- table lamp

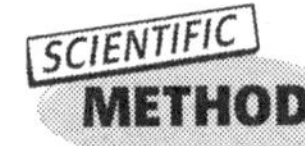

Ask a Question

How do snails respond to different stimuli?

Make a Prediction

1. How will the slope of the glass affect the distance a snail travels?

____

____

____

Conduct an Experiment

2. Tape one side of a picture frame to a table. Place the frame flat on the table, as shown below. Label the tape "Start."

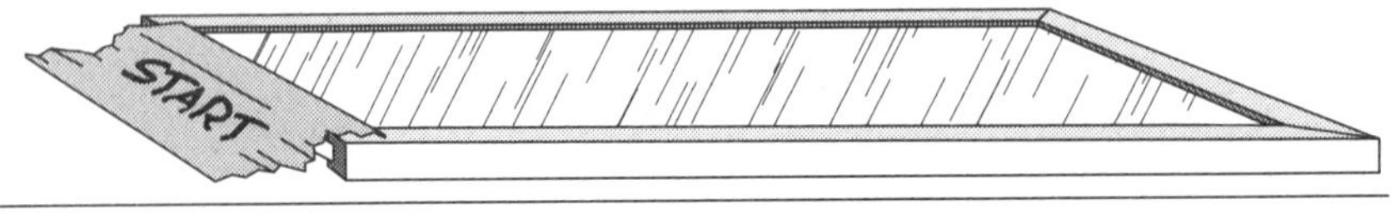

____

____

Name ______________________ Date __________ Class __________

SNAIL SAFETY

Wash your hands before and after handling the snails. Treat snails gently and with respect. To pick up a snail, wet your fingers and carefully roll the snail from the front to the back. Touch only the shell of the snail. Touching the soft tissues could injure the snail.

3. Gently place the snail on the starting spot. Start timing when the snail comes out of its shell and begins to move.
4. After two minutes, mark the snail's position on the glass with a washable marker. Measure the distance traveled, and record it in the table below. Gently remove the snail. Clean the glass with water, and dry it thoroughly.
5. Use a book to raise the picture frame to a 30° angle. Check the angle with a protractor. Repeat steps 3–4.
6. Repeat step 3–4 for 45°, 60°, and 90° angles. You should either hold the frame or wedge it between two solid, sturdy objects at the 90° angle.

Snail Response Data: Angle of Incline

Angles	Distance traveled	Observations
0°		
30°		
45°		
60°		
90°		

Analyze the Results

7. Was your prediction correct? Explain your answer.

____

____

____

8. Why do you think the snail responded as it did?

____

____

____

Communicate Results

9. Graph your results below. What is the shape of the graph?

____

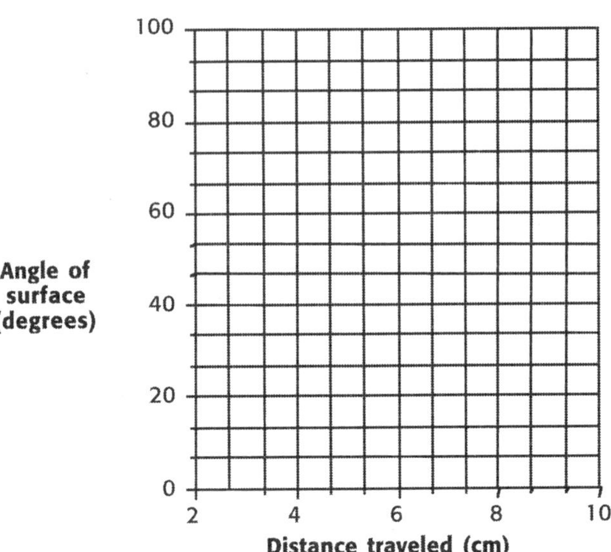

Make a Prediction

10. How will your snail respond to temperature?

____

____

Conduct an Experiment

11. Label a 20 cm length of tape "Start." Place a picture frame in ice water. After one minute, remove and dry the glass.

12. Place the picture frame flat on the table, and use the tape to anchor one edge of the frame to the table. Use books to raise the frame to a 60° angle. Verify the angle with a protractor.

13. Gently place the snail on the starting point. Start timing when the snail comes out of its shell and moves.

14. After two minutes, mark the snail's position on the glass with a washable marker. Measure the distance traveled, and record it in the table on the next page. Repeat steps 11–13 using warm water.

Snail Response Data: Temperature

Temperature	Distance traveled	Observations
Cool		
Warm		

Analyze the Results

15. Was your prediction correct? Explain your answer.

Make a Prediction

16. How will your snail respond to light or darkness?

Conduct an Experiment

17. Create a 60° ramp as you did in step 12. Focus the light from a lamp onto the ramp. Position the lamp far enough from the glass so it doesn't heat up the glass or the snail. Fold the cardboard in half, and place it over the ramp like a tent. The snail should be able to travel up the ramp by passing under the cardboard tent.

18. Gently place the snail on the starting point. Start timing when the snail begins to move.

19. After two minutes, mark the snail's position on the glass with a washable marker. Measure and record the distance traveled in the table below.

20. Repeat steps 18–19 without the cardboard tent.

Snail Response Data: Light

Conditions	Distance traveled	Observations
Light		
Dark		

Analyze the Results

21. Was your prediction correct? Explain your answer.

____

____

____

22. What general conclusions can you make about the movement of the snail in light compared with its movement in darkness?

____

____

____

23. Based on your results, where are you more likely to find snails—in cool, dark areas or warm, bright areas? Explain your answer.

____

____

____

____

____

____

24. Snails that move toward a stimulus show a positive response. Snails that move away from a stimulus show a negative response. What type of responses did the snails exhibit in each experiment?

____

____

____

____

____

____

____

Draw Conclusions

25. Were your snail's responses similar to those of your classmates' snails? Explain your answer.

____

____

____

____

____

____

26. Why is it important to collect data on more than one test subject?

____

____

____

____

Critical Thinking

27. If you were going to test a moth's response to different stimuli, what type of stimulus might cause a positive response?

____

____

____

Going Further 

Test the snail with other stimuli:

- Tickle the snail with a feather near its antennae.
- Place the snail on various surfaces.
- Place the snail near a piece of lettuce.
- Provide soothing music or sounds.

Name ______________________ Date ____________ Class ____________

CHAPTER 2

STUDENT PROJECT WORKSHEET

Creepy, Crawly Food?

How about having ants for lunch? Or maybe you prefer fried grasshoppers for dinner? Although insects may not be your idea of a great meal, they are an important food source in many parts of the world. Insect larvae, locusts, crickets, termites, and grasshoppers are just a few of the many insects that are eaten by humans. Dig in!

Bugs for Dinner?

1. Research several cultures in which insects are part of people's regular diet. Why do they eat insects? How are the insects prepared? What is their nutritional value? Discuss your findings in a report, and include at least two recipes that contain insects as ingredients.

Research Ideas

2. What does a mollusk have to do with photography? For centuries, people have made products from mollusks. Pearls and mother-of-pearl are used in jewelry, and octopuses release a black fluid that was once used to make ink. Discover the connections between mollusks and photography, and then research at least nine other mollusk products. Make a poster display of your findings, and include samples, photos, or illustrations of the products.
3. The Great Barrier Reef, off the coast of Australia, supports an incredible variety of marine life. It takes an incredible number of coral skeletons, and sometimes millions of years, to build a coral reef. Find out how coral reefs are formed and why they are endangered. Present your research in the form of a news article.
4. Most people try to avoid leeches, little wormlike creatures that suck blood. But did you know that leeches were used to treat illnesses in the eighteenth and nineteenth centuries? Use library resources to find out how and why leeches were used and how they are being used today. Write a report about your findings.
5. If a scorpion stung you, would you know what to do? Research how the sting or bite of an arachnid, such as a scorpion or spider, affects the human body. How dangerous are these animals to humans? What do they use their poison for? Find out what you should do if you are bitten, and write a safety brochure outlining your findings.

Name ______________________ Date ____________ Class ____________

CHAPTER 2 INVERTEBRATES

Chapter 2 Test

USING VOCABULARY

To complete the following sentences, choose the correct term from each pair of terms listed, and write the term in the blank.

1. The body parts of some invertebrates are controlled by individual groupings of nerve cells called ________________. (ganglia or coelom)
2. The body form of a jellyfish is the ________________, which looks like a bell with tentacles hanging underneath. (polyp or medusa)
3. In ________________ circulatory systems, blood is pumped through vessels that empty into sinuses. (closed or open)
4. Insects have a rigid ________________ made of chitin. (endoskeleton or exoskeleton)
5. Many arthropods have feelers called ________________ that respond to touch or taste. (mandibles or antennae)

UNDERSTANDING CONCEPTS

Multiple Choice

Circle the correct answer.

6. The phylum Mollusca includes
   - **a.** octopuses, nematodes, and snails.
   - **b.** slugs, flukes, and clams.
   - **c.** slugs, clams, and octopuses.
   - **d.** squids, annelid worms, and oysters.
7. The word *arthropod* means
   - **a.** "large brain."
   - **b.** "jointed foot."
   - **c.** "spiny skin."
   - **d.** "paralyzing toxin."
8. The ________ of crustaceans make them different from all other arthropods.
   - **a.** segmented bodies
   - **b.** head capsules
   - **c.** double antennae
   - **d.** chitinous skeletons
9. The organs of more-complex invertebrates such as the earthworm are contained in a body cavity called the
   - **a.** gut.
   - **b.** coelom.
   - **c.** abdominal hollow.
   - **d.** visceral mass.
10. Digestion of food particles in a sponge takes place in its
    - **a.** gut.
    - **b.** ampulla.
    - **c.** osculum.
    - **d.** collar cells.

Short Answer

11. Name three of the four distinguishing characteristics of arthropods.

____

____

____

____

____

____

12. Sponges move too slowly to escape predators. What adaptation do some sponges have that protects them from being eaten by predators?

____

____

____

CRITICAL THINKING AND PROBLEM SOLVING

13. People who eat raw oysters or clams taken from polluted waters can develop mild to serious illnesses. Think about how oysters and other bivalves eat; then develop a hypothesis to explain why some people get sick from eating them.

____

____

____

____

____

____

MATH IN SCIENCE

14. Wood ants, which are common in North America, work together to feed their colony. A typical colony can bring as many as 28 dead insects to their nest per minute. How many dead insects could a colony of wood ants bring to the nest if they worked for 24 hours without stopping? Show your work.

____

____

INTERPRETING GRAPHICS

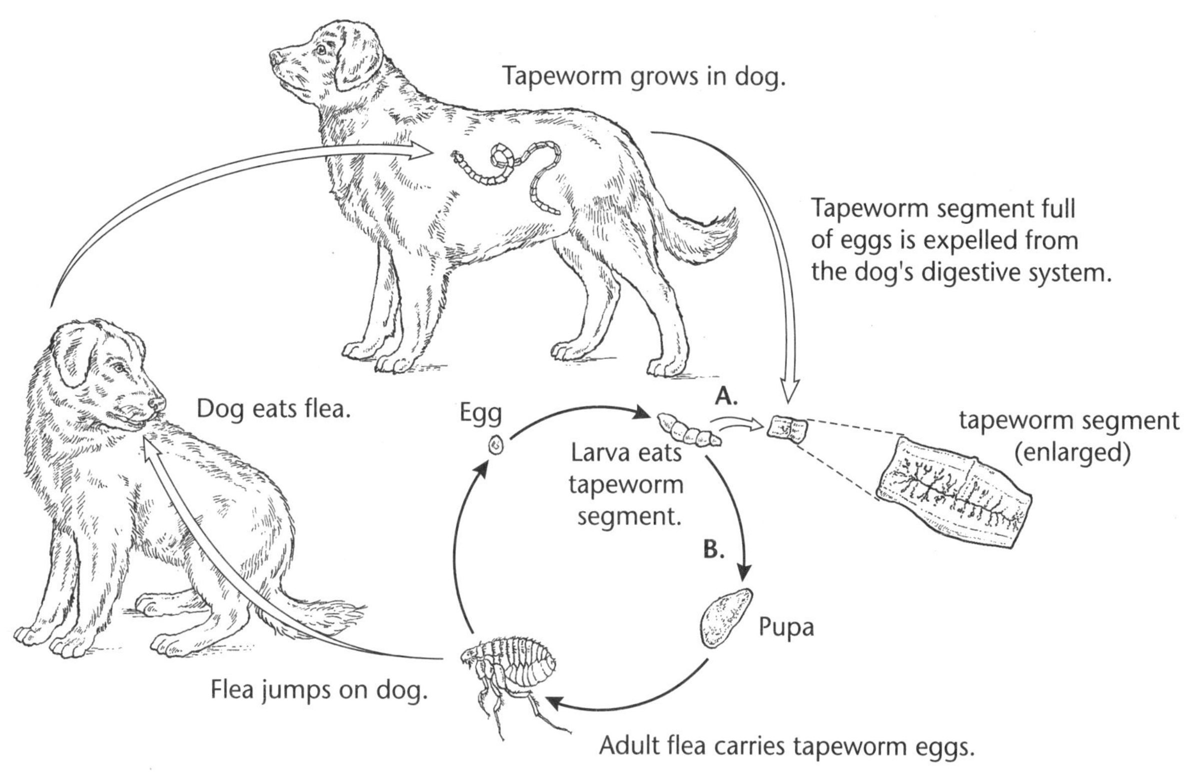
Tapeworm grows in dog.
Tapeworm segment full of eggs is expelled from the dog's digestive system.
Dog eats flea.
Egg
A.
Larva eats tapeworm segment.
tapeworm segment (enlarged)
B.
Pupa
Flea jumps on dog.
Adult flea carries tapeworm eggs.

15. Analyze the diagram above. Identify two main similarities between the flea and the tapeworm that set them apart from the dog.

____

____

____

16. Does the diagram show the flea undergoing simple or complete metamorphosis? Use the diagram to support your conclusion. (Be sure to refer to stages *A* and *B* in your explanation.)

____

____

____

____

____

____

CONCEPT MAPPING

17. Use the following words to complete the concept map below: bilateral, nematocysts, endoskeleton, radial, exoskeleton, cnidarians, echinoderms.

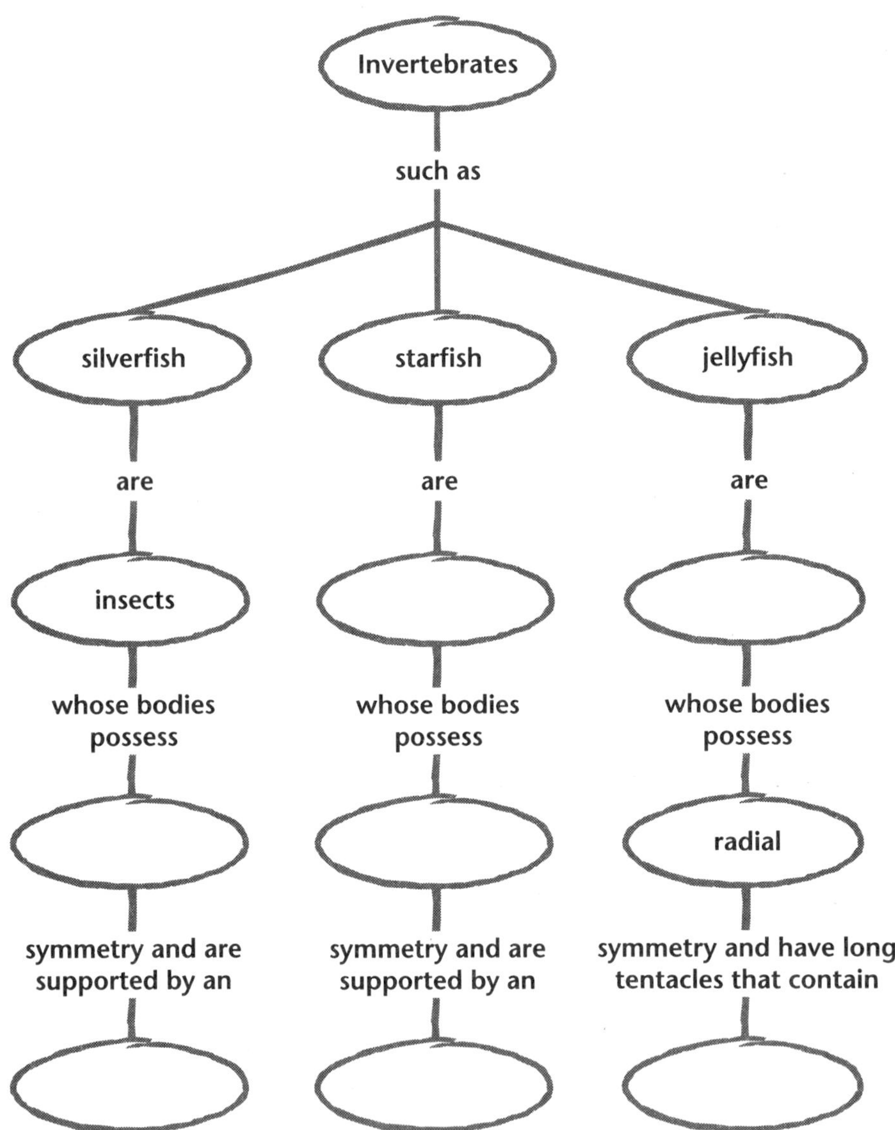

Chapter 2 Performance-Based Assessment

TEACHER'S PREPARATORY GUIDE

Purpose

Students will research and report the properties of various invertebrates in the context of an employment agency.

Time Required

One 45-minute class period

P. B. A. Ratings

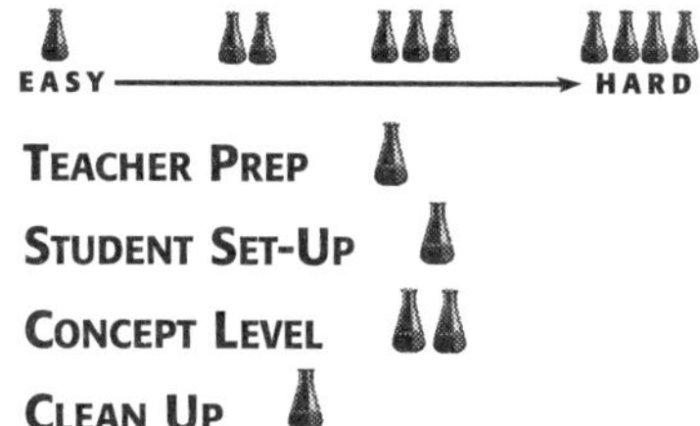

Advance Preparation

Gather reference materials on invertebrates. Secure access to the Internet, if possible.

Teaching Strategies

This activity works best in groups of 2–3 students.

Evaluation Strategies

Use the following rubric to evaluate student performance.

CLASSROOM TESTED & APPROVED

Susan Gorman
Northridge Middle School
North Richland Hills, Texas

Rubric for Chapter 2 Assessment

Possible points	Completion of activity (100 points possible)
100–90	Demonstrates exceptional creativity; understanding of animal is thorough and accurate; presentation is clear and readable; high level of detail
89–80	Demonstrates some creativity; understanding of animal may be somewhat unfocused; presentation is somewhat unclear; moderate level of detail
79–70	Demonstrates lack of creativity; understanding of animal is questionable; presentation is unclear; low level of detail; activity not complete
69–1	Demonstrates no creativity; understanding of animal is flawed; serious lack of detail; activity not taken seriously

Name ______________________ Date ____________ Class ____________

CHAPTER 2 INVERTEBRATES

Chapter 2 Performance-Based Assessment

MATERIALS

- reference materials on invertebrates
- Internet access

Objective

You will use what you already know as well as what you learn by doing research to help an invertebrate get a job.

Know the Score!

As you work through the activity, keep in mind that you will be earning a grade for the following:

- how thoroughly you complete the activity (100%)

Procedure

1. What type of invertebrate has your teacher assigned you?

____

2. Imagine that you work for an employment agency. The invertebrate that you have been assigned is your client. Read about your client using the reference materials that your teacher has provided. Write a paragraph about your client and his special traits, such as medicinal uses, agricultural uses, regenerative abilities, etc.

____

____

____

____

____

____

____

____

3. Think about what types of companies could use this invertebrate. Make up a name for such a company and describe it below. How will your client "fit in" there?

____

____

____

____

Module B
Chapter 3: Fishes, Amphibians, and Reptiles
Lesson Plan
Section 1: What Are Vertebrates?

Pacing

1 Block = 45 minutes

Regular Schedule:	**with Lab(s):** N/A	**without Lab(s):** 2 Days
Block Schedule:	**with Lab(s):** N/A	**without Lab(s):** 1 Day

Objectives

1. List the four characteristics of chordates.
2. Describe the main characteristics of vertebrates.
3. Explain the difference between an exotherm and an endotherm.

Standards Covered

Unifying Concepts and Processes (UCP)

1. Systems, order and organization
2. Evidence, models, and explanation
3. Change, constancy, and measurement
4. Evolution and equilibrium
5. Form and function

Science As Inquiry (SAI)

1. Abilities necessary to do scientific inquiry

Life Science (LS)
Structures and Functions of Living Systems (LS 1)

1a. Living system at all levels of organization demonstrate the complementary nature of structure and function. Important levels of organization from structure and function include cells, tissues, organs, organ systems, whole organs, and ecosystems.

1d. Specialized cells perform specialized functions in multicellular organisms. Groups of specialized cells cooperate to form a tissue, such as a muscle. Different tissues are in turn grouped together to form larger function units, called organs. Each type of cell, tissue, and organ has a distinct structure and a set of functions that serve the organism as a whole.

Regulation and Behavior (LS 3)

3a. All organisms must be able to obtain and use resources, grow, reproduce, and maintain stable internal conditions while living in a constantly changing external environment.

3b. Regulations of an organism's internal environment involves sensing the internal environment and changing physiological activities to keep conditions in the range required for the organism to survive.

Name ______________________ Date __________ Class __________

3c. Behavior is one kind of response an organism can make to an internal or environmental stimulus. A behavior response requires coordination and communication at many levels, including cells, organ systems, and whole organisms. A behavioral response is a set of actions determined in part by heredity and in part from experience.

3d. An organisms behavior evolves through adaptation to its environment. How a species moves, obtains food, reproduces, and responds to danger are all based on the species' evolutionary history.

Diversity and Adaption of Organisms (LS 5)

5a. Millions of species of animals, plants, and microorganisms are alive today. Although different species might look dissimilar, the unity among organisms becomes apparent from an analysis of internal structures, the similarity of the chemical processes, and their evidence of common ancestry.

Key
PE = Pupil's Edition
ATE = Annotated Teacher's Edition
An asterisk indicates the item is part of the Unit Resource booklet for this unit.

Block 1

Focus *5 minutes*

______ **Bellringer,** ATE p. 60. While you are taking attendance, ask students to ponder this question: What are some of the physical characteristics shared by dinosaurs and people? Have each student jot down two or three ideas. Then briefly discuss students' lists before beginning the section.

Motivate *15 minutes*

______ **Demonstration,** "Assembling Skeletons," ATE p. 60. As an introduction to vertebrates, have students reassemble small mammal skeletons. Obtain owl pellets (the bones of animals eaten by owls) from a nature center or biological supply company. Provide students with a simple illustration of a small mammal skeleton as a reference. In groups of two or three, have students break apart pellets and sort the bones, reconstructing an "exploded view" of whatever small mammal skeletons they find. This activity supports STANDARDS LS1a and 5a.

Teach *25 minutes*

______ **Math and More,** ATE p. 61. Using the figures below, have students construct a pie graph to show the relative numbers of the species in the different classes of vertebrates. Fish: 25,000; Amphibians: 4,500; Reptiles: 6,000; Birds: 9,000; Mammals: 4,300.

______ **Science Skills Worksheet Chapter 3,*** "Grasping Graphing." Students learn how to construct bar, line, and pie graphs.

______ **Teaching Transparency 59,*** "Chordates." This transparency illustrates the four chordate characteristics in a lancelet: a tail, a notochord, a hollow nerve cord, and pharyngeal pouches.

Homework

______ **Directed Reading Worksheet Chapter 3,* Section 1.** This worksheet reinforces the main concepts in the section while developing students' reading skills, and supports STANDARDS 5 and 5c.

Block 2

Teach *15 minutes*

______ **Real World Connection,** ATE p. 61. Have students research the field of paleontology and report their findings to the class. The report could be part of a special "career day" on which students present reports on a variety of scientific fields. Suggest that students answer questions such as the following: What do paleontologists do? What type of education do they need? What types of career opportunities exist for paleontologists?

Extend *20 minutes*

______ **Activity,** ATE p. 62. Invite a paleontologist or fossil enthusiast to speak with the class about fossil hunting in your area.

Close *10 minutes*

______ **Alternative Assessment,** ATE p.62. Have small groups of students compile lists of three or four questions related to the content in this section. Then have students use their questions to quiz each other.

Homework

______ **Review,** PE p. 62. Students answer three questions that review the lesson content.

Additional Resource Options

______ **Science Puzzlers, Twisters & Teasers, Worksheet Chapter 3.*** These worksheets offer puzzles, games, and logic problems that use vocabulary and concepts from the chapter.

______ **Weird Science,** "Warm Brains in Cold Water," PE p. 85. Students read a passage about certain species of "brain-warming" fish, then contact a local pet store for further information about the water temperatures that best suit fish from different regions.

______ **Quiz,** ATE p. 62. Students answer two questions about vertebrates.

Name ______________________ Date ____________ Class ____________

_____ **Module B Guided Reading Audio CD Program, Disc 16, Tracks 1-2.** The audio reading of the chapter provides essential chapter content for ESL students, auditory learners, and struggling readers.

_____ **NSTA *sci*LINKS:** *Vertebrates, sci*LINKS number HSTL380. Students research Internet resources related to vertebrates.

Module B
Chapter 3: Fishes, Amphibians, and Reptiles
Lesson Plan
Section 2: Fishes

Pacing
1 Block = 45 minutes
Regular Schedule: **with Lab(s):** 3 Days **without Lab(s):** 2 Days
Block Schedule: **with Lab(s):** 1 1/2 Days **without Lab(s):** 1 Day

Objectives
1. Describe the three classes of living fishes, and give an example of each.
2. Describe the function of a swim bladder and an oily liver.
3. Explain the difference between internal fertilization and external fertilization.

Standards Covered
UCP 1 Systems, order, and organization
UCP 2 Evidence, models, and explanation
UCP 3 Change, constancy, and measurement

SAI 1 Abilities necessary to do scientific inquiry

Science and Technology (ST)
1. Abilities of technological design
2. Understandings about science and technology

Science in Personal and Social Perspectives (SPSP)
5. Science and technology in society

History and Nature of Science (HNS)
1. Science as a human endeavor

Structures and Functions of Living Systems (LS 1)

LS 1a. Living system at all levels of organization demonstrate the complementary nature of structure and function. Important levels of organization from structure and function include cells, tissues, organs, organ systems, whole organs, and ecosystems.

LS 1d. Specialized cells perform specialized functions in multicellular organisms. Groups of specialized cells cooperate to form a tissue, such as a muscle. Different tissues are in turn grouped together to form larger functional units, called organs. Each type of cell, tissue, and organ has a distinct structure and a set of functions that serve the organism as a whole.

Name ______________________________ Date ____________ Class ____________

Reproduction and Heredity (LS2)

LS 2a. Reproduction is a characteristic of all living systems; because no individual organism lives forever, reproduction is essential to the continuation of every species. Some organisms reproduce asexually while other organisms reproduce sexually.

Regulation and Behavior (LS 3)

LS 3a. Behavior is one kind of response an organism can make to an internal or environmental stimulus. A behavior response requires coordination and communication at many levels, including cells, organ systems, and whole organisms. A behavioral response is a set of actions determined partially by heredity and partially from experience.

LS 3d. An organism's behavior evolves through adaptation to its environment. How a species moves, obtains food, reproduces, and responds to danger are all based on the species' evolutionary history.

LS 5a. Millions of species of animals, plants, and microorganisms are alive today. Although different species might look dissimilar, the unity among organisms becomes apparent from an analysis of internal structures, the similarity of the chemical processes, and their evidence of common ancestry.

LS 5c. Extinction of a species occurs when the environment changes and the adaptive characteristics of a species are insufficient to allow for its survival. Fossils indicate that many organisms that lived long ago are extinct. Extinction of a species is common; most of the species that have lived on earth no longer exist.

Block 1

Focus *5 minutes*

______ **Bellringer,** ATE p. 63. Have students write a book-title pun on the subject of fishes. Write a few titles on the board to get students' creative juices flowing, such as the following: *I Like Fishes, by Ann Chovie; Life on a Limb,* by Anna Perch; *Fish Story,* by Rod Enreel.

Motivate *15 minutes*

______ **Group Activity,** ATE p. 63. Have students turn the classroom or hallway into a fantasy sea world. Using books, magazines, and other media, students should draw, accurately color, and cut out two or three different fish each. Before posting the fish around the room, have students make a card with the name of the fish, its range, and its size.

Teach *25 minutes*

______ **Reading Strategy,** "Prediction Guide," ATE p. 65. Ask students: What are the three types of fishes alive in the world today?

______ **Whiz-Bang Demonstrations, Chapter 3,*** "The Fish in the Abyss." This demonstration introduces students to the role of camouflage, and protective coloration, and supports STANDARDS Ls 1a and 3d.

______ **Discussion,** "Aquarium Presentations," ATE p. 64, Encourage students who have aquariums to share information about their fish with the class. Discuss the importance of providing oxygen-rich water and other care requirements.

Homework

______ **Homework,** ATE p. 65. Have students indicate which class (or classes) of fishes have the following characteristics: *J* for jawless, *C* for cartilaginous, and *B* for bony: gills, denticles, cartilage skeleton, swim bladder, scales.

Block 2

Teach *25 minutes*

______ **QuickLab,** PE p. 67. Supply each group of students with water, cooking oil, a balloon, and a bowl. Have students follow the steps of the QuickLab to learn through a model how an oily liver keeps a shark afloat.

______ **MathBreak,** PE p. 66. Students calculate how many species of bony fishes there are given the total number of fish species and the percentage that are bony.

______ **Teaching Transparency 269,*** "How a Cell Produces an Electric Current." This transparency, which links to physical science, illustrates the process through which a cell produces electric current.

Extend *10 minutes*

______ **Math and More,** ATE p. 66. *Carcharodon megalodon* shark teeth are as much as 17.5 cm long. Based on its tooth length, scientists estimate that the Miocene-era shark was probably 12 m long, which is about twice as long as today's great white shark. Have students imagine that they discovered some shark teeth with the following lengths: 35 cm, 70 cm, and 8.75 cm. Have them use ratios to estimate the sizes of the sharks these teeth came from.

Close *10 minutes*

______ **Quiz,** ATE p. 67. Students answer two questions about bony fishes and sharks.

______ **Review,** PE p. 67. Students answer four questions that review the lesson content.

Homework

______ **Alternative Assessment,** "Concept Mapping," ATE p. 67. Create a concept map using the following terms (students may also supply the connecting words linking the terms): vertebrate, chordate, notochord, tail, hollow nerve chord, pharyngeal pouches.

Block 3

Lab Days *45 minutes*

______ **Making Models,** "Floating a Pipe Fish," page 78. Students make a model of a fish with a swim bladder, and then make the fish float in a container of water halfway between the top of the water and the bottom of the container. This lab supports STANDARDS UCP 5, SAI 2, and HNS 2.

Name ______________________________ Date ______________ Class ______________

______ **Datasheets for LabBook, Chapter 3,*** "Floating a Pipe Fish." This blackline master makes progressing through the lab easier for students and grading easier for you.

Additional Resource Options

______ **Directed Reading Worksheet Chapter 3,* Section 2.** This worksheet reinforces the main ideas in the section while developing students' reading skills.

______ **Across the Sciences,** "Robot Fish," PE p. 84. Students read a passage about a robotic fish designed by scientists at MIT, then conduct a brief experiment to view vortices in a roasting pan.

______ **Homework,** "Researching Fishes," ATE p. 63, Students choose one type of fish sold at a local supermarket and research its natural habitat and the amount harvested each year.

______ **Module B Guided Reading Audio CD Program, Disc 16, Track 3.** The audio reading of the chapter provides essential chapter content for ESL students, auditory learners, and struggling readers.

______ **NSTA *sci*LINKS:** *Fishes, sci*LINKS number HSTL385. Students research Internet resources related to fishes.

Name ______________________ Date ____________ Class ____________

Module B
Chapter 3: Fishes, Amphibians, and Reptiles
Lesson Plan
Section 3: Amphibians

Pacing
1 Block = 45 minutes

Regular Schedule:	**with Lab(s):** N/A	**without Lab(s):** 2 Days
Block Schedule:	**with Lab(s):** N/A	**without Lab(s):** 1 Day

Objectives
1. Understand the importance of amphibians in evolution.
2. Explain how amphibians breathe.
3. Describe metamorphosis in amphibians.

Standards Covered
UCP1 Systems, order, and organization
UCP2 Evidence, models, and explanation
UCP3 Change, constancy, and measurement
UCP4 Evolution and equilibrium
UCP5 Form and function

SAI1 Abilities necessary to do scientific inquiry

Structures and Functions of Living Systems (LS 1)

LS 1a. Living systems at all levels of organization demonstrate the complementary nature of structure and function. Important levels of organization from structure and function include cells, tissues, organs, organ systems, whole organs, and ecosystems.

LS 3c. Behavior is one kind of response an organism can make to an internal or environmental stimulus. A behavior response requires coordination and communication at many levels, including cells, organ systems, and whole organisms. A behavioral response is a set of actions determined partially by heredity and partially from experience.

LS 3d. An organisms behavior evolves through adaptation to its environment. How a species moves, obtains food, reproduces, and responds to danger are based in the species' evolutionary history.

LS 4d. The number of organisms an ecosystem can support depends on the resources available and the abiotic factors, such as quantity of light and water, range of temperatures, and soil composition. Given adequate biotic and abiotic resources and no disease or predators, populations (including humans) increase at rapid rates. Lack of resources and other factors, such as predation and climate, limit the growth if population in specific niches in the ecosystem.

Name ______________________ Date ____________ Class ____________

LS 5b. Biological evolution accounts for the diversity of species developed through gradual processes over many generations. Species acquire many of their unique characteristics through biological adaptation, which involves the selection of naturally occurring variations in populations. Biological adaptations include changes of structure, behavior, or physiology that enhance survival and reproductive success in a particular environment.

LS 5c. Extinction of a species occurs when the environment changes and the adaptive characteristics of a species are insufficient to allow for its survival. Fossils indicate that many organisms that lived long ago are extinct. Extinction of a species is common; most of the species that have lived on earth no longer exist.

Block 1

Focus *5 minutes*

______ **Bellringer,** ATE p. 68. On the board or overhead projector, instruct the students to answer the following questions in their ScienceLog: What is an advantage to the thin, moist skin of amphibians? What is the primary disadvantage to such skin?

Motivate *10 minutes (+ 5 minutes the following day)*

______ **Demonstration,** "Illustrating Fossilization," ATE p. 68. Show students how fossils are formed. Fill a small bucket halfway with sand. Place a kitchen sponge on top of the sand. Pour sand on top of the sponge until the bucket is nearly filled. Next, pour table salt in a small bucket of warm water, and stir until the salt no longer dissolves. Pour the solution over sand in the bucket, and leave overnight. On the next day, uncover the sponge. The water should have evaporated, and the salt should have hardened the sponge. Explain to students that fossils are formed in a similar manner. (Dissolved minerals enter openings or spaces in plant or animal material and harden.)

Teach *30 minutes*

______ **Activity,** "Observing Development," ATE p. 70. Obtain frog or salamander eggs either locally or from a biological supply company. Set up an aquarium, and allow students to observe the metamorphosis that follows. Students should sketch the process each step of the way. This activity supports STANDARD UCP1-3.

______ **Teaching Transparency 60,*** "Metamorphosis of a Frog." This transparency illustrates the steps of metamorphosis for a frog, and supports STANDARD 2a.

______ **Reteaching,** "Poster Project," ATE p. 70. Have students create a poster with captions showing how a tadpole changes into a frog.

Homework

______ **Directed Reading Worksheet Chapter 3,* Section 3.** This worksheet reinforces the main concepts in the section while developing students' reading skills.

______ **Homework,** "Research Cloning," ATE p. 69. Tell students that the African clawed frog *(Xenopus laevis)* was the first vertebrate to be successfully cloned. Have students use library or Internet resources to locate information about this event and report their findings to the class.

Name ______ Date ______ Class ______

Block 2

Teach *10 minutes*

______ **Self-Check,** PE p. 69. Students answer a question about the relationship between amphibian skin and a lung.

______ **Apply,** PE p. 71. Students apply their knowledge of amphibians to formulate a hypothesis about why amphibians are sensitive to air and water pollution.

Extend *20 minutes*

______ **Research,** ATE p. 72. Have interested students conduct research about the field of herpetology, the branch of zoology that deals with amphibians and reptiles. Students could prepare reports and present them to the class. As an alternative, invite a herpetologist or other zoologist from the area to speak with the class about herpetology.

Close *15 minutes*

______ **Quiz,** ATE p. 72. Students answer three questions about amphibians

______ **Alternative Assessment,** ATE p. 72. Have students compose a song or poem accurately describing the life cycle of an amphibian of their choice.

Homework

______ **Review,** PE p. 72. Students answer five questions that review the lesson content.

Additional Resource Options

______ **Skill Builder,** "A Prince of a Frog," p. 128. Students observe a live frog in a dry container and in water, then use their observations to write a report about amphibian anatomy and behavior. This lab supports STANDARDS UCP2, 4,5, SAI 1, LS1a,3c,3d,5b.

______ **Datasheets for LabBook, Chapter 3,*** "A Prince of a Frog." This blackline master makes progressing through the lab easier for students and grading easier for you.

______ **Module B Guided Reading Audio CD Program, Disc 16, Track 4.** The audio reading of the chapter provides essential chapter content for ESL students, auditory learners, and struggling readers.

______ **NSTA *sci*LINKS:** *Amphibians, sci*LINKS number HSTL390. Students research Internet resources related to amphibians.

Name ________________________________ Date ______________ Class______________

Module B
Chapter 3: Fishes, Amphibians, and Reptiles
Lesson Plan
Section 4: Reptiles

Pacing

1 Block = 45 minutes

Regular Schedule:	**with Lab(s):** N/A	**without Lab(s):** 2 Days
Block Schedule:	**with Lab(s):** N/A	**without Lab(s):** 1 Day

Objectives

1. Explain the adaptations that allow reptiles to live on land.
2. Name the three main groups of vertebrates that evolved from reptiles.
3. Describe the characteristics of an amniotic egg.
4. Name the three orders of modern reptiles.

Standards Covered

UCP1 Systems, order, and organization
UCP2 Evidence, models, and explanation
UCP4 Evolution and equilibrium
UCP5 Form and function

Structures and Functions of Living Systems (LS 1)

LS 1a. Living systems at all levels of organization demonstrate the complementary nature of structure and function. Important levels of organization from structure and function include cells, tissues, organs, organ systems, whole organisms, and ecosystems.

Reproduction and Heredity (LS 2)

LS 2a. Reproduction is a characteristic of all living systems; because no individual organism lives forever, reproduction is essential to the continuation of every species. Some organisms reproduce asexually. Others reproduce sexually.

LS 2b. In many species, including humans, females produce eggs and males produce sperm. Plants also reproduce sexually—the egg and sperm are produced in the flowers of flowering plants. An egg and sperm unite to begin development of a new individual. The new individual receives genetic information from its mother (via the egg) and its father (via the sperm). Sexually produced offspring are never identical to either of their parents.

LS 2e. The characteristics of an organism can be described in terms of a combination of traits. Some traits are inherited and others result from interactions with the environment.

Name ____________ Date ________ Class ________

Regulation and Behavior (LS 3)

LS 3a. All organisms must be ale to obtain and use resources, grow, reproduce, and maintain stable internal conditions while living in a constantly changing external environment.

LS 3c. Behavior is one kind of response an organism can make to an internal or environmental stimulus. A behavior response requires coordination and communication at many levels, including cells, organ systems, and whole organisms. A behavioral response is a set of actions determined in part by heredity and in part from experience.

LS 3d. An organisms behavior evolves through adaptation to its environment. How a species moves, obtains food, reproduces, and responds to danger are based in the species' evolutionary history.

Diversity and Adaption of Organisms (LS 5)

LS 5a. Millions of species of animals, plants, and microorganisms are alive today. Although different species might look dissimilar, the unity among organisms becomes apparent from an analysis of internal structures, the similarity of the chemical processes, and their evidence of common ancestry.

LS 5b. Biological evolution accounts for the diversity of species developed through gradual processes over many generations. Species aquire many of their unique characteristics through biological adaptation, which involves the selection of naturally occurring variations in populations. Biological adaptations include changes of structure, behavior, or physiology that enhance survival and reproductive success in a particular environment.

LS 5c. Extinction of a species occurs when the environment changes and the adaptive characteristics of a species are insufficient to allow for its survival. Fossils indicate that many organisms that lived long ago are extinct. Extinction of a species is common; most of the species that have lived on earth no longer exist.

Block 1

Focus *5 minutes*

_____ **Bellringer,** ATE p. 73. Have students list three adjectives they associate with reptiles. They should record their responses in their ScienceLog under the heading *First Impressions*. After they read the section, have them record three more adjectives under the heading *Second Impressions.*

Name ______________________________ Date ____________ Class ____________

Motivate *10 minutes*

______ **Discussion,** "Exploring Fears," ATE p. 73. Ask students to list the five most fearsome creatures on Earth. Likely, many of the named animals will be reptiles, especially snakes. Ask students: Why is this so? Is their reputation deserved?

Teach *30 minutes*

______ **Teaching Transparency 61,*** "Reptile History." This transparency shows that early reptiles were the ancestors of modern reptiles, birds, and mammals.

______ **Demonstration,** "Reptile Exhibit," ATE p. 75. Invite a reptile expert from the local zoo or an amateur reptile enthusiast to bring several reptiles to the class for a hands-on presentation. Afterward, have students describe in their ScienceLog their impressions of the reptiles, including the reptiles' physical characteristics and the way the reptiles felt to the touch.

______ **Self-Check,** p.75. Students answer two questions about reptiles.

Homework

______ **Homework,** "Reporting on Reptiles," ATE p. 76. Have students choose their favorite reptile and write a brief report about the animal. Students should include the following information: size, appearance, range (where is it found in the world?), habitat, diet, adaptations to its particular way of life (i.e. what tricks or tools does it use to survive), relationship to people, and its status in the world (is it endangered? rare? common?).

Block 2

Teach *20 minutes*

______ **Reinforcement Worksheet Chapter 3,*** "Cold-blooded Critters." Students complete a chart of cold-blooded critters (reptiles, fishes, and amphibians) using a list of characteristics.

______ **Critical Thinking Worksheet Chapter 3,*** "Frogs Aren't Breathing Easy." Students read a passage from *The Frog Killer* that explains how a fungus that attacks frogs' skin may be responsible for declining populations. Students then apply critical thinking skills to answer two conceptual questions about this topic.

Extend *15 minutes*

______ **Research,** ATE p. 77. Have students investigate and write a report on the differences between the diet of an alligator and that of a similarly sized carnivorous mammal (a lion or tiger). Which of these animals eats more? Why?

Name ______________________________ Date ____________ Class ____________

Close *10 minutes*

_____ **Quiz,** ATE p. 77. Students answer two questions about reptiles.

Homework

_____ **Review,** ATE p.77. Students answer three questions that review the lesson content.

Additional Resource Options

_____ **Long-Term Projects and Research Ideas, Chapter 3,*** "Go Fish!". Research ideas: illegal hunting of reptiles, lampreys in the Great Lakes; surviving a venomous snake bite; Project idea: observing the schooling behavior of fish.

_____ **Directed Reading Worksheet Chapter 3,* Section 4.** This worksheet reinforces the main ideas in the section and develops students' reading skills.

_____ **Teaching Transparency 62,*** "Amniotic Egg." This transparency illustrates the parts of an amniotic egg: albumen, shell, amniotic sac, yolk, and allantois.

_____ **Math Skills for Science Worksheet Chapter 3,*** "Using Temperature Scales." Students learn how to convert between degrees Celsius and degrees Fahrenheit.

_____ **Math and More,** ATE p. 75. Students convert temperatures from Celsius to Fahrenheit.

_____ **Alternative Assessment,** ATE p. 77. Students imagine they are reptile restaurateurs, and prepare accurate menus that will please their ectothermic thick-skinned customers.

_____ **Module B Guided Reading Audio CD Program, Disc 16, Track 5.** The audio reading of the chapter provides essential chapter content for ESL students, auditory learners, and struggling readers.

_____ **NSTA *sci*LINKS:** *Reptiles, sci*LINKS number HSTL395. Students research Internet resources related to reptiles.

Name ______________________________ Date ______________ Class ______________

End of Chapter Review and Assessment

_____ **Study Guide,*** Vocabulary, Notes, and Chapter Review

_____ **Chapter Tests with Performance-Based Assessment, Chapter 3 Test***

_____ **Chapter Tests with Performance-Based Assessment, Performance-Based Assessment 3***

_____ **Concept Mapping Transparency 16***

Name ______________________ Date ____________ Class ____________

CHAPTER 3 DIRECTED READING WORKSHEET

Fishes, Amphibians, and Reptiles

Chapter Introduction

As you begin this chapter, answer the following.

1. Read the title of the chapter. List three things that you already know about this subject.

____

____

____

____

____

2. Write two questions about this subject that you would like answered by the time you finish this chapter.

____

____

____

Section 1: What Are Vertebrates? (p. 60)

3. What does a dinosaur skeleton have in common with your skeleton?

____

____

____

Chordates (p. 60)

Mark each of the following statements *True* or *False*.

4. __________ Animals with a backbone belong to the phylum Chordata.
5. __________ The largest group of chordates are vertebrates.
6. __________ Lancelets do not have a backbone and therefore are not true chordates.
7. __________ An organism must have all four of the special chordate body parts as an adult in order to belong to the phylum Chordata.

Use Figure 3 on page 61 to choose the term in Column B that best matches the definition in Column A. Then write the corresponding letter in the space provided.

Column A	Column B
____ **8.** In vertebrates this structure is filled with spinal fluid.	**a.** notochord
____ **9.** This structure is located behind the anus.	**b.** pharyngeal pouch
____ **10.** In most vertebrates this structure disappears and a backbone grows in its place.	**c.** tail
____ **11.** This structure develops into a gill or other body part as an embryo matures.	**d.** hollow nerve cord

Getting a Backbone (p. 61)

12. Vertebrates are different from other chordates because

a. tunicates and lancelets have pharyngeal pouches.
b. they have a notochord.
c. they do not have a postanal tail.
d. they have a backbone and a skull.

13. A segmented column of bones called ____________________ protects the nerve cord, and a ____________________ protects the head.

14. The name of the tough material in the flexible parts of your nose and ears is called cartilage. True or False? (Circle one.)

15. Why do you think we know more about the evolution of vertebrates than any other group of organisms?

____

____

____

____

____

Are Vertebrates Warm or Cold? (p. 62)

16. There is an ideal temperature range for the chemical reactions that take place inside an animal's body cells. True or False? (Circle one.)

17. How does an endotherm stay warm when it's cold outside?

____

____

____

18. An endotherm's body temperature ______________ when the temperature of the environment changes. (changes a lot or stays about the same)

19. Which of the following statements is NOT true?

a. Ectotherms include most fish, amphibians, and reptiles.
b. Ectotherms' body temperature does not fluctuate.
c. Ectotherms' body temperature depends on their environment.
d. Ectotherms are sometimes called "coldblooded."

Review (p. 62)

Now that you've finished Section 1, review what you learned by answering the Review questions in your ScienceLog.

Section 2: Fishes (p. 63)

1. Which of the following statements is NOT true?

a. Fish can live almost anywhere except in cold arctic waters.
b. The first vertebrates appeared about 500 million years ago.
c. There are more species of fishes today than all other vertebrates combined.
d. More than 25,000 species of fishes exist.

2. Take a look at the fishes in Figure 6. Why do you think a seahorse is considered a fish?

____

____

____

Fish Characteristics (p. 63)

3. What parts of a fish's body help the fish move, steer, stop, and balance?

____

____

4. The lateral line system in fish enables them to keep track of information. True or False? (Circle one.)

Name ______________________________ Date ____________ Class____________

5. How do fish use their gills to breathe?

____

____

____

____

6. In external fertilization, the male fish drops sperm onto the unfertilized eggs in the water. True or False? (Circle one.)

7. After internal fertilization takes place, fish always give birth to live young. True or False? (Circle one.)

Types of Fishes (p. 65)

8. There are ____________________ different classes of fishes alive today. Two other classes of fishes are now ____________________.

9. Which is NOT true of jawless fishes?
   a. They are eel-like.
   b. They have backbones.
   c. They have round mouths.
   d. They were the first fishes.

10. The skeleton of a cartilaginous fish, such as a ray, never changes from cartilage to bone. True or False? (Circle one.)

11. A cartilaginous fish has a jaw and is an expert ____________________.

12. How can a shark's skin hurt you?

____

____

____

13. In order to stay afloat, a cartilaginous fish stores oil in its ____________________ and keeps swimming.

14. How does a cartilaginous fish keep from suffocating? (Circle all that apply.)
   a. It keeps swimming.
   b. It goes to the surface for air.
   c. It pumps water across its gills.
   d. It swims at certain depths.

15. All bony fishes have a _______________ made of bone instead of cartilage.

16. Bony fishes have a body covered by scales. True or False? (Circle one.)

17. Which is NOT true of a swim bladder?

a. It's found in bony fishes.
b. It's filled with gases from the bloodstream.
c. It gives the fish buoyancy.
d. It helps fishes steer against wave action.

18. Most bony fishes are _______________-finned fishes.

19. _______________-finned fishes, such as coelacanths, have thick, muscular fins.

20. Lungfishes, like the one shown in Figure 15 at the bottom of page 381, can gulp air. True or False? (Circle one.)

Review (p. 67)

Now that you've finished Section 2, review what you learned by answering the Review questions in your ScienceLog.

Section 3: Amphibians (p. 68)

1. 350 million years ago, what made the land such a wonderful place for vertebrates?

____

____

Moving to Land (p. 68)

2. The lungs of lungfishes became an adaptation for walking. True or False? (Circle one.)

3. What did the first amphibians look like?

____

____

4. Early amphibians needed to return to the water from time to time. True or False? (Circle one.)

Characteristics of Amphibians (p. 69)

5. How do amphibians lead a "double-life"?

____

____

____

____

____

Mark each of the following statements *True* or *False*.

6. __________ Amphibians do not drink water.

7. __________ An amphibian's skin makes it easy for the animal to become dehydrated.

8. __________ Some amphibians breathe only through their skin.

9. __________ All amphibians with brightly colored skin are deadly.

10. Amphibian embryos must develop in a wet environment because

a. their eggs lack shells.
b. they begin life as fish.
c. they are ectotherms.
d. the water is less polluted than the air.

11. When an amphibian goes through ______________________, it changes from its larval form, a tadpole, into its adult form.

12. Where does the embryo of the Darwin frog finish developing?

____

____

Kinds of Amphibians (p. 71)

13. Frogs and toads belong to the same group of amphibians.

True or False? (Circle one.)

14. How are caecilians different from most other amphibians? (Circle all that apply.)

a. They don't have legs.
b. Some have bony scales.
c. They are shaped like snakes.
d. They have thin, moist skin.

15. How are salamanders similar to their prehistoric amphibian ancestors?

____

____

16. A good place to look for a salamander in North America is under a

______________________ or a ______________________.

17. All salamanders go through metamorphosis. True or False? (Circle one.)

18. Frogs and toads are found only in temperate parts of the world.

True or False? (Circle one.)

Use the information on page 72 to mark each of the following phrases *F* if it is characteristic of a frog, *T* if it is characteristic of a toad, or *B* if it is characteristic of both a frog and a toad.

19. _____ extendible, sticky tongue

20. _____ dry, bumpy skin

21. _____ spends more time in the water

22. _____ vocal chords

23. _____ powerful leg muscles

24. _____ well-developed ears

25. _____ moist skin

26. Frogs have a special structure called a vocal sac that humans don't have. What does this structure do?

____

____

____

____

Review (p. 72)

Now that you've finished Section 3, review what you learned by answering the Review questions in your ScienceLog.

Section 4: Reptiles (p. 73)

1. After ______________________ years, some amphibians evolved into animals that could live on dry land.

2. Which of the following traits allowed the first reptiles to live completely out of the water? (Circle all that apply.)

a. an egg that could be laid on dry land
b. stronger, more vertical legs
c. thick, dry skin
d. teeth

Reptile History (p. 73)

3. Some prehistoric reptiles could fly. True or False? (Circle one.)

4. Mammals had reptile ancestors called ______________________ that are now extinct.

Characteristics of Reptiles (p. 74)

5. How is a reptile's skin an important adaptation for life on land?

____

____

____

____

6. Reptiles are less active when the environment is ______________________ and more active when the environment is ______________________.

7. Most reptiles live in mild climates because they usually cannot maintain a constant body temperature. True or False? (Circle one.)

8. What are the advantages of an amniotic egg?

____

____

____

____

____

Choose the part of the amniotic egg in Column B that best matches the definition in Column A, and write the corresponding letter in the space provided.

Column A	Column B
____ **9.** supplies the embryo with food	**a.** yolk
____ **10.** stores waste from the embryo and passes oxygen to the embryo	**b.** albumen
____ **11.** keeps the egg from drying out	**c.** amniotic sac
____ **12.** fluid-filled structure that protects the embryo from injury	**d.** allantois
____ **13.** provides the embryo with protein and water	**e.** shell

14. Which of the following are true of reptiles? (Circle all that apply.)

a. Reptiles don't undergo metamorphosis.
b. Reptile embryos develop directly into tiny reptiles.
c. All reptiles lay eggs.
d. Reptiles don't have a larval stage.

Types of Reptiles (p. 75)

15. Most of the reptiles that have ever lived are now

______________________.

16. List the three groups of modern reptiles.

____

____

17. Which of the following is NOT true of both turtles and tortoises?

a. They are only distantly related to the other reptiles.
b. They spend all of their lives on land.
c. Their armorlike shells protect them from predators.
d. They are slow and inflexible.

18. All crocodiles and alligators are ______________________. (carnivores or herbivores)

19. In Figure 32 at the bottom of page 76, how can you tell the difference between a crocodile and an alligator?

____

____

____

Mark each of the following statements *True* or *False*.

20. ________ Lizards include skinks, chameleons, alligators, and geckos.

21. ________ On rare occasions, the largest lizards, one of which is shown in Figure 33, have been known to eat humans.

22. ________ Snakes move on smooth surfaces by using suckers on their bellies to grip the surface and pull forward.

23. ________ Snakes are not herbivores.

24. ________ Snakes have special, five-jointed jaws that allow them to swallow their prey whole.

25. ________ Snakes have an acute sense of hearing.

26. How does a snake use its tongue to smell?

____

____

____

____

____

____

____

Review (p. 77)

Now that you've finished Section 4, review what you've learned by answering the Review questions in your ScienceLog.

Name ________________ Date ________ Class ________

CHAPTER 3 VOCABULARY & NOTES WORKSHEET

Fishes, Amphibians, and Reptiles

By studying the Vocabulary and Notes listed for each section below, you can gain a better understanding of this chapter.

SECTION 1

Vocabulary

In your own words, write a definition for each of the following terms in the space provided.

1. vertebrate ________________

2. vertebrae ________________

3. endotherm ________________

4. ectotherm ________________

Notes

Read the following section highlights. Then, in your own words, write the highlights in your ScienceLog.

- At some point during their development, chordates have a notochord, a hollow nerve cord, pharyngeal pouches, and a tail.
- Chordates include lancelets, tunicates, and vertebrates. Most chordates are vertebrates.
- Vertebrates differ from the other chordates in that they have a backbone and skull made of bone or cartilage.
- The backbone is composed of units called vertebrae.
- Vertebrates may be ectotherms or endotherms.
- Endotherms control their body temperature through the chemical reactions of their cells. Ectotherms do not.

Name ______________________ Date ____________ Class ____________

SECTION 2

Vocabulary

In your own words, write a definition for each of the following terms in the space provided.

1. fins ________________________________

2. scales ________________________________

3. lateral line system ________________________________

4. gills ________________________________

5. denticles ________________________________

6. swim bladder ________________________________

Notes

Read the following section highlights. Then, in your own words, write the highlights in your ScienceLog.

- There are three groups of living fishes: jawless fishes, cartilaginous fishes, and bony fishes.
- The cartilaginous fishes have an oily liver that helps them float.
- Most bony fishes have a swim bladder. The swim bladder is a balloonlike organ that gives bony fishes buoyancy.
- In external fertilization, eggs are fertilized outside the female's body. In internal fertilization, eggs are fertilized inside the female's body.

SECTION 3

Vocabulary

In your own words, write a definition for each of the following terms in the space provided.

1. lung ____

____

____

____

____

____

2. tadpole ____

____

____

____

____

____

3. metamorphosis ____

____

____

____

____

____

Notes

Read the following section highlights. Then, in your own words, write the highlights in your ScienceLog.

- Amphibians were the first vertebrates to live on land.
- Amphibians breathe by gulping air into their lungs and by absorbing oxygen through their skin.
- Amphibians start life in water, where they breathe through gills. During metamorphosis, they lose their gills and develop lungs and legs that allow them to live on land.
- Modern amphibians include caecilians, salamanders, and frogs and toads.

SECTION 4

Vocabulary

In your own words, write a definition for each of the following terms in the space provided.

1. therapsid ____

____

____

____

____

____

2. amniotic egg ____

____

____

____

____

____

Notes

Read the following section highlights. Then, in your own words, write the highlights in your ScienceLog.

- Reptiles evolved from amphibians by adapting to life on dry land.
- Reptiles have thick, scaly skin that protects them from drying out.
- A tough shell keeps the amniotic egg from drying out and protects the embryo.
- Amniotic fluid surrounds and protects the embryo in an amniotic egg.
- Vertebrates that evolved from early reptiles are reptiles, birds, and mammals.
- Modern reptiles include turtles and tortoises, lizards and snakes, and crocodiles and alligators.

Name ______________________ Date ____________ Class ____________

CHAPTER 3

CHAPTER REVIEW WORKSHEET

Fishes, Amphibians, and Reptiles

USING VOCABULARY

To complete the following sentences, choose the correct term from each pair of terms listed below, and write the term in the space provided.

1. At some point in their development, all chordates have ______________________. (lungs and a notochord or a hollow nerve cord and a tail)
2. Mammals evolved from early ancestors called ______________________. (therapsids or dinosaurs)
3. Fish are ______________________. (endotherms or ectotherms)
4. When a frog lays eggs that are later fertilized by sperm, it is an example of ______________________ fertilization. (internal or external)
5. The vertebrae wrap around and protect the ______________________ of vertebrates. (notochord or hollow nerve cord)

UNDERSTANDING CONCEPTS

Multiple Choice

6. Which of the following is NOT a vertebrate?
   - **a.** tadpole
   - **b.** lizard
   - **c.** lamprey
   - **d.** tunicate
7. Tadpoles change into frogs by the process of
   - **a.** evolution.
   - **b.** internal fertilization.
   - **c.** metamorphosis.
   - **d.** temperature regulation.
8. The swim bladder is found in
   - **a.** jawless fishes.
   - **b.** cartilaginous fishes.
   - **c.** bony fishes.
   - **d.** lancelets.
9. The amniotic egg first evolved in
   - **a.** bony fishes.
   - **b.** birds.
   - **c.** reptiles.
   - **d.** mammals.

10. The yolk holds
- **a.** food for the embryo.
- **b.** amniotic fluid.
- **c.** wastes.
- **d.** oxygen.

11. Both bony fishes and cartilaginous fishes have
- **a.** denticles.
- **b.** fins.
- **c.** an oily liver.
- **d.** a swim bladder.

12. Reptiles are adapted to a life on land because
- **a.** they can breathe through their skin.
- **b.** they are ectotherms.
- **c.** they have thick, moist skin.
- **d.** they have an amniotic egg.

Short Answer

13. How do amphibians breathe?

____

____

____

____

____

14. What characteristics allow fish to live in the water?

____

____

____

____

15. How does an embryo in an amniotic egg get oxygen?

____

____

____

____

CONCEPT MAPPING

16. Use the following terms to create a concept map: *dinosaur, turtle, reptiles, amphibians, fishes, shark, salamander, vertebrates.*

CRITICAL THINKING AND PROBLEM SOLVING

Write one or two sentences to answer each of the following questions:

17. Suppose you have found an animal that has a backbone and gills, but you can't find a notochord. Is it a chordate? How can you be sure?

18. Suppose you have found a shark that lacks the muscles needed to pump water over its gills. What does that tell you about the shark's lifestyle?

19. A rattlesnake does not see very well, but it can detect a temperature change of as little as three-thousandths of a degree Celsius. How is this ability useful to a rattlesnake?

20. It's 43°C outside, and the normal body temperature of a velociraptor is 38°C. Would you most likely find the raptor in the sun or in the shade? Explain.

MATH IN SCIENCE

21. A Costa Rican viper can eat a mouse that has one-third more mass than the viper. How much can you eat? Write down your mass in kilograms. To find your mass in kilograms, divide your mass in pounds by 2.2. If you were to eat a meal with a mass one-third larger than your mass, what would the mass of the meal be in kilograms?

CHAPTER 3

INTERPRETING GRAPHICS

Examine the graph of body temperatures below, and answer the questions that follow.

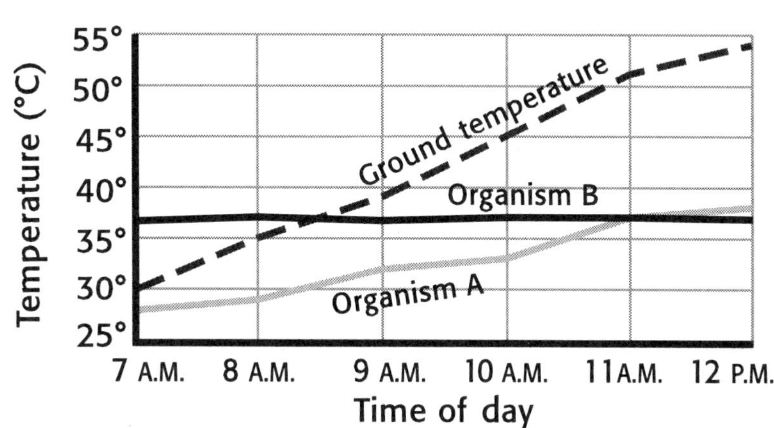

22. How do the body temperatures of organism A and organism B change with the ground temperature?

____

____

____

____

____

____

23. Which of these organisms is most likely an ectotherm? Why?

____

____

____

____

____

____

24. Which of these organisms is most likely an endotherm? Why?

____

____

____

____

____

____

READING CHECK-UP

Take a minute to review your answers to the ScienceLog questions at the beginning of the chapter. Have your answers changed? If necessary, revise your answers based on what you have learned since you began this chapter. Record your revisions in your ScienceLog.

Name ______________________ Date ____________ Class ____________

CHAPTER 3 SCIENCE PUZZLERS, TWISTERS & TEASERS

Fishes, Amphibians, and Reptiles

Chordate Code

1. Use the clue that is given to help you find several terms found in this chapter. Write your answers in the spaces provided.

   If the phrase:

   V E R T E B R A T E S A R E C H O R D A T E S

   is represented as:

   3 8 1 6 8 10 1 5 6 8 4 5 1 8 2 20 9 1 7 5 6 8 4

   what are the following vertebrate-related terms?

   a. 18 9 6 9 2 20 9 1 7 ____________________

   b. 6 5 12 14 ____________________

   c. 2 5 1 6 12 14 5 11 8 ____________________

   d. 8 2 6 9 6 20 8 1 15 ____________________

   e. 10 5 2 22 10 9 18 8 ____________________

   f. 4 19 12 18 5 14 2 9 1 7 ____________________

Scrambled Eggs

2. Below you will find several different reptilian eggs. The reptiles have begun to hatch, so all of the eggs have cracked open. The same letter has been lost out of each one. Unscramble the letters found within each egg and combine them with the missing letter to find what type of reptile is hatching from each egg. Write the names of the reptiles in the spaces provided.

   The missing letter is: ________

O L T G
L A A I

a. ____________________ **b.** ____________________

c. ____________________

d. ____________________ **e.** ____________________

Name ______________________ Date ____________ Class ____________

Who's Who

3. For each lettered statement below, decide if the statement best describes fishes, amphibians, or reptiles. If the statement describes fishes, place the capital letter in the box labeled *Fishes*. If the statement best describes amphibians, place the capital letter in the *Amphibians* box, and so on. Then unscramble the letters in each box to find the name of a reptile, fish, or amphibian. Write the name of the animal on the line beneath the box.

a. first vertebrates on Earth (K)
b. have a thick dry skin which helps them live on land (E)
c. obtain oxygen by gulping air into their lungs or by absorbing it through their skin (D)
d. all use lungs to breathe air (U)
e. most have a lateral line (A)
f. live part of their life in the water and part on land (O)
g. thought to be the ancestors of modern birds and mammals (T)
h. have three classes: jawless, cartilaginous, and bony (R)
i. undergo metamorphosis to change from larval to adult form (T)
j. lay eggs surrounded by a shell to protect them from drying out (T)
k. most use gills to breathe throughout their life (S)
l. live in almost every water environment (H)
m. often called ecological indicators due to their sensitivity to air and water pollution (A)
n. have stronger, more vertical legs (R)
o. eggs contain an amniotic sac filled with amniotic fluid (L)

Fishes	Amphibians	Reptiles

x. ______________ **y.** ______________ **z.** ______________

Name ______________________ Date ______________ Class ______________

CHAPTER 3 REINFORCEMENT WORKSHEET

Coldblooded Critters

Complete this worksheet after you read Chapter 3, Section 4.

1. Take a look at each of the illustrations in the chart on the next page. Label each illustration "Reptiles," "Fishes," or "Amphibians."
2. Read over the characteristics listed below. Then on the next page, write each characteristic in the box next to the group of animals that commonly have that characteristic. Some characteristics may be used more than once.

thin, moist skin

ectotherms

external or internal fertilization

amniotic egg

many have scales

some have young born live

only internal fertilization

fins

gills

most lay eggs on land

metamorphosis

eggs laid in water

no scales

vertebrates

thick, dry skin

mostly external fertilization

breathe through skin and lungs

some have swim bladders

"double life"

lateral line system

breathe through lungs

some have skeletons of cartilage

many have bright colors to scare predators

almost all adults have lungs

Name ______________________________ Date ______________ Class ______________

Coldblooded Critter Chart

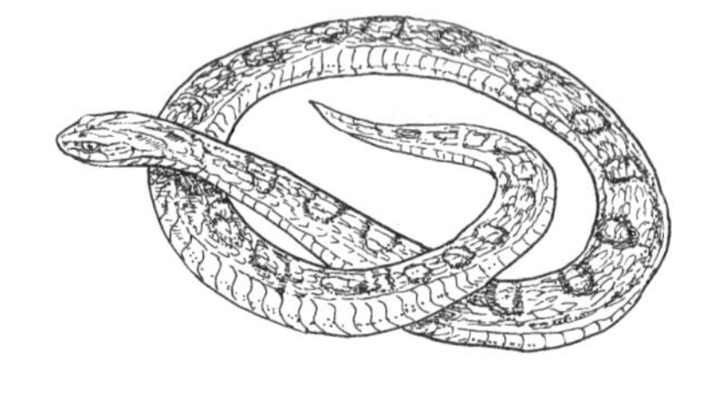 	

Name ______________________ Date ____________ Class ____________

CHAPTER 3 VOCABULARY REVIEW WORKSHEET

Fishin' for Vertebrates

Complete this puzzle after you finish reading Chapter 3.

ACROSS

1. crocodiles, turtles, and snakes

6. system of tiny rows of sense organs along the sides of a fish's body

8. cartilaginous fishes store oil here to stay afloat

9. group of fishes with skeletons made of bone and swim bladders

10. aquatic larva of an amphibian

11. balloonlike organ that gives bony fish buoyancy

14. an animal that maintains a constant body temperature

16. bony structures covering the skin of bony fishes

21. body parts of a fish that remove oxygen from water and carbon dioxide from blood

22. prehistoric reptile ancestor of mammals

23. frogs use a vocal sac to do this

24. structures made of bone contained in the fins of perch, minnows, and eels

25. hard-shelled reptiles that live only on land

DOWN

2. fertilization of an egg that occurs inside the female's body

3. fertilization of an egg that occurs outside the female's body

4. the first fishes were this type of fish

5. an animal with a body temperature that fluctuates with the temperature of its environment

7. an egg that is usually surrounded by a hard shell

12. small, toothlike structures on the skin of cartilaginous fishes

13. a change from a larval form to an adult form

15. sharks and skates are this type of fish

17. saclike organs that take oxygen from the air and deliver it to the blood

18. an animal with a skull and a backbone

19. these fishes have air sacs and can gulp air

20. fanlike structures that help fish move, steer, stop, balance

Name ______________________ Date ____________ Class __________

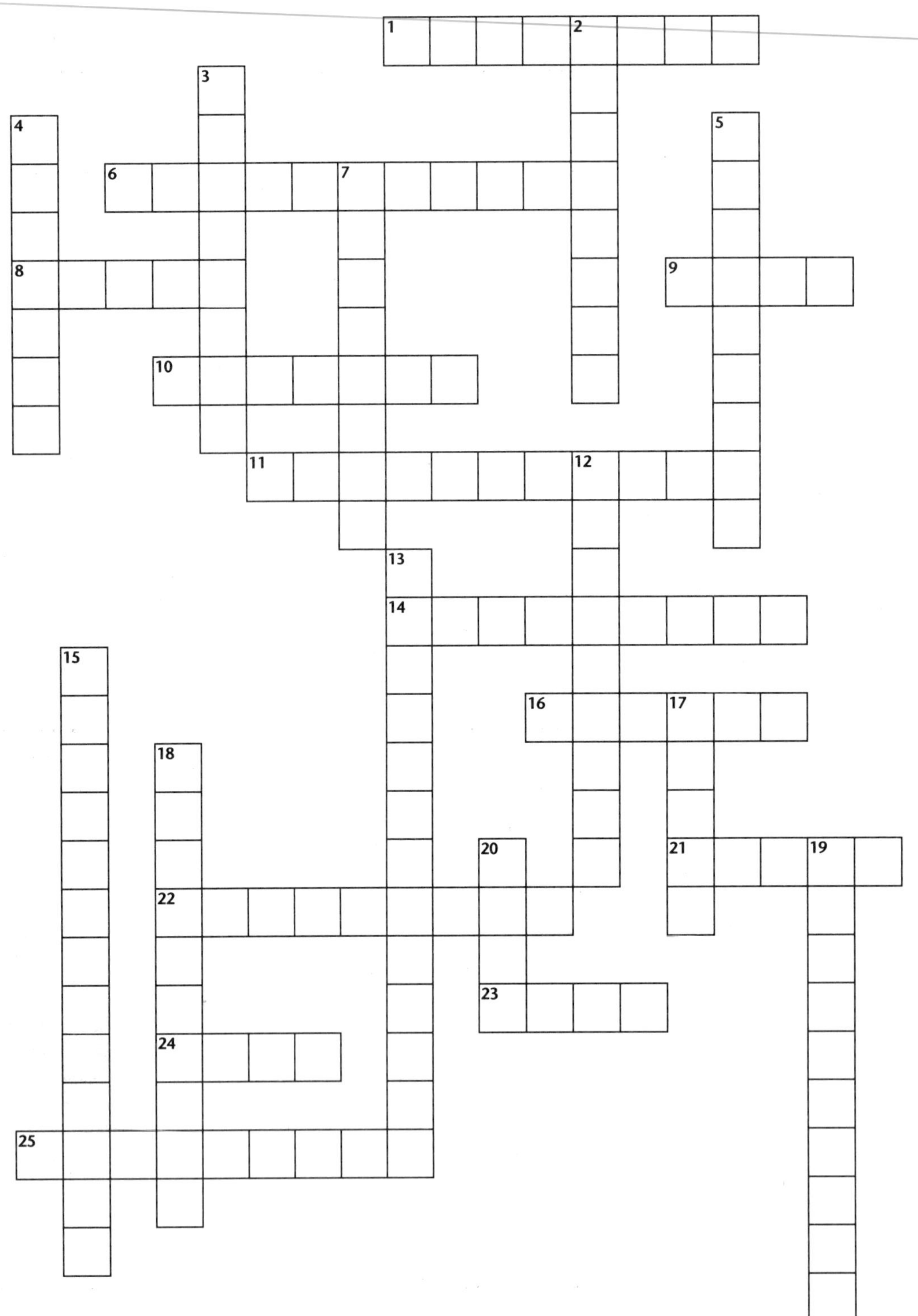

Name ______________________ Date ______________ Class ______________

CHAPTER 3 ▶▶▶

CHAPTER 3 CRITICAL THINKING WORKSHEET

Frogs Aren't Breathing Easy

Something is killing frogs all over the world. The list of suspects includes acid rain, pollution, and vanishing wetlands. But the real killer may be none of the above. A team of biologists suspects that a previously unknown fungus may be at least partly responsible for the global decline of frogs. . . .

To date the researchers have found the fungus in about 30 frog species from Australia, Central America, and the United States and have shown that it kills frogs in laboratory trials. The fungus attacks the frogs' skin . . .

The fungus, apparently a new species of aquatic chytrid fungi, has yet to be named.

USEFUL TERMS

fungus
a multicellular organism that gets food by breaking down other substances and absorbing the nutrients

chytrid
belonging to the phylum Chytridiomycota

Comprehending Ideas

1. Why would a fungus that affects skin be especially deadly to frogs?

____

____

____

____

____

Making Comparisons

2. Are fish or reptiles more likely to be affected by this fungus? Explain your answer.

____

____

____

____

____

____

____

____

Name ______________________ Date ______________ Class ____________

Predicting Consequences

3. Complete the chart below by stating how the factors in the left column could affect the frog population and lead to fungal infection.

Factors Contributing to Fungal Infection

Possible factors	Effect on frog population
increased pollution	
a foreign material or species in the frogs' habitat	
vanishing wetlands	

HELPFUL HINTS

Think about the effects of various treatments on other plants and animals.

Demonstrating Reasoned Judgment

4. If a substance were made that could rid the frogs of this killer fungus, how might it be given to the frogs?

____

____

____

____

____

____

HELPFUL HINTS

Because of their "double life," amphibians are easily affected by small environmental changes in water or on land.

Making Inferences

5. The Declining Amphibian Population Task Force was created in 1990. An estimated 500 environmental groups joined the force. Why do you think declining amphibian populations caused this much concern?

____

____

____

____

____

Name ______________________ Date ____________ Class ____________

CHAPTER 3 MATH IN SCIENCE: INTEGRATED SCIENCE

Using Temperature Scales

MATH SKILLS USED
Addition
Multiplication
Fractions
Decimals
Scientific Notation

Convert between degrees Fahrenheit and degrees Celsius.

Do you remember the last time you had your temperature taken? Your body temperature is usually about 98.6°F. This temperature is in degrees Fahrenheit (°F). The Fahrenheit temperature scale is a common temperature scale. In science class, however, a scale known as the Celsius (°C) scale is used. Temperatures in one scale can be mathematically converted to the other system using one of the equations below.

EQUATIONS: Conversion from Fahrenheit to Celsius: $\frac{5}{9} \times (°F - 32) = °C$

Conversion from Celsius to Fahrenheit: $\frac{9}{5} \times °C + 32 = °F$

SAMPLE PROBLEMS:

A. Convert 59°F to degrees Celcius.

$$°C = \frac{5}{9} \times (°F - 32)$$

$$°C = \frac{5}{9} \times (59 - 32)$$

$$°C = \frac{5}{9} \times 27$$

$$°C = \mathbf{15°C}$$

B. Convert 112°C to degrees Fahrenheit.

$$°F = \frac{9}{5} \times °C + 32$$

$$°F = \frac{9}{5} \times 112 + 32$$

$$°F = 201\frac{3}{5} + 32$$

$$°F = \mathbf{233\frac{3}{5}°F}$$

Turn Up the Temperature!

1. Convert the following temperatures from degrees Fahrenheit to degrees Celsius:

   a. 98.6°F ______________________

   b. 482°F ______________________

   c. −4°F ______________________

2. Convert the following temperatures from degrees Celsius to degrees Fahrenheit:

   a. 24°C ______________________

   b. 17°C ______________________

   c. 0°C ______________________

Challenge Yourself!

3. Convert 2.7×10^4°C to degrees Fahrenheit. ______________________

Name ______________________ Date ____________ Class ____________

CHAPTER 3 COMMUNICATING SKILLS

Grasping Graphing

When you bake cookies, you must use the right ingredients to make the cookies turn out right. Graphs are the same way. They require the correct ingredients, or components, to make them readable and understandable.

Bar and Line Graphs

- First, set up your graphs with an *x*-axis and a *y*-axis. The ***x*-axis** is horizontal, and the ***y*-axis** is vertical as shown in the example at right. The axes represent different variables in an experiment.

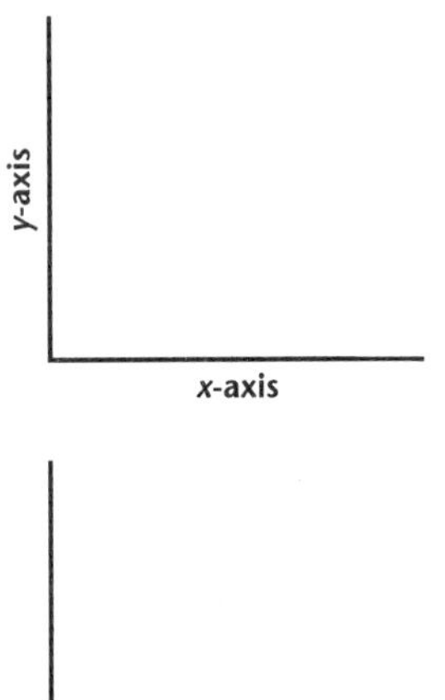

- The *x*-axis represents the independent variable. The **independent variable** is the variable whose values are chosen by the experimenter. For example, the range of grades is the independent variable.

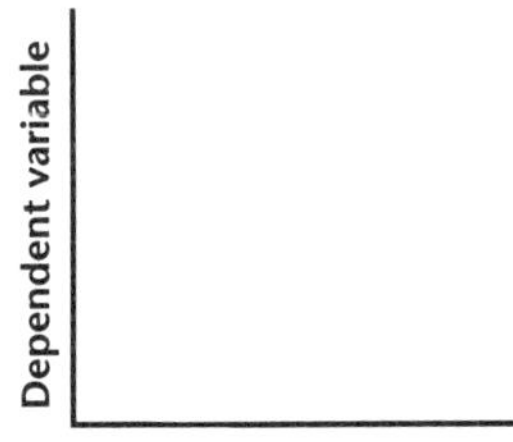

- The *y*-axis represents the dependent variable. The values for the **dependent variable** are determined by the independent variable. If you are grouping students by grades, the number of students in each group **depends** on the grade they get.

- Next choose a **scale** for each of the axes. Select evenly spaced intervals that include all of your data, as shown on the grade-distribution bar graph. When you label the axes, be sure to write the appropriate units where they apply.

- Next, plot your data on the graph. Make sure you double-check your numbers to ensure accuracy.

- Finally, give your graph a title. A **title** tells the reader what he or she is studying. A good title should explain the relationship between the variables. Now your graph is complete!

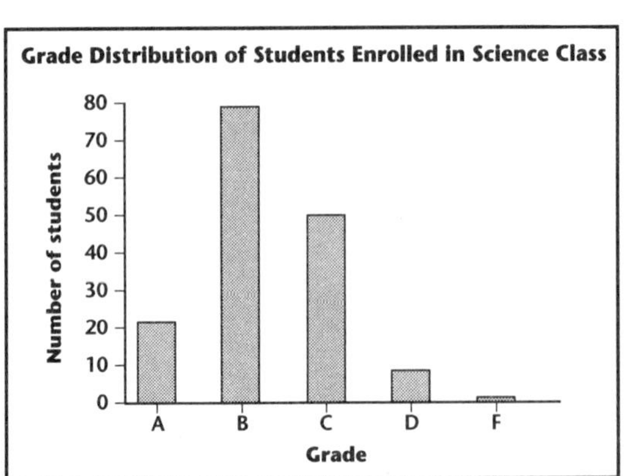

Pie Graphs

When you convert data to show percentages, you can use a pie graph. Pie graphs are shaped like a circle. The size of each "pie slice" is determined by the percentage it will represent. A full pie is equal to 100 percent, half a pie is equal to 50 percent, and so on.

Like bar and line graphs, pie graphs have independent and dependent variables. The independent variable is whatever the pie or slice of pie represents. The dependent variable is the size of the pie slice, the percentage of the whole it represents.

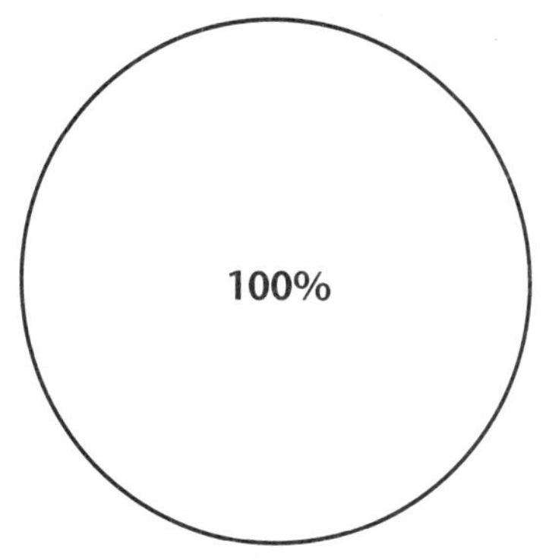

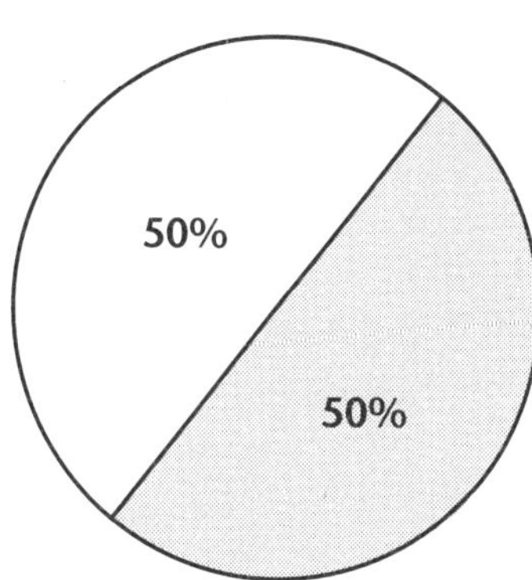

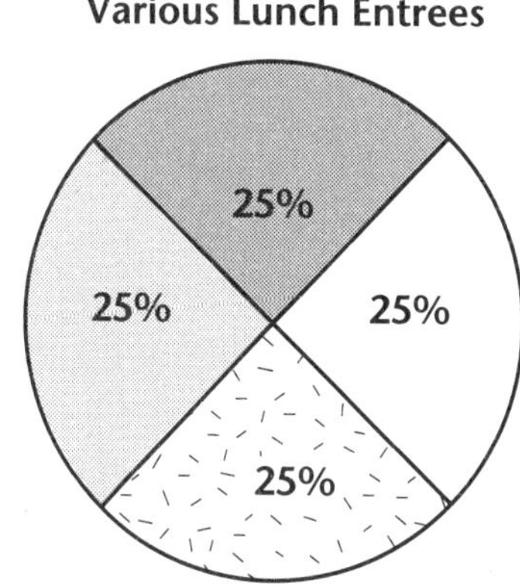

Your Turn

For each table (a) identify the independent and dependent variable, (b) determine the type of graph to use, and (c) provide a title.

1.

Amount of daily sunlight exposure (min)	Average height of plants (cm)
50	14.8
60	14.9
95	15.2
75	15.1
110	16.5
135	17.3
100	16.1
30	11.0

a. ____

b. ____

c. ____

2.

Student	Number of jelly beans consumed
Anthony	15
Keiko	28
Leigh Ann	58
Adam	22
Katie	12
Juan	17

a. ______________________________

b. ______________________________

c. ______________________________

Give It a Try

Graph the data below in your ScienceLog. Don't forget to do the following:

- Select the appropriate graph type.
- Identify the independent and the dependent variable.
- Choose an appropriate scale.
- Label the axes.
- Give your graph a title.

Amount of fertilizer added to soil (g)	Average height of plants (cm)
5	13.2
10	14.1
15	14.9
20	15.4
25	16.5
30	17.3
35	16.1
40	11.0

Name ______________________ Date ______________ Class ______________

CHAPTER 3 LAB DATASHEET

Floating a Pipe Fish

Bony fishes control how deep or shallow they swim with a special structure called a swim bladder. As gases are absorbed and released by the swim bladder, the fish rises or sinks in the water. In this activity, you will make a model of a fish with a swim bladder. Your challenge will be to make the fish float halfway between the top of the water and the bottom of the container. It will probably take several tries and a lot of observing and analyzing along the way.

MATERIALS

- water
- container for water at least 15 cm deep
- slender balloon
- small cork
- 12 cm length of PVC pipe, 3/4 in. diameter
- rubber band

Procedure

1. Estimate how much air you will need in the balloon so that your pipe fish will float halfway between the top of the water and the bottom of the container. Will you need to inflate the balloon halfway, just a small amount, or all the way? (It will have to fit inside the pipe, but there will need to be enough air to make the pipe float.)

____

2. Inflate your balloon. Hold the neck of the balloon so that no air escapes, and push the cork into the end of the balloon. If the cork is properly placed, no air should leak out when the balloon is held underwater.
3. Place your swim bladder inside the pipe, and place a rubber band along the pipe as shown. The rubber band will keep the swim bladder from coming out of either end.

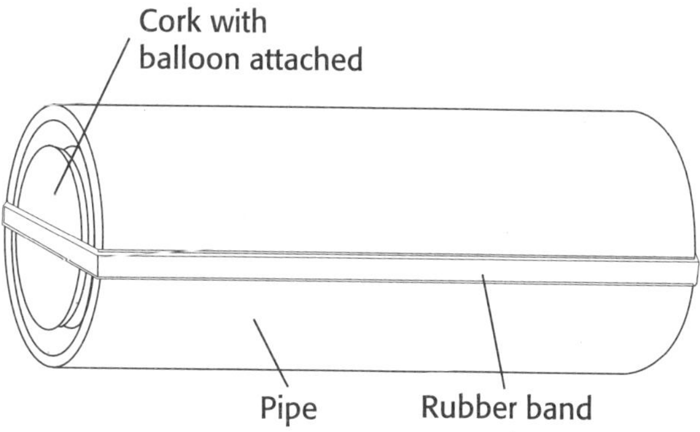

4. Place your pipe fish in the water, and note where the fish floats. Record your observations.

____

CHAPTER 3

5. If the pipe fish does not float where you want, take it out of the water, adjust the amount of air in the balloon, and try again.
6. You can release small amounts of air from the bladder by carefully lifting the neck of the balloon away from the cork. You can add more air by removing the cork and blowing more air into the balloon. Keep adjusting and testing until your fish floats halfway between the bottom of the container and the top of the water.

Analysis

7. Was the estimate you made in step 1 correct? Explain your answer.

   ____

8. In relation to the length and volume of the entire pipe fish, how much air was needed to make the fish float? State your answer as a percentage.

   ____

   ____

   ____

9. Based on the amount of space the balloon took up inside the pipe in your model, how much space do you estimate is taken up by a swim bladder inside a living fish? Explain.

   ____

   ____

   ____

   ____

   ____

Going Further

Some fast-swimming fishes, such as sharks, and marine mammals, such as whales and dolphins, do not have a swim bladder. Find out from the library or the Internet how these animals keep from sinking to the bottom of the ocean. Create a poster, and explain your results on index cards. Include drawings of the fish or marine mammals you have researched.

Name ______________________ Date ____________ Class ____________

CHAPTER 3 LAB DATASHEET

A Prince of a Frog

Imagine that you are a scientist interested in amphibians. You have heard in the news about amphibians disappearing all over the world. What a great loss it will be to the environment if all amphibians become extinct! Your job is to learn as much as possible about how frogs normally behave so that you can act as a resource for other scientists who are studying the problem.

In this activity, you will observe a normal frog in a dry container and in water.

MATERIALS

- live frog in a dry container
- live crickets
- 600 mL beaker
- container half-filled with dechlorinated water
- large rock
- protective gloves

Procedure

1. Use the data table below to record your observations in steps 3–11.

Observations of a Live Frog

Characteristic	Observation
Breathing	
Eyes	
Legs	
Response to food	
Response to noise	
Skin texture	
Swimming behavior	
Skin coloration	

2. Observe a live frog in a dry container. Draw the frog in the space on the next page. Label the eyes, nostrils, front legs, and hind legs.

3. Watch the frog's movements as it breathes air with its lungs. Write a description of the frog's breathing in the data table.

4. Look closely at the frog's eyes and note their location. Examine the upper and lower eyelids as well as the transparent third eyelid. Which of these three eyelids actually moves over the eye? Record your observation.

5. Study the frog's legs. Note in your data table the difference between the front and hind legs.

6. Place a live insect, such as a cricket, in the container. Observe and record how the frog reacts.

7. Carefully pick up the frog, and examine its skin. How does it feel? Record your observations. **Caution:** Remember that a frog is a living thing and deserves to be handled gently and with respect.

8. Place a 600 mL beaker in the container. Place the frog in the beaker. Cover the beaker with your hand and carry it to a container of dechlorinated water. Tilt the beaker and gently submerge it in the water until the frog swims out of the beaker.

9. Watch the frog float and swim in the water. How does the frog use its legs to swim? Notice the position of the frog's head. Record your observations.

10. As the frog swims, bend down and look up into the water so that you can see the underside of the frog. Then look down on the frog from above. Compare the color on the top and the underside of the frog. Record your observations.

Analysis

11. From the position of the frog's eyes, what can you infer about the frog's field of vision?

____

____

How might the position of the frog's eyes benefit the frog while it is swimming?

____

____

12. How can a frog "breathe" while it is swimming in water?

____

13. How are the hind legs of a frog adapted for life on land and in water?

____

14. What differences did you notice in coloration on the frog's top side and its underneath side? What advantage might these color differences provide?

____

____

____

____

15. How does the frog eat? What senses are involved in helping the frog catch its prey?

____

____

Going Further

Observe another type of amphibian, such as a salamander. How do the adaptations of other types of amphibians compare with those of the frog you observed in this investigation?

The Fish in the Abyss

Purpose

This demonstration introduces students to the role of camouflage, or protective coloration.

Time Required

10–15 minutes

Lab Ratings

EASY → HARD

TEACHER PREP 2
CONCEPT LEVEL 1
CLEAN UP 1

MATERIALS
• 2 sheets of construction paper, both the same dark color • scissors • correction fluid or crayon • plastic transparency sheet

Advance Preparation

- Cut a fish shape from one piece of construction paper. Leave a handle protruding from the bottom.
- Using the correction fluid or crayon, mark a random pattern of dots on the fish and on the second piece of paper.
- Cover the fish and the paper with the transparency sheet. The plastic should hold the edges of the cutout flat against the paper background.
- Hold the setup in the front of the classroom, or tape the background and transparency to the wall or blackboard. Be sure that students will not be able to see the edges.

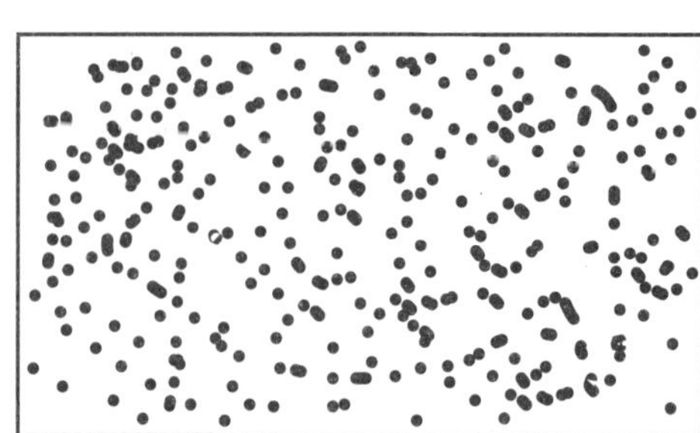

What to Do

1. Challenge students to distinguish the animal from the background. Ask them if they know what kind of animal it is.
2. It should be very difficult for students to see the fish. Tell them that the animal is well-camouflaged to protect itself from predators.
3. Move the fish under the plastic. Students should be able to see it more clearly.
4. Ask students for examples of animals that use camouflage for defense. Discuss different patterns and colors used for camouflage.

Explanation

Many fish and other animals have coloring that protects them from detection. The yellow perch, for example, is camouflaged by underwater vegetation. It is difficult to detect these fish when they are still. When they move, it is easier to distinguish them from the background because humans and many other animals use specialized brain cells to perceive motion. Information is relayed to these cells from light-sensitive cells at the back of the eye.

James Chin
Frank A. Day Middle School
Newtonville, Massachusetts

Name ______________________ Date ____________ Class ____________

Go Fish!

You're wading at the edge of a lake when suddenly you see a silvery streak dart through the water—a fish! And it looks like a big one! Slowly and quietly, you wade closer. Wait a minute! That streak of silver isn't one big fish after all—it's a large group of tiny fish swimming together in a school. Because the small fish turn together, they appear to be a single, larger fish.

Back to School

1. Visit a local aquarium and observe the schooling behavior of different fishes. You will need to observe a large tank that contains at least 10 fish each of two different species. How does a lone fish act toward members of its own species? How does a lone fish react to members of a different species? Research how the fish behave in the wild. Are there differences between their schooling behavior in the wild and their schooling behavior in the aquarium? If so, what do you think would account for those differences? Create a poster display to present your findings.

Research Ideas

2. Wear those fabulous alligator-skin boots, and you could be breaking the law! Many reptiles are protected species, and killing them is illegal. Find out about protected reptile species. How are they hunted illegally, and what is being done to protect them? Present the information in the form of an article for a hunting or environmental magazine.

3. It's an invasion! Lampreys from the Atlantic Ocean have invaded the Great Lakes! "But that's impossible," you say. "The Atlantic isn't even connected to the Great Lakes!" Find out how the lampreys got into the lakes, the problems lampreys are causing, and what scientists are doing to fix the problems. Report your findings to the class in a special news report.

4. Watch out for those fangs! Although only a few of the 3,000 known species of snakes are poisonous, it takes only one snake to endanger a human life. Surviving a venomous snake bite may require an injection of *antivenin,* an antitoxin for snake venom. Many antivenins are manufactured in unusual ways. Investigate how antivenins are made, how they work, and how effective they are. Write a science news article about your findings.

Name ______________________________ Date ______________ Class ______________

CHAPTER 3 FISHES, AMPHIBIANS, AND REPTILES

Chapter 3 Test

USING VOCABULARY

To complete the following sentences, choose the correct term from each pair of terms listed, and write the term in the blank.

1. In some chordates, pharyngeal pouches develop into ______________________ as the embryo matures. (vertebrae or gills)

2. ______________________ make up the largest group of chordates. (Vertebrates or Invertebrates)

3. ______________________ help a fish move, steer, stop, and balance. (Fins or Denticles)

4. The ______________________ allows fish to detect vibrations in the surrounding water. (swim bladder or lateral line system)

5. ______________________ can regulate their internal temperature. (Ectotherms or Endotherms)

UNDERSTANDING CONCEPTS

Multiple Choice

Circle the correct answer.

6. The flexible ________ is an embryonic structure that is usually replaced by a backbone.
   - **a.** nerve cord
   - **b.** notochord
   - **c.** alimentary canal
   - **d.** postanal tail

7. Which of the following is a member of the largest class of fishes?
   - **a.** perch
   - **b.** lamprey
   - **c.** shark
   - **d.** skate

8. Fish first appeared on Earth about
   - **a.** 1 billion years ago.
   - **b.** 500 million years ago.
   - **c.** 65 million years ago.
   - **d.** 400 billion years ago.

9. The life cycle of a salamander involves
   - **a.** eggs with protective shells.
   - **b.** a land-based larval stage.
   - **c.** internal fertilization.
   - **d.** All of the above

10. Which statement is false?
    - **a.** All mammals are vertebrates.
    - **b.** Most vertebrates have an open circulatory system.
    - **c.** Vertebrates have a well-developed head with a skull.
    - **d.** The skeletons of all vertebrate embryos are made of cartilage.

Short Answer

11. Identify and describe the stages in the metamorphosis of an ordinary frog.

12. Reptiles are entirely adapted for life on land. Describe these adaptations.

CRITICAL THINKING AND PROBLEM SOLVING

13. At the zoo you see an unusual four-legged, hairless animal. It is smaller than your hand and lives in a hole in the ground in a darkened display case. One of the zoo assistants allows you to reach into the display and touch the animal. Although the ground and air in the display are cool, the animal feels warm to the touch. Is this strange animal likely to be an ectotherm or an endotherm? Why do you think so?

14. Suppose you put one goldfish in a relatively warm aquarium and another goldfish of equal size and age in a relatively cold aquarium. If you put equal amounts of food in each tank, which goldfish would eat the most food? Explain your choice.

____

____

____

____

____

____

INTERPRETING GRAPHICS

Examine the graph below and answer the questions that follow.

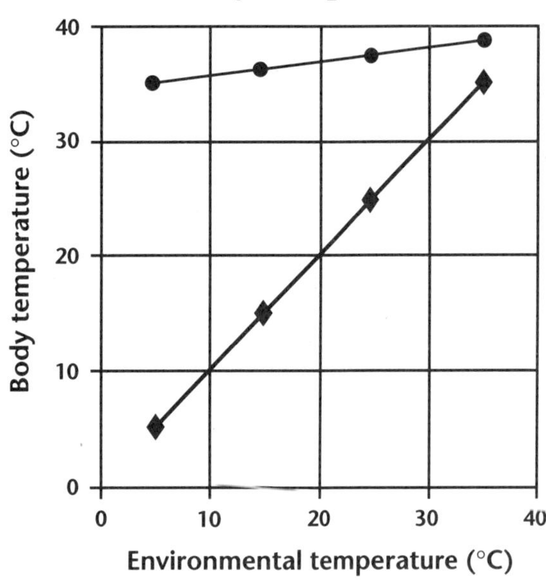

15. Compare the relationship of body temperature to environmental temperature in ectotherms with that of endotherms.

____

____

____

____

____

CONCEPT MAPPING

16. Use the following terms to complete the concept map below: skin with denticles, jawless fishes, hard scales, cartilaginous fishes, bony fishes, smooth and slimy skin.

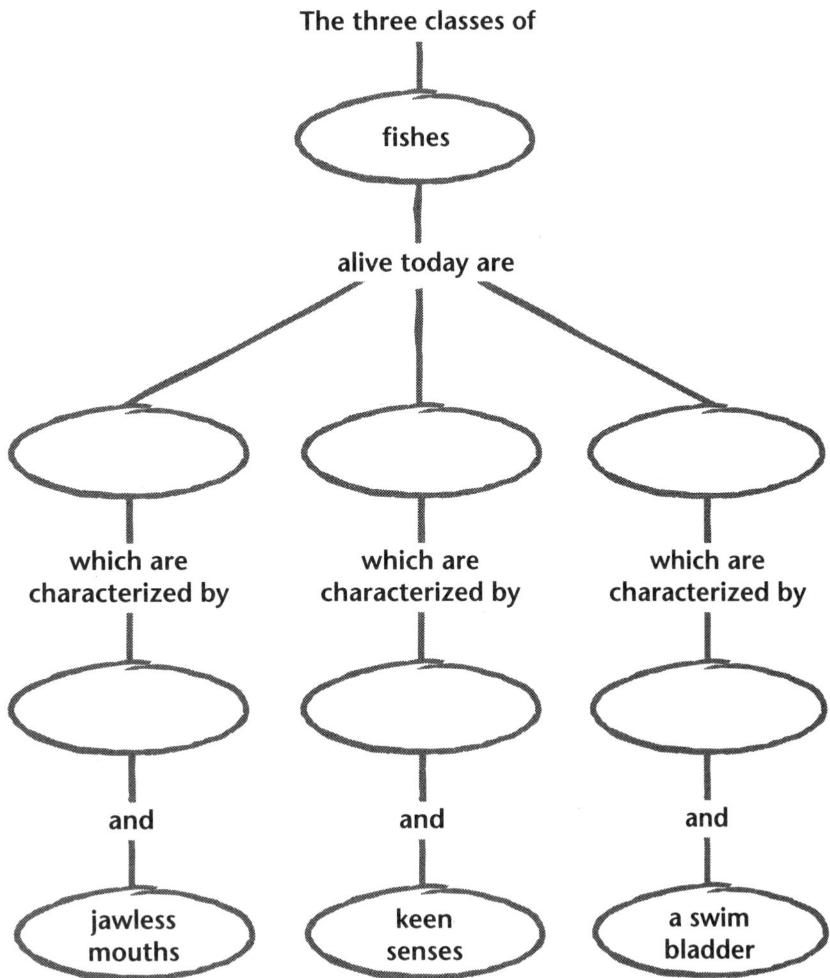

Name ______________________ Date ____________ Class ____________

CHAPTER 3 FISHES, AMPHIBIANS, AND REPTILES

Chapter 3 Performance-Based Assessment

TEACHER'S PREPARATORY GUIDE

Purpose
Students will observe a live goldfish and use it as a guide to illustrate the external features of a bony fish. They will then draw conclusions about a fish's form as it relates to function.

Time Required
35 minutes

Students will need 30 minutes to perform the activity and 5 minutes to answer the analysis questions.

P. B. A. Ratings
EASY → HARD

TEACHER PREP: 2

STUDENT SET-UP: 1

CONCEPT LEVEL: 2

CLEAN UP: 1

Advance Preparation
Secure enough goldfish for the class. Equip each student activity station with the necessary materials.

Safety Information
Remind students to follow the directions carefully and to be respectful of their subject. Mop up spills immediately.

Teaching Strategies
This activity works best in groups of 2–3 students.

Background Information
Fish are vertebrates that belong to the phylum Chordata. All fish have strong bodies, well-developed senses, and a brain. Three classes of fish alive today are jawless fishes, cartilaginous fishes, and bony fishes. The goldfish is an example of a bony fish, the largest class of fishes. Other examples include tuna, trout, salmon, and catfish. Bony fishes have skeletons of bone, paired fins and a swim bladder; and most bony fishes' bodies are covered by bony scales. The two types of bony fishes are ray-finned fish and lobe-finned fish. Almost all bony fishes are ray-finned fish.

Kathy LaRoe
East Valley Middle School
East Helena, Montana

Evaluation Strategies

Use the following rubric to evaluate student performance.

Rubric for Chapter 3 Assessment

Possible points	Quality and clarity of observations (50 points possible)
50–38	Excellent degree of accuracy and detail in drawing of external anatomical structures; superior understanding of external fish anatomy and characteristics
37–25	Good degree of accuracy and detail in drawing of external anatomical structures; good understanding of external fish anatomy and characteristics
24–12	Mostly accurate drawing of external anatomical structures; some understanding of external fish anatomy and characteristics
11–1	Accuracy and detail lacking in drawing of external anatomical structures; little or no understanding of external fish anatomy and characteristics
	Explanation of observations (50 points possible)
50–38	Clear, detailed explanations that show superior knowledge of bony fish characteristics; uses excellent examples to support explanations
37–25	Good explanations that show understanding of bony fish characteristics; uses some examples to support explanations
24–12	Explanations show unclear or incorrect understanding of bony fish characteristics; no examples to support explanations

Chapter 3 Performance-Based Assessment

Objective

You've read about bony fishes. Now you can use what you have learned—together with the observations you will make of your own fish—to identify anatomical structures of a bony fish.

Know the Score!

As you work through the activity, keep in mind that you will be earning a grade for the following:

- the quality and clarity of your observations (50%)
- your explanation of these observations (50%)

MATERIALS

- goldfish in a fishbowl or other clear container
- ruler
- colored pencils or markers

Procedure

1. Get at eye level with your fish. Remember not to tap the container because fish are particularly sensitive to vibrations. Observe your fish closely. Most aquarium goldfish are 5–10 cm long. Estimate the length of your fish from its mouth to the tip of its caudal fin, or tail. How long is your fish in centimeters?

   ____

2. In the space provided, draw just the body of your goldfish, including the caudal fin, or tail.

3. All bony fishes have paired fins, both pectoral and pelvic. Pectoral fins are located just behind the gills. Pelvic fins are located below the pectoral fins. Add fins to your fish and label them with the appropriate names. Observe closely how your fish uses its fins to move forward and maneuver.

4. Draw and label the median (dorsal and anal) fins. The dorsal fin is along the backbone, and the anal fin is near the tail, along the belly.

5. Locate the gills. The gills are covered by a structure called the operculum. Draw and label the gills on your fish. Observe the opening and closing of the mouth and relate this to the movement of the gills. Does this gill movement occur only when the fish is moving?

____

6. Look at the fish from above and from below as best you can. Color your fish drawing with colored pencils. Make note of the difference in color between the top and bottom of your fish.

7. Locate the lateral line system on your fish. It appears as a line of tiny dots. Draw and label this feature on your drawing. What is the function of the lateral line system?

____

____

____

8. Draw eyes on your fish.

Analysis

9. How does the location of the eyes increase the field of vision?

____

____

____

10. Fish cannot swim backward. What about their body structure prevents them from doing this?

____

____

____

____

____

____

Name ______________________ Date ____________ Class ____________

Module B
Chapter 4: Birds and Mammals
Lesson Plan
Section 1: Birds

Pacing

1 Block = 45 minutes

Regular Schedule:	**with Lab(s):** 3 Days	**without Lab(s):** 2 Days
Block Schedule:	**with Lab(s):** 1 1/2 Days	**without Lab(s):** 1 Day

Objectives

1. Name two characteristics that birds share with reptiles.
2. Describe the characteristics of birds that make them well suited for flight.
3. Explain lift.
4. List some advantages of migration.

Standards Covered

Unifying Concepts and Processes (UCP)

UCP 1. Systems, order, and organization
UCP 2. Evidence, models, and explanation
UCP 3. Change, constancy, and measurement
UCP 5. Form and function

Science As Inquiry (SAI)

SAI 1. Abilities necessary to do scientific inquiry

Science and Technology (ST)

ST 2. Understandings about science and technology

Science and Personal and Social Perspectives (SPSP)

SPSP 5. Science and technology in society

Life Science (LS)
Structures and Functions of Living Systems (LS 1)

1a. Living systems at all levels of organization demonstrate the complementary nature of structure and function. Import levels of organization from structure and function includes cells, organs, tissues, organs systems, whole organisms, and ecosystems.

1d. Specialized cells perform specialized functions in multicellular organisms. Groups of specialized cells cooperate to form a tissue, such as the muscle. Different tissues are in turn grouped together to form larger functional units, called organs. Each type of cell, tissue, an organ has a distinct structure and set of functions that serves the organism as a whole.

Regulation and Behavior (LS 3)

LS 3a. All organisms must be able to obtain and use resources, and grow, reproduce, and maintain stable internal conditions while living in a constantly changing external environment.

LS 3b. Regulation of the organism's internal environment involves sensing its internal environment and changing physiological activities is to keep conditions within the range required for the organism to survive.

LS 3c. Behavior is one kind of response an organism can make to an internal or environmental stimulus. A behavioral response requires coordination and communication at many levels, including cells, organ systems, and whole organisms. A behavioral response is a set of actions determined in part by heredity and in part from experience.

Diversity and Adaption of Organisms (LS 5)

LS 5a. Millions of species of animals, plants, and microorganisms are alive today. Although different species might look dissimilar, the unity among organisms becomes apparent from an analysis of internal structures, the similarity of their chemical processes, and the evidence of common ancestry.

LS 5b. Biological evolution accounts for the diversity of species developed through gradual processes over many generations. Species acquire many of their unique characteristics through biological adaptation, which involves the selection of naturally occurring variations in population. Biological adaptations include changes in structures, behavior, or physiology that enhance survival and reproductive success in a particular environment.

Key
PE = Pupil's Edition
ATE = Annotated Teacher's Edition
An asterisk indicates the item is part of the Unit Resource booklet for this unit.

Block 1

Focus *5 minutes*

______ **Bellringer,** ATE p. 88. Pose this question to students on the board or an overhead projector: What are some ways that birds are beneficial to people?

Motivate *15 minutes*

______ **Activity,** "Light as a Feather," ATE p. 88. Divide the class into small groups. Provide each group with a feather (preferably a wing feather), a paper clip, a small scale, and a meterstick. Tell students to weigh the feather and the paper clip. Next tell the class to let group members take turns dropping the feather and the paper clip from a height of 1 m. Challenge groups to brainstorm about the differences they observe and about the role of feather shape in bird flight.

Teach *25 minutes*

______ **Guided Practice,** "Making Models," ATE p. 89. Provide each group of students with pipe cleaners and straws. Use the board to illustrate how a contour feather is constructed of a main shaft, projecting barbs, barbules, and barbule hooks. Tell students to insert one or two pipe cleaners into a straw to make it stiff. Then tell them to follow the illustration to construct a model of a feather with at least three barbs and accompanying barbules and hooks.

______ **Teaching Transparency 63,*** "The Digestive System of a Bird." This transparency illustrates the digestive system of a bird: gizzard, intestine, and crop.

______ **Teaching Transparency 64,*** "Flight Adaptations of Birds." This transparency illustrates adaptations that enable birds to fly, including air sacs, a fast-beating heart, large eyes, wing shape, compact skeletons, hollow bones, and powerful flight muscles.

______ **Self-Check,** PE p. 90. Students answer two questions about bird feathers and the eating habits of birds.

Homework

______ **Homework,** "Researching Bird Breeding," ATE p. 88. Tell students that biologists have used their understanding of parent-offspring relationships in birds to breed birds in captivity. Tell students to research how scientists mimic parent birds to feed and support newborn chicks. Encourage them to research the success of these captive breeding efforts.

Block 2

Teach *25 minutes*

______ **Demonstration,** "Observing Bird Bones," ATE p. 91. Obtain several bones from a chicken or a turkey, such as the lower leg bones (drumsticks) and thigh bones, that have been cooked and thoroughly cleaned. Carefully break open the bones so that students can examine the air spaces inside.

______ **Teaching Transparency 227,*** "Wing Shape Creates Differences in Air Speed." This transparency, which links to physical science, illustrates the effects of wing shape on air pressure.

______ **QuickLab,** "Bernoulli Effect," PE p. 92. Provide each student with a drinking straw, a push or straight pin, and tissue paper. Have students follow the steps of the QuickLab to observe that fast-moving air creates low pressure.

Extend *15 minutes*

______ **Debate,** "Is it Okay to Destroy Wildlife to Save It?" ATE p. 96. The artist John James Audubon (1785-1851) painted pictures of birds that he shot. This was the only way he could get close enough to see the level of detail he needed in his paintings. Although modern cameras and binoculars provide researchers with excellent detail, scientists still sometimes kill birds for study and museum collections. This allows them to place the birds in proper evolutionary context. The results allow scientists to confirm the discovery of new species and develop specific conservation measures. Ask students to debate the pros and cons of this scientific technique.

Close *5 minutes*

______ **Quiz,** ATE p. 97. Students answer four questions about birds.

Homework

______ **Review,** PE p. 94 and p. 97. Students answer eight questions that review the lesson content.

______ **Critical Thinking Worksheet Chapter 4,*** "A Puzzling Piece of Paleontology." Students read a fictional episode about the discovery of a bird skeleton, then apply their knowledge of birds to answer conceptual questions about the passage.

Block 3

Lab Days *45 minutes*

______ **Labs You Can Eat, Chapter 4,*** "Why Birds of a Beak Eat Together." Students model the beak adaptations of birds and study how effective the adaptations are in obtaining various types of food.

Additional Resource Options

______ **Making Models,** "What? No Dentist Bills?" p. 112. Students design and build a model of a bird's digestive system to learn why birds don't require teeth to break down food like humans do. This lab supports STANDARDS UCP 2, UCP 5, SAI 1, LS1a, and LS1d.

______ **Datasheets for LabBook, Chapter 4,*** "What? No Dentist Bills?" This blackline master makes progressing through the lab easier for students and grading easier for you.

______ **Science Puzzlers, Twisters & Teasers, Worksheet Chapter 4.*** These worksheets offer puzzles, games, and logic problems that use vocabulary and concepts from the chapter.

______ **Directed Reading Worksheet Chapter 4,* Section 1.** This worksheet reinforces the main ideas in the section while developing students' reading skills.

______ **Across the Sciences,** "The Aerodynamics of Flight," p. 118. Students read a passage about the aerodynamics of flight, then conduct research about aerodynamics.

______ **Homework,** ATE p. 91. Students research the history of falconry and write a report on the subject.

______ **Going Further,** ATE p. 91. Students research the primary migration corridors in North America and illustrate them on a map.

______ **Alternative Assessment,** ATE p. 97. Students make a display with pictures of birds from nature magazines.

______ **Module B Guided Reading Audio CD Program, Disc 17, Tracks 1-2.** The audio reading of the chapter provides essential chapter content for ESL students, auditory learners, and struggling readers.

______ **NSTA *sci*LINKS:** *Bird Characteristics, sci*LINKS number HSTL405. Students research Internet resources related to the characteristics of birds. *Kinds of Birds, sci*LINKS number HSTL410. Students research Internet resources related to the kinds of birds.

Name ______________________ Date ____________ Class ____________

Module B
Chapter 4: Birds and Mammals
Lesson Plan
Section 2: Mammals

Pacing

1 Block = 45 minutes

Regular Schedule:	**with Lab(s):** N/A	**without Lab(s):** 2 Days
Block Schedule:	**with Lab(s):** N/A	**without Lab(s):** 1 Day

Objectives

1. Describe the common characteristics of mammals.
2. Explain the differences between monotremes, marsupials, and placental mammals.
3. Give some examples of each type of mammal.

Standards Covered

UCP 1. Systems, order, and organization
UCP 2. Evidence, models, and explanation
UCP 3. Change, constancy, and measurement
UCP 4. Evolution and equilibrium
UCP 5. Form and function

SAI 1. Abilities necessary to do scientific inquiry

HNS 2. Nature of science

Structures and Functions of Living Systems (LS 1)

LS 1a. Living systems at all levels of organization demonstrate the complementary nature of structure and function. Important levels of organization from structure and function include cells, tissues, organs, organ systems, whole organisms, and ecosystems.

LS 1d. Specialized cells perform specialized functions in multicellular organisms. Groups of specialized cells cooperate to form a tissue, such as a muscle. Different tissues are in turn grouped together to form larger functional units, called organs. Each type of cell, tissue, and organ has a distinct structure and set of functions that serves the organism as a whole.

Reproduction and Heredity (LS2)

LS 2a. Reproduction is a characteristic of all living systems; because no individual organism lives forever, reproduction is essential to the continuation and every species. Some organisms reproduce asexually. Others reproduce sexually.

LS 3a. All organisms must be able to obtain and use resources, and grow, reproduce, and maintain stable internal conditions while living in a constantly changing external environment.

LS 3c. Behavior is one kind of response an organism can make to an internal or environmental stimulus. A behavioral response requires coordination and communication at many levels, including cells, organ systems, and whole organisms. A behavioral response is a set of actions determined in part by heredity and in part from experience.

LS 5a. Millions of species of animals, plants, and microorganisms are alive today. Although different species might look dissimilar, the unity among organisms becomes apparent from an analysis of internal structures, the similarity of their chemical processes, and evidence of common ancestry.

LS 5c. Extinction of species occurs when the environment changes and the adaptive characteristics of the species are insufficient to allow for its survival. Fossils indicate that many organisms that lived long ago are extinct. Extinction of a species is common; most of the species that have lived on Earth no longer exist.

Block 1

Focus *5 minutes*

_____ **Bellringer,** ATE p. 98. Write the following on the board or overhead on a transparency: In the next 5 minutes, list as many characteristics of mammals as you can think of. After the 5 minutes are up, ask students what characteristics they have listed, and put their answers on the board. Use their answers as a springboard for discussion about what mammals are and where they live.

Motivate *10 minutes*

_____ **Discussion,** "Domestication of Animals," ATE p. 98. Ask students to describe how humans have interacted with wild mammals over time. Then ask students how the domestication of mammals, such as horses, cattle, pigs, and dogs, changed the lives of early humans. Students should indicate that it became easier to obtain food, to cultivate crops, to catch wild game, and to control pests.

Teach *30 minutes*

_____ **Demonstration,** "Comparing Skulls," ATE p. 100. Display the skulls of several species for students to study. Ideally, include several mammal skulls, a reptile skull, a bird skull, and an amphibian skull. Tell students to carefully examine the skulls, paying close attention to the similarities and differences between classes (major groups) and within the mammal class. Ask them to describe differences in dentition (tooth structure and arrangement) and speculate about advantages and disadvantages of the arrangements they observe.

_____ **Independent Practice,** "Concept Mapping," ATE p. 104. Have students create a concept map that compares the development and life histories of monotremes, marsupials, and placental mammals. Some terms and concepts students can use include: type of egg with a shell, incubation, gestation, nest, uterus, mammary glands, and method of nursing.

_____ **MathBreak,** "Ants for Dinner," p. 104. Students calculate how many hours a day an anteater would need to spend eating, given a certain rate of catching ants and a required daily caloric intake.

______ **Self-Check,** p. 104. Students answer a question about the differences between a monotreme, a marsupial, and a placental mammal.

Homework

______ **Homework,** "Create a Timeline," ATE p. 99. Have students use library references to create a timeline of mammalian evolution from their first appearance in the Triassic period (Mesozoic era) some 230 million years ago through the Cenozoic era to the present. Encourage students to illustrate their timelines with original drawings or pictures from books or magazines.

Block 2

Teach *25 minutes*

______ **Apply,** p. 106. Students apply their knowledge of bat echolocation to answer a question about submarine navigation with sonar.

______ **Activity,** "Comparing Footprints," ATE p. 107. Have students compare footprints or foot casts of two common carnivores, the domestic dog and the domestic cat. Students can make footprints by having a pet step on damp, claylike soil. They can make casts by pouring plaster of paris in a dried footprint. Have them study the casts and hypothesize about the reasons for the features and differences they notice.

______ **Self-Check,** PE p. 109. Students answer two questions about mammal classifications.

Extend *15 minutes*

______ **Going Further,** p. 109. The ears of African and Asian elephants are the most noticeable difference between the two species. Have students explain the evolutionary significance of this difference by exploring how the ears differ and researching the environments in which the animals live.

Close *5 minutes*

______ **Quiz,** ATE p.111. Students answer three questions about mammals.

Homework

______ **Review**, p. 111. Students answer four questions that review the main content of the lesson.

Additional Resource Options

______ **Long-Term Projects & Research Ideas, Chapter 4,*** "Look Who's Coming to Dinner." *Research ideas:* whooping crane courtship; decline of the American buffalo; poisonous mammals; illegal feathers; hibernation; *Project ideas:* building a bird feeder; designing a bat house; observing hamster families; breeding animals in captivity.

______ **Directed Reading Worksheet Chapter 4,* Section 2.** This worksheet reinforces the main concepts in the section and develops students' reading skills.

_____ **Math Skills for Science Worksheet Chapter 4,*** "The Unit Factor and Dimensional Analysis." Students learn how to use unit factors in dimensional analysis through sample and practice problems.

_____ **Reinforcement Worksheet Chapter 4,*** "Mammals Are Us." Students use a given list of orders and examples of mammals in each order to complete a chart that lists characteristics and an interesting fact for each order.

_____ **Math and More,** ATE p. 102. Given the maximum speed of red kangaroos and their stride for short distances, students calculate how far a red kangaroo could travel in 2 minutes and how many strides it would take.

_____ **Weird Science,** "Naked Mole-Rats," p. 119. Students read a feature about a unique mammal, naked mole rats, then conduct further research to find out why these animals are classified as mammals.

_____ **Homework,** "Researching Mammals," ATE p. 102. Students look up the word *amphibious* in a dictionary and list examples of amphibious mammals in their ScienceLog.

_____ **Review,** p. 101. Students answer three questions that review the content of the lesson.

_____ **Alternative Assessment,** ATE p. 111. Students make a poster that visually summarizes the information they have learned about birds and mammals.

_____ **Module B Guided Reading Audio CD Program, Disc 17, Track 3.** The audio reading of the chapter provides essential chapter content for ESL students, auditory learners, and struggling readers.

_____ **NSTA *sci*LINKS:** *The Origin of Mammals, sci*LINKS number HSTL415. Students research Internet resources related to the origin of mammals. *Characteristics of Mammals, sci*LINKS number HSTL420. Students research Internet resources related to mammal characteristics.

End of Chapter Review and Assessment

_____ **Study Guide,*** Vocabulary, Notes, and Chapter Review

_____ **Chapter Tests with Performance-Based Assessment, Chapter 4 Test***

_____ **Chapter Tests with Performance-Based Assessment, Performance-Based Assessment 4***

_____ **Concept Mapping Transparency 17***

Name ______________________________ Date ______________ Class ______________

CHAPTER 4 **DIRECTED READING WORKSHEET**

Birds and Mammals

Chapter Introduction

As you begin this chapter, answer the following.

1. Read the title of the chapter. List three things that you already know about this subject.

____

____

____

____

2. Write two questions about this subject that you would like answered by the time you finish this chapter.

____

____

____

3. How does the title of the Start-Up Activity relate to the subject of the chapter?

____

____

____

Section 1: Birds (p. 88)

4. If a living animal has ______________________, it's a bird.

Bird Characteristics (p. 88)

5. Which of the following characteristics do birds share with modern-day reptiles? (Circle all that apply.)
   - **a.** They have thick, dry scales on their legs and feet.
   - **b.** They have vertebrae.
   - **c.** They have amniotic eggs.
   - **d.** They lay eggs with hard eggshells.
6. When bird feathers get old, they fall out, and new feathers grow in their place. True or False? (Circle one.)
7. Down feathers help keep birds from losing ______________________.

8. The main function of contour feathers is to
   a. form a streamlined flying surface.
   b. attract a mate.
   c. provide protection.
   d. provide warmth.

9. How does preening make a bird's feathers water-repellent?

____

____

10. How do birds cool off on hot days?
   a. They fly higher in the atmosphere, where the air is cooler.
   b. They lay their feathers flat and pant like dogs.
   c. They shed feathers.
   d. They sweat.

11. Birds eat and digest their food quickly because their metabolisms require a lot of energy. True or False? (Circle one.)

12. How does a gizzard help a bird digest food?

____

____

____

____

____

Up, Up, and Away (p. 90)

Choose the bird characteristic in Column B that best matches the use in Column A, and write the corresponding letter in the space provided.

Column A	Column B
____ **13.** ensuring flight muscles get as much oxygen as possible	**a.** keen eyesight
____ **14.** maneuvering rapidly	**b.** air sac
____ **15.** finding food from a distance	**c.** short wing
____ **16.** soaring	**d.** rigid skeleton
____ **17.** increasing the bird's oxygen intake	**e.** rapid heart rate
____ **18.** moving wings powerfully and efficiently	**f.** long, narrow wing

Getting off the Ground (p. 92)

19. The upward pressure on the wing that keeps a bird in the air is called ______________________.

Mark each of the following statements *True* or *False.*

20. __________ The top of a bird's wing is curved so air flowing under the wing moves faster than the air flowing over the wing.

21. __________ The larger the wings, the greater the lift.

22. __________ Birds must flap their wings constantly to stay in the air.

Fly Away (p. 93)

23. Why do some birds migrate for the winter?

____

____

____

Bringing Up Baby (p. 93)

24. Which of the following is NOT true about brooding?
    - **a.** It keeps a bird's eggs warm.
    - **b.** All birds share the responsibility between males and females.
    - **c.** A bird does this until its eggs hatch.
    - **d.** Birds sit on their eggs.

25. How do cuckoos and cowbirds make other birds work for them?

____

____

____

26. Precocial chicks depend on their parents to feed and protect them. True or False? (Circle one.)

27. Altricial chicks hatch with their eyes closed. True or False? (Circle one.)

Review (p. 94)

Now that you've finished the first part of Section 1, review what you learned by answering the Review questions in your ScienceLog.

Kinds of Birds (p. 95)

28. One of the smallest birds is the 1.6 g

bee ______________________.

29. Look at the description of Flightless Birds on page 95. Describe an adaptation that helps each of the following flightless birds get around.

a. Ostriches ______________________

____

b. Penguins ______________________

____

30. Look at the description of Water Birds on page 96. Water birds,

also known as ______________________, usually have

______________________ feet.

31. What is the the blue-footed booby known for?

a. remaining underwater for long periods of time
b. attracting females with beautiful plumage
c. courting females by raising one foot at a time

32. Look at the description of Birds of Prey at the bottom of page 96. Which of the following is NOT helpful to birds of prey?

a. keen vision
b. sharp claws and beaks
c. strong muscles
d. webbed feet

33. Most birds of prey, such as eagles, falcons, and hawks, eat meat and

hunt during the ______________________.

34. Look at the description of Perching Birds on page 97. Why don't perching birds fall off their perches when they fall asleep?

____

____

35. Chickadees sometimes hunt while dangling upside down.

True or False? (Circle one.)

Review (p. 97)

Now that you've finished Section 1, review what you learned by answering the Review questions in your ScienceLog.

Section 2: Mammals (p. 98)

1. There are more species of ______________________ than there are species of ______________________.
(mollusks or mammals, mollusks or mammals)

2. The largest animal that has ever lived is a mammal. True or False? (Circle one.)

The Origin of Mammals (p. 98)

3. Many scientists believe mammals are descended from reptiles called ______________________.

4. Which of the following statements is NOT true about the first mammals?

a. They appear in the fossil record about 200 million years ago.
b. They foraged for food at night.
c. They existed only after dinosaurs became extinct.
d. They were endotherms.

Characteristics of Mammals (p. 99)

5. Mammary glands are special organs that only female mammals have. True or False? (Circle one.)

6. The milk of mammals is made up of fat, water, ______________________, and ______________________.

7. A mammal's body temperature never changes, even when hibernating. True or False? (Circle one.)

8. Name two adaptations that help keep mammals warm.

____

____

____

Match the type of tooth in Column B to its use in Column A, and write the corresponding letter in the space provided.

Column A	Column B
____ **9.** cutting	**a.** canine
____ **10.** grinding	**b.** incisor
____ **11.** stabbing	**c.** molar

12. The shape of a mammal's teeth reflects the

    ______________________ of the mammal. (size or diet)

13. Mammals have ______________________ sets of teeth.

14. The main purpose of the diaphragm muscle is to
    - **a.** bring air into the lungs.
    - **b.** separate blood with oxygen from blood without oxygen.
    - **c.** provide as much oxygen as possible to the heart.
    - **d.** help mammals make sounds necessary for communication.

15. Mammals use their well-developed senses and large brains to respond quickly to their environment. True or False? (Circle one.)

16. Which of the following statements are true of young mammals? (Circle all that apply.)
    - **a.** They result from sexual reproduction.
    - **b.** They are protected by their parent(s).
    - **c.** They have milk teeth.
    - **d.** They nurse.

Review (p. 101)

Now that you've finished the first part of Section 2, review what you learned by answering the Review questions in your ScienceLog.

Kinds of Mammals (p. 102)

17. Why are monotremes considered mammals even though they lay eggs?

    ____

    ____

    ____

18. The duckbilled platypus and the ______________________ are the only living monotremes. Monotremes are found only in Australia and ______________________.

19. A baby platypus gets milk from its mother by licking the milk from the skin and hair around its mother's nipples. True or False? (Circle one.)

20. Marsupials lay eggs just like monotremes do. True or False? (Circle one.)

21. Marsupials use their pouches for
    - **a.** storing food in the winter.
    - **b.** giving birth to their young.
    - **c.** carrying and protecting young.
    - **d.** digesting food for their young.

22. The ____________________ is the only marsupial living in North America north of Mexico.

23. Female placental mammals do NOT
    - **a.** have a uterus.
    - **b.** supply food and oxygen to their embryo through a placenta.
    - **c.** have a gestation period lasting from a few weeks to many months.
    - **d.** lay eggs.

Kinds of Placental Mammals (p. 104)

24. Look at the description of Toothless Mammals on page 104. All toothless mammals, such as armadillos, pangolins, and sloths, have no teeth. True or False? (Circle one.)

25. Most toothless mammals catch insects with a long, sticky tongue. True or False? (Circle one.)

26. Look at the description of Insect Eaters on page 105. Insectivores are tiny mammals that live on every continent except ____________________ and ____________________. Most of them dig in the soil with their long, pointed ____________________.

27. Look at the description of Rodents on page 105. Rodents gnaw so much that they grow several sets of teeth. True or False? (Circle one.)

28. Look at the description of Lagomorphs on page 106. Which of the following is NOT a characteristic of a lagomorph?
    - **a.** sensitive nose
    - **b.** large ears
    - **c.** two sets of incisors
    - **d.** long tail

29. Look at the description of Flying Mammals on page 106. Explain how bats use sound to find their dinner.

____

____

____

____

30. Look at page 107. Animals that eat almost only meat are called ______________________. Meat-eaters have large canines and special ______________________ for slicing meat.

31. Some carnivores eat ______________________ as well as meat.

32. Look at page 108. Hoofed mammals are divided into groups based on the thickness of their hooves. True or False? (Circle one.)

33. Giraffes are the tallest living mammals. True or False? (Circle one.)

34. Look at page 109. Elephants use their trunk the same way we use our nose, ______________________, and ______________________.

35. Look at the description of Cetaceans on page 110. Sperm whales are cetaceans that use echolocation to stun their food as well as to find it. True or False? (Circle one.)

36. Look at the description of Sirenia on page 110. Which of the following characteristics does NOT describe Sirenia, such as manatees or dugongs?

a. plant-eaters
b. completely aquatic
c. quiet
d. make up the largest group of mammals

Look at the description of Primates on page 111. Then mark each of the following statements *True* or *False*.

37. __________ Monkeys, humans, and prosimians are all primates.

38. __________ Primates have large brains in proportion to their body size.

39. __________ In primates, the eyes face forward.

40. __________ All primates have five fingers on each hand and five toes on each foot.

41. __________ All primates live on the ground.

42. __________ Primates have claws.

Review (p. 111)

Now that you've finished Section 2, review what you learned by answering the Review questions in your ScienceLog.

Name ______________________ Date ____________ Class ____________

CHAPTER 4

VOCABULARY & NOTES WORKSHEET

Birds and Mammals

By studying the Vocabulary and Notes listed for each section below, you can gain a better understanding of this chapter.

SECTION 1

Vocabulary

In your own words, write a definition for each of the following terms in the space provided.

1. down feather ______________________________

____

2. contour feather ______________________________

____

3. preening ______________________________

____

4. lift ______________________________

____

____

5. brooding ______________________________

____

Notes

Read the following section highlights. Then, in your own words, write the highlights in your ScienceLog.

- Like reptiles, birds lay amniotic eggs and have thick, dry scales.
- Unlike reptiles, birds are endotherms and are covered with feathers.
- Because flying requires a lot of energy, birds must eat a high-energy diet and breathe efficiently.
- Birds' wings are shaped so that they generate lift. Lift is air pressure beneath the wings that keeps a bird in the air.
- Birds are lightweight. Their feathers are strong but lightweight, and their skeleton is relatively rigid, compact, and hollow.
- Because birds can fly, they can migrate great distances. They can nest in one habitat and winter in another. Migrating birds can take advantage of food supplies and avoid predators.

SECTION 2

Vocabulary

In your own words, write a definition for each of the following terms in the space provided.

1. mammary glands ______________________________

2. diaphragm ______________________________

3. monotreme ______________________________

4. marsupial ______________________________

5. placental mammal ______________________________

6. gestation period ______________________________

Notes

Read the following section highlights. Then, in your own words, write the highlights in your ScienceLog.

- All mammals have mammary glands; in females, mammary glands produce milk. Milk is a highly nutritious fluid fed to the young.
- Like birds, mammals are endotherms.
- Mammals maintain their high metabolism by eating a lot of food and breathing efficiently.

- Mammals have a diaphragm that helps them draw air into their lungs.
- Mammals have highly specialized teeth for chewing different kinds of food. Mammals that eat plants have incisors and molars for cutting and grinding plants. Carnivores have canines for seizing and tearing their prey.
- Mammals are the only vertebrates that have mammary glands, fur, and two sets of teeth.
- Mammals are divided into three groups: monotremes, marsupials, and placental mammals.
- Monotremes lay eggs instead of bearing live young. Monotremes produce milk but do not have nipples or a placenta.
- Marsupials give birth to live young, but the young are born as embryos. The embryos climb into their mother's pouch, where they drink milk until they are more developed.
- Placental mammals develop inside of the mother for a period of time called a gestation period. Placental mothers nurse their young after birth.

Name ______________________ Date __________ Class __________

CHAPTER

4 CHAPTER REVIEW WORKSHEET

Birds and Mammals

USING VOCABULARY

To complete the following sentences, choose the correct term from each pair of terms listed below, and write the term in the space provided.

1. ______________________ chicks can run after their mother soon after they hatch. ______________________ chicks can barely stretch their neck out to be fed when they first hatch. (Altricial or Precocial)
2. The ______________________ helps mammals breathe. (diaphragm or air sac)
3. The ______________________ allows some mammals to supply nutrients to young in the mother's uterus. (mammary gland or placenta)
4. Birds take care of their feathers by ______________________. (brooding or preening)
5. A lion belongs to a group of mammals called ______________________. (carnivores or primates)
6. ______________________ are fluffy feathers that help keep birds warm. (Contour feathers or Down feathers)

UNDERSTANDING CONCEPTS

Multiple Choice

7. Both birds and reptiles
   a. lay eggs.
   b. brood their young.
   c. have air sacs.
   d. have feathers.
8. Flight requires
   a. a lot of energy and oxygen.
   b. a lightweight body.
   c. strong flight muscles.
   d. All of the above
9. Only mammals
   a. have glands.
   b. nurse their young.
   c. lay eggs.
   d. have teeth.
10. Monotremes do NOT
   a. have mammary glands.
   b. care for their young.
   c. have pouches.
   d. have fur.

Name ______________________ Date __________ Class __________

11. Lift

a. is air that travels over the top of a wing.
b. is provided by air sacs.
c. is the upward force on a wing that keeps a bird in the air.
d. is created by pressure from the diaphragm.

12. Which of the following is not a primate?

a. a lemur
b. a human
c. a pika
d. a chimpanzee

Short Answer

13. How are marsupials different from other mammals? How are they similar?

____

____

____

____

____

14. Both birds and mammals are endotherms. How do they stay warm?

____

____

____

____

15. What is the Bernoulli effect?

____

____

____

____

16. Why do some bats have large ears?

____

____

____

____

Name ______________________ Date ____________ Class ____________

CONCEPT MAPPING

17. Use the following terms to create a concept map: *monotremes, endotherms, birds, mammals, mammary glands, placental mammals, marsupials, feathers, hair.*

CRITICAL THINKING AND PROBLEM SOLVING

Write one or two sentences to answer each of the following questions:

18. Unlike bird and monotreme eggs, the eggs of placental mammals and marsupials do not have a yolk. How do developing embryos of marsupials and placental mammals get the nutrition they need?

19. Most bats and cetaceans use echolocation. Why don't these mammals rely solely on sight to find their prey and examine their surroundings?

20. Suppose you are working at a museum and are making a display of bird skeletons. Unfortunately, the skeletons have lost their labels. How can you separate the skeletons of flightless birds from those of birds that fly? Will you be able to tell which birds flew rapidly and which birds could soar? Explain your answer.

MATH IN SCIENCE

21. A bird is flying at a speed of 35 km/h. At this speed, its body consumes 60 Calories per gram of body mass per hour. If the bird has a mass of 50 g, how many Calories will it use if it flies for 30 minutes at this speed?

INTERPRETING GRAPHICS

Endotherms use a lot of energy when they run or fly. The graph below shows how many Calories a small dog uses while running at different speeds. Use this graph to answer the questions below.

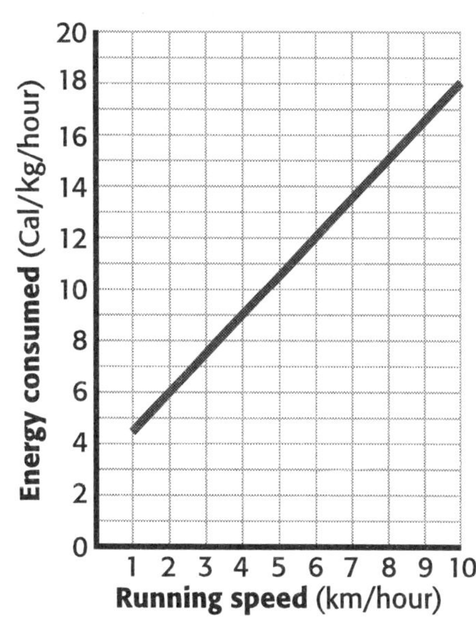

22. As the dog runs faster, how does the amount of energy it consumes per hour change?

____

____

23. How much energy per hour will this dog consume if it is running at 4 km/h? at 9 km/h?

____

____

24. Energy consumed is given in Calories per kilogram of body mass per hour. If the dog has a mass of 6 kg and is running at 7 km/h, how many Calories per hour will it use?

____

____

READING CHECK-UP

Take a minute to review your answers to the ScienceLog questions at the beginning of the chapter. Have your answers changed? If necessary, revise your answers based on what you have learned since you began this chapter. Record your revisions in your ScienceLog.

Name ______________________ Date ____________ Class ____________

CHAPTER 4 SCIENCE PUZZLERS, TWISTERS & TEASERS

Birds and Mammals

Flying Without a Spare

1. You've borrowed your next-door neighbor's space cruiser to visit a cousin who lives on Mars. But on the way there, one of your engines blows out. The contraption won't fly without all six engines, and now only five work. Your neighbor never keeps a spare and the escape pod appears to be out of whack. Being your resourceful self, you tinker about until you get the escape pod in semi-decent shape. Have you ever driven a rickety old escape pod? Well, it's difficult to steer. You land on various continents on Earth in your search for home. Looking out the porthole, determine—by what you see—where you've landed.

   a. 1st landing: You see a large animal—a huge rodent. It must weigh over 70 kg! What is it, and where have you landed?

   ____

   b. 2nd landing: Immediately after landing, you spot a smaller furry animal. It seems to have small copies of itself hugging onto its belly. The mammal sees you too, and it stops moving. Perhaps it died of fright. What is this creature, and where are you?

   ____

   c. 3rd landing: This time you see a flat-nosed, large-eared mammal. You pry open your portal and stick your head out. This animal's breath smells of eucalyptus, like a cough drop. What is it? Where are you?

   ____

   d. 4th landing: Now something strikes at the glass of the porthole. It's the beak of a large (almost 125 kg!), bad-tempered bird. Its feet look like hooves! What is it?

   ____

   e. 5th landing: Another bird! This time it's a shy one with soft, hairy feathers and a long, pointed beak. It doesn't look like it does much flying. What bird is this? Where are you?

   ____

The Wedding Reception

2. Many animals will attend Elephant's wedding reception. His mother is trying to arrange the guests so that each sits next to another animal with whom it shares something in common. In particular, there are four guests who are giving Elephant's mom a headache. Who will sit next to whom? The guests in question are:

Spider Monkey—Mrs. Elephant remembers how Spider Monkey embarrassed everyone at Ostrich's picnic last year by insisting on shaking hands. Really, *hands*! Good gracious!

Bat—With all his talk of moving around in the dark, and how those of us with good eyesight are supposedly "missing out," Bat can be such an awful bore!

Mole—He means well, Elephant's mom admits, but it is kind of creepy having Mole always smelling you and touching you with his nose.

Archaeopteryx—Frankly, everyone is tired of Archaeopteryx's talk of the "good old days."

Here are the guests that Elephant's mother can choose from: Swordfish, Manatee, Therapsids, Whale, Platypus, Orangutan. Match one of these guests up with each of our "problem" guests, and explain your choice.

a. Spider Monkey: ______________________________

____

____

b. Bat: ______________________________

____

____

c. Mole: ______________________________

____

____

d. Archaeopteryx: ______________________________

____

____

Name ______________________ Date ______________ Class ____________

CHAPTER 4

REINFORCEMENT WORKSHEET

Mammals Are Us

Complete this worksheet after you finish reading Chapter 4, Section 2.

Each of the following terms is either an order of animals or an example of a particular order. Use the characteristics and facts in the table below to identify the order and one example of each group of animals, and record the corresponding terms in the spaces provided.

dolphin	cetaceans	hoofed mammals	sirenia
rabbit	human	carnivores	rodents
porcupine	aardvark	cow	toothless mammals
primates	manatee	Siberian tiger	
insectivores	lagomorphs	hedgehog	

Order	Characteristic	Example	An interesting fact
______	generally eat insects and have long, sticky tongues	______	only one is truly "toothless"
______	tend to have pointed noses for digging	______	live on all continents but Australia
______	small animals that have sharp front teeth for gnawing	______	front teeth never stop growing
______	have strong legs for jumping, sensitive noses, and big ears	______	some gather plants and shape them in "haystacks" to dry
______	have eyes that face forward and opposable thumbs	______	considered the most intelligent mammals
______	eat mostly meat	______	most have special teeth for slicing meat
______	generally fast runners; they have flat teeth for chewing plants	______	divided into groups according to the number of toes
______	water-dwelling mammals that resemble fish	______	use echolocation like bats do
______	eat seaweed and water plants	______	only four species in this order

Name ______________________ Date ____________ Class __________

CHAPTER 4 **VOCABULARY REVIEW WORKSHEET**

Is It a Bird or a Mammal?

Complete this worksheet after you finish reading Chapter 4.
Match each description in the second column with the correct term in the first column, and write the corresponding letter in the space provided.

_____ **1.** primates
_____ **2.** contour feathers
_____ **3.** carnivores
_____ **4.** down feathers
_____ **5.** gestation period
_____ **6.** preening
_____ **7.** placenta
_____ **8.** lift
_____ **9.** placental mammals
_____ **10.** brooding
_____ **11.** marsupials
_____ **12.** precocial chicks
_____ **13.** monotremes
_____ **14.** altricial chicks
_____ **15.** therapsids
_____ **16.** mammary glands
_____ **17.** diaphragm

a. a large muscle at the bottom of the rib cage that helps bring air into the lungs
b. a mammal that nourishes its unborn offspring with a special organ inside the uterus
c. the time during which an embryo develops within the mother
d. a group of mammals that have opposable thumbs and binocular vision; includes humans, apes, and monkeys
e. chicks that hatch weak, naked, and helpless
f. a special organ of exchange that provides a developing fetus with nutrients and oxygen
g. mammals that lay eggs
h. prehistoric reptile ancestors of mammals
i. consumers that eat animals
j. feathers made of a stiff central shaft with many side branches called barbs
k. fluffy, insulating feathers that lie next to a bird's body
l. glands that secrete a nutritious fluid called milk
m. the upward pressure on the wing of a bird that keeps a bird in the air
n. when a bird uses its beak to spread oil on its feathers
o. chicks that hatch fully active
p. when a bird sits on its eggs until they hatch
q. a mammal that gives birth to partially developed, live young that develop inside the mother's pouch or skin fold

Name ______________________ Date ____________ Class ____________

CHAPTER 4 CRITICAL THINKING WORKSHEET

A Puzzling Piece of Paleontology

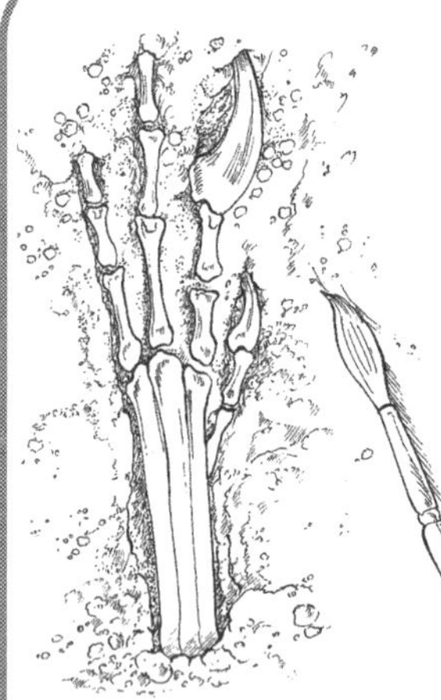

In today's episode, we find Outback Jack and his trusty partner, Diego, on the exotic island of Madagascar, off the east coast of Africa. After a dozen dusty days of digging in the dirt, Diego declares with delight, "Jack, I've found something! It's part of a skeleton!"

Jack sprints to his partner's side to see the bounty of bones. "Great Scott!" exclaims Jack. "It's a bird! An ancient bird! Look at these wing bones, Diego. See these bumps? That's where the flight feathers were attached."

Diego, however, notices something nearby and nudges his partner. "But look over here, Jack," he says, pointing to a hole in the ground several centimeters away. "It's the rear half of the skeleton. And look at the second toe on the left foot!"

Jack examines the foot and jumps back. "Can they be sickle-shaped claws like those found on dromaeosaurs?" he wonders out loud. "It looks like a velociraptor claw!"

"But the first toe is pointing backward, like a bird's foot!" exclaims Diego. "I think we may have found an important piece of the puzzle! It must be from an animal that is closely related to both birds and dinosaurs."

Outback Jack and Diego quickly take their discovery to Professor Pronk at the university. "These are definitely bird wings," Professor Pronk proclaims, "and these look an awful lot like dinosaur feet. But, my fine friends, I'm still not convinced that you've found a meaningful piece of evidence."

USEFUL TERMS

dromaeosaurs
a group of dinosaurs that included the velociraptor

Establishing Connections

1. When Diego says, "I think we may have found an important piece of the puzzle," which puzzle is he referring to?

____

____

____

____

____

____

____

____

____

2. Why are toes that point backward useful to birds?

Demonstrating Reasoned Judgment

3. Professor Pronk is not totally convinced that Jack and Diego have found a meaningful piece of evidence. Why do you think he is skeptical?

Identifying Relationships

4. If Jack and Diego's hypothesis is correct, which ancient animal could this creature be closely related to?

CHAPTER 4 MATH SKILLS

The Unit Factor and Dimensional Analysis

The measurements you take in science class, whether for time, mass, weight, or distance, are more than just numbers—they are also units. To make comparisons between measurements, it is convenient to have your measurements in the same units. A mathematical tool called a **unit factor** is used to convert back and forth between different kinds of units. A unit factor is a ratio that is equal to 1. Because it is equal to 1, multiplying a measurement by a unit factor changes the measurement's units but does not change its value. The skill of converting with a unit factor is known as **dimensional analysis.** Read on to see how it works.

Part 1: Converting with a Unit Factor

PROCEDURE: To convert units with a unit factor, determine the conversion factor between the units you have and the units you want to convert to. Then create the unit factor by making a ratio, in the form of a fraction, between the units you want to convert to in the numerator and the units you already have in the denominator. Finally, multiply your measurement by this unit factor to convert to the new units.

SAMPLE PROBLEM A: Convert 3.5 km to millimeters.

Step 1: Determine the conversion factor between kilometers and millimeters.

$$1 \text{ km} = 1{,}000{,}000 \text{ mm}$$

Step 2: Create the unit factor. Put the units you want to convert to in the numerator and the units you already have in the denominator.

$$\frac{1{,}000{,}000 \text{ mm}}{1 \text{ km}} = 1$$

Step 3: Multiply the unit factor by the measurement. Notice that the original unit of the measurement cancels out with the unit in the denominator of the unit factor, leaving the units you are converting to.

$$3.5 \cancel{\text{km}} \times \frac{1{,}000{,}000 \text{ mm}}{1 \cancel{\text{km}}} = \mathbf{3{,}500{,}000 \text{ mm}}$$

On Your Own!

1. Convert the following measurements using a unit factor:

Conversion	Unit factor	Answer
a. 2.34 cm = ? mm		
b. 54.6 mL = ? L		
c. 12 kg = ? g		

Part 2: Working with Square Units

Many times in your science class, you will work with units of two dimensions, such as square centimeters (cm^2) or square kilometers (km^2). Dimensional analysis is especially useful when working with these types of units because it can help you to avoid confusing the different dimensions of your units. Carefully follow the steps in Sample Problem B to see how it works.

SAMPLE PROBLEM B: 1 km^2 is how many square meters?

Step 1: Simplify the units you are converting.	**Step 2:** Create the unit factor for converting meters to kilometers. As in Sample Problem A, put the units you are converting *to* in the numerator.
$1\ km^2 = 1\ km \times 1\ km$	$\frac{1000\ m}{1\ km} = 1$

Step 3: Multiply the measurement you are converting by the unit factor. Because 1 km^2 = 1 km × 1 km, you will need to multiply the measurement you are converting from by *two* unit factors. Notice that the original unit of measurement cancels the units in the denominator. This leaves the units you are converting *to*.

$$1\ \cancel{km}^2 \times \frac{1000\ m}{1\ \cancel{km}} \times \frac{1000\ m}{1\ \cancel{km}} = 1{,}000{,}000\ m \times m$$

$$1\ km^2 = \mathbf{1{,}000{,}000\ m^2}$$

Practice Your Skills!

2. Convert the following measurements:

Conversion	Unit factor	Answer
a. 3 cm^2 = ? m^2		
b. 12,000 m^2 = ? km^2		
c. 980 cm^2 = ? mm^2		

3. An Olympic-sized soccer field has an area of 0.007776 km^2. How many square meters does a soccer field cover?

____

____

Working with Cubic Dimensions

Because volume can be measured by multiplying length times height times width, volume is expressed in units of three dimensions, or cubic units. Volume is often expressed in cubic millimeters (mm^3) or cubic centimeters (cm^3), but larger volumes may be expressed in cubic meters (m^3) or cubic kilometers (km^3). A cubic centimeter (cm^3) is equal to one milliliter (mL), and a cubic decimeter (dm^3) is equal to one liter (L). Doing dimensional analysis with cubic units is much like doing dimensional analysis with square units, except that with cubic units you will multiply the measurement you are converting by three unit factors instead of two. Follow the steps in Sample Problem C to see how it is done.

SAMPLE PROBLEM C: A certain plant needs about 525 cm^3 of soil to grow properly. How many cubic meters of soil is this?

Step 1: Simplify the units you are converting.

$$cm^3 = cm \times cm \times cm$$

Step 2: Create the unit factor for converting centimeters to meters, putting the units you are converting *to* in the numerator.

$$\frac{1\ m}{100\ cm}$$

Step 3: Multiply the measurement you are converting by the unit factors. Because $cm^3 = cm \times cm \times cm$, you will need to multiply the measurement you are converting from by *three* unit factors.

$$525\ \cancel{cm^3} \times \frac{1\ m}{100\ \cancel{cm}} \times \frac{1\ m}{100\ \cancel{cm}} \times \frac{1\ m}{100\ \cancel{cm}} = 0.000525\ m \times m \times m$$

$$525\ cm^3 = \mathbf{0.000525\ m^3}$$

Try It Yourself!

4. Convert the following measurements:

Conversion	Unit factor	Answer
a. 30 m^3 = ? cm^3		
b. 9000 mm^3 = ? m^3		
c. 4 km^3 = ? m^3		

Challenge Yourself!

5. The Mississippi River has an average water discharge of 17,000 m^3 per second. How many cubic kilometers of water does the river discharge in 1 hour? Show your work.

____

____

____

Name ______________________ Date ____________ Class ____________

CHAPTER 4 LAB DATASHEET

What? No Dentist Bills?

When you eat, you must chew your food well. Chewing food into small bits is the first part of digestion. But birds don't have teeth. How do birds make big chunks of food small enough to begin digestion? In this activity, you will develop a hypothesis about how birds digest their food. Then you will build a model of a bird's digestive system to test your hypothesis.

MATERIALS

- several sealable plastic bags of various sizes
- birdseed
- aquarium gravel
- water
- string
- drinking straw
- transparent tape
- scissors or other materials as needed

Ask a Question

1. How are birds able to begin digestion without having any teeth?

Form a Hypothesis

2. Look at the diagram below of a bird's digestive system. Form a hypothesis that answers the question above. Write your hypothesis below.

____

____

Test the Hypothesis

3. Design a model of a bird's digestive system using the materials listed at left. Include in your design as many of these parts as possible: esophagus, crop, gizzard, intestine, cloaca.

4. Using the materials you selected, build your model.

5. Test your model with the birdseed. Record your observations.

____

____

____

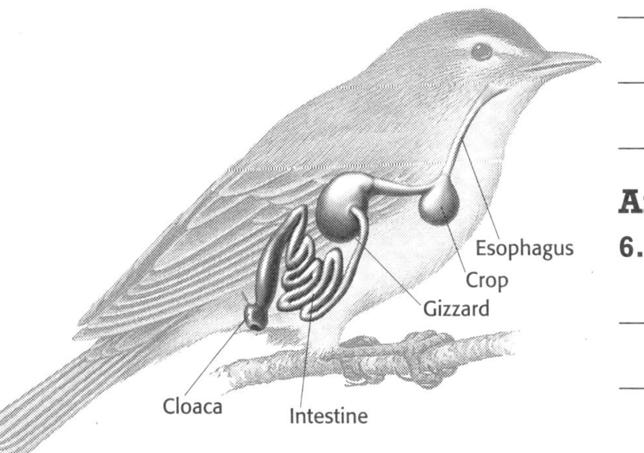

Analyze the Results

6. Did your "gizzard" grind the food?

____

____

Name ____________________ Date __________ Class __________

7. What do you think *gizzard stones* are? How do you think they help a bird?

____

____

8. Does the amount of material added to your model gizzard change its ability to work effectively? Explain your answer.

____

____

9. Birds can break down food particles without teeth. What conclusions can you draw about how they do this?

____

____

Draw Conclusions

10. Analyze the strengths and weaknesses of your hypothesis based on your results. Was your hypothesis correct? Explain your answer.

____

____

11. What are some limitations of your model? How do you think you could improve it?

____

____

Going Further

Did you know that "gizzard stones" have been found at the sites of fossilized dinosaur skeletons? Look in the library or on the Internet for information about the evolutionary relationship between dinosaurs and birds. List the similarities and differences you find.

____

____

____

DISCOVERY LAB

Why Birds of a Beak Eat Together

Cooperative Learning Activity

Group size: 4–6 students

Group goal: To use models of various bird beaks to study how adaptations help birds survive in a particular habitat

Positive interdependence: Each group member should choose a role, such as timer, recorder, feeder, and presenter.

Individual accountability: After the activity, each group member should be able to explain which habitat their beak was best suited for and why.

Time Required

One 45-minute class period

Lab Ratings

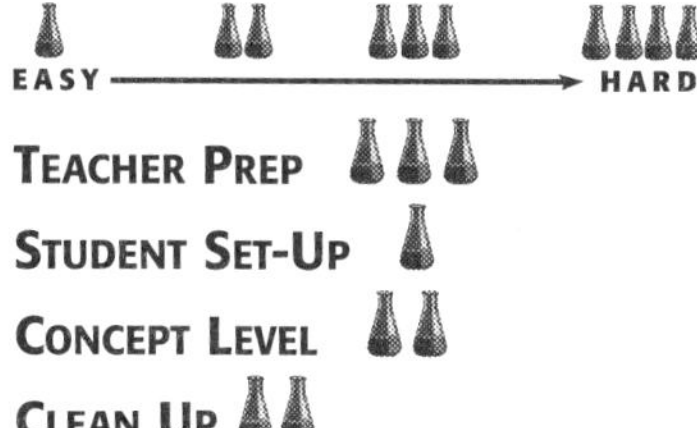

Advance Preparation

Set up six stations around the room. Each station will serve as one of the habitats described in the chart on page 230. At each table, provide the listed materials and display a card describing the habitat. You will also need to provide six kitchen implements to model six beak adaptations, as follows. Label each utensil with the name of the corresponding bird.

Bird Information

Model beak	Bird
1. spoon with slots or holes	duck
2. large tongs	heron
3. short straw or an eyedropper	hummingbird
4. small tweezers	warbler
5. fork	hawk
6. pliers	finch

Safety Information

Caution students not to eat any food at any of the stations. Students should also exercise caution when working with sharp objects, such as the tweezers, fork, or pliers.

Before beginning this activity, ask students if they are allergic to any of the foods used in this lab. Students should avoid contact with any such foods. Instruct students to notify you as soon as possible if they have an allergic reaction.

Teaching Strategies

This activity is designed to accommodate a total of six groups. If a large class size dictates that you must have groups of more than four students, you can include additional habitats and beaks. For example, a small plastic cup could be used to represent the beak of a whippoorwill, which eats flying insects. The insects could be represented by popcorn thrown into the air.

continued...

Elizabeth Rustad
Crane Junior High
Yuma, Arizona

Before beginning the activity, you may wish to discuss with your students the concepts of natural selection and adaptation. Natural selection is the process by which organisms that are best suited to their environment survive and reproduce. Adaptation is a change in an organism's structure that helps it live and reproduce successfully in its environment.

Assign each flock to an initial station. Tell the flocks that they will be given two minutes at each station to obtain as much food as they can from the station. They should start only on your signal.

You may wish to have extra food samples available for the students to enjoy after completing the activity.

Evaluation Strategies

Request that students hand in their feeding charts upon completion of the activity. This chart will provide an indication of the critical thinking each student applied in this activity.

For help evaluating this lab, see the Group Evaluation of Cooperative Group Activity in the *Assessment Checklists & Rubrics*. This checklist is also available in the *One-Stop Planner CD-ROM.*

Station Information

Station	Materials	Habitat description
1	Cereal flakes in a large bowl of milk (water may be substituted for milk)	Small plants floating in a lake
2	Bran flakes and raisins moistened with milk (or water) in a large bowl	Small animals buried in mud
3	Jar filled halfway with juice or powdered drink mix; cap on jar removed	A flower filled with nectar
4	Jelly beans buried in crumpled aluminum foil	Small insects living in tree bark
5	Cubes of cheese or bread	Small rodents
6	Peanuts covered with cereal flakes in a shallow bowl	Leaves and nuts buried on the forest floor

Name ______________________ Date __________ Class __________

CHAPTER 4 STUDENT WORKSHEET

CHAPTER 4

Why Birds of a Beak Eat Together

You are part of a group of hungry birds looking for a good place to eat. How do you know how to find such a place? Well, it depends on the type of food available in the area and how easily you can get to the food.

Luckily, there are many types of feeding habitats nearby. In this activity, you and your flock will fly to each one of the habitats and try to obtain food.

Happy flying and good eating!

MATERIALS

- One of the following tools: spoon with slots or holes, large tongs, short straw or eyedropper, small tweezers, fork, or pliers
- plastic cup

Objective

To model the beak adaptations of birds and study how effective the adaptations are in obtaining various types of food

Let's Get Pecking, Birds!

1. Your teacher will provide your flock with a model of a beak and a plastic cup. Six different feeding "habitats" are arranged around the room. Your flock's job is to determine the habitat your beak is best suited for. First walk around the room and examine each habitat. Then predict in which habitat you think it will be easiest to obtain food. Record your prediction below.

____

____

____

SAFETY ALERT!

Exercise caution when working with sharp objects such as tweezers, forks, or pliers.

WARNING

Do not eat the food you collect!

2. Move to your first habitat, and designate one student to obtain the food.
3. When your teacher signals to begin, have this student use the "beak" to collect as much food as possible in the time allotted. The collected food should be transferred to the plastic cup.
4. When your teacher signals to stop, discuss with your flock how easy it was to get food in this habitat. Record your results in the Feeding Chart on page 232.
5. Return the collected food to the station, leaving the station for the next group in the same condition as you found it.
6. Move around the room to each habitat. At each habitat, repeat steps 3–4. Be sure that every student contributes to the discussions.

Name ______________________ Date __________ Class __________

Feeding Chart

Habitat	Feeding results
1	
2	
3	
4	
5	
6	
7	

Beak-ause All Birds Are Different

7. In which habitat was it easiest for your flock to obtain food? Explain.

____

____

____

8. How does your answer compare with your prediction at the beginning of this activity?

____

____

____

____

____

____

9. Based on the results of this activity, why do you think beaks have adapted the way they have?

____

____

____

____

Critical Thinking

10. What would happen if the habitat to which your flock were best suited were destroyed? Are there any other habitats in which your flock could easily survive? Justify your answer.

____

____

____

____

Going Further

Watch a video about the eating habits of birds that live in different habitats. Then discuss with the rest of the class what you learned from the video.

Name ______________________ Date ______________ Class ____________

CHAPTER 4 STUDENT PROJECT WORKSHEET

Look Who's Coming to Dinner

"Please pass the sunflower seeds." "Stop spitting!" "Would you PLEASE close your beak while you eat?" You can learn a lot about birds by watching them eat together. A good place to observe bird behavior is at a bird feeder. Some animals other than birds like to eat bird seed, so a bird feeder can also be a good place to see how birds interact with other animals.

Fly-Through Restaurant

1. Use bird field guides or identification books to find out which birds are common in your area. What do these birds eat? Use empty milk cartons or plastic soda bottles to build a bird feeder. Fill your bird feeder and hang it from a low tree limb, a balcony, or a porch. Make sure to keep the feeder full.

Observe your feeder at the same time each day for 30 minutes. Record the number and name of each bird species that you see. Also note any other animals that visit the bird feeder. Write down the behavior you observe between members of the same species and members of different species. Is the behavior you observe the same behavior that is described in the bird identification books? Present your findings as a scientific journal article.

INTERNET KEYWORDS

- bats
- bat house
- Bat Conservation International

Other Long-Term Project Ideas

2. Many people build bird houses, but what about bat houses? Use the library or Internet resources to find out how to build your own bat house. What kinds of bats live in your area? How high off the ground should the house be? What temperature do bats prefer? What color should you paint the house? After you put up the bat house, keep track of how long it takes to attract bats. Present your findings to the class. Why might building a bat house in your area be a good idea?

3. Can you imagine baby-sitting eight children? Eight is the average litter size for a Syrian hamster. Observe a small female mammal, such as a hamster or a mouse, that has recently had babies. For several weeks, take notes on the behavior of the mother and the babies. How do the mother and the babies interact? How do the babies interact with each other? What are their sleeping and eating patterns? How do those patterns change as the babies get older? Share your findings with your classmates in a poster display.

4. Why have Tamarin monkeys been bred successfully in captivity, while other animals have not? Visit a zoo and talk to the scientists about the challenges of creating a successful breeding program. Why are certain species easier to breed in captivity? Make a display that shows 8–10 species of birds and mammals, describes the breeding programs for each, and lists the reasons for the success or failure of each program.

Research Ideas

5. Bobbing and weaving on their long, thin legs, whooping cranes perform an elaborate dance before mating. Why do the cranes dance? Investigate the courtship behaviors of five bird species, and create a poster display comparing the species' courtship behaviors.

6. Over 60 million American buffalo, or bison, once ruled the Great Plains. Today, only about 200,000 bison remain. Research the decline of the bison. What caused it? How were bison important to the Native Americans that lived on the Great Plains? What effect did the decline of bison have on the Native Americans? Write a report that summarizes what you learned.

7. You'd probably go to the hospital if you were bitten by a rattlesnake or a black widow spider, but what if you were bitten by a shrew? The shrew and three other mammals—the platypus, the echidna, and the solendon—are poisonous! Find out more about these mammals. How strong is their poison? How is it used? Write an article about these four poisonous mammals.

8. Warning: Possession of feathers could be a felony. Believe it or not, it is illegal to buy or sell the feathers of some species of birds. Research the laws that control which feathers can be used under what conditions. What kinds of feathers can people legally own? Are exceptions made for certain uses? Why? Create a brochure about the legal and illegal uses of feathers.

9. When you touch or pick up a hibernating Arctic ground squirrel, it won't wake up. But don't try that with a hibernating grizzly bear! Find out more about animals that hibernate. What makes the hibernation of arctic ground squirrels different from the hibernation of bears? What changes occur in an animal's body during hibernation? What other animals hibernate, and why? Write an article about these animals, and explain your findings.

Name ______________________________ Date ______________ Class ______________

CHAPTER 4 BIRDS AND MAMMALS

Chapter 4 Test

USING VOCABULARY

To complete the following sentences, choose the correct term from each pair of terms listed, and write the term in the blank.

1. ______________________ is a behavior among birds in which they spread oil on their feathers. (Preening or Brooding)

2. A mammal's ______________________ helps the mammal draw air into its lungs. (placenta or diaphragm)

3. ______________________ distinguish mammals from all other animals. (Lungs or Mammary glands)

4. ______________________ are the reptilian ancestors of mammals. (Marsupials or Therapsids)

5. ______________________ chicks quickly learn to feed themselves after they hatch. (Precocial or Altricial)

UNDERSTANDING CONCEPTS

Multiple Choice

Circle the correct answer.

6. A bird's streamlined body surface is the result of
   a. down feathers.
   b. thick scales.
   c. contour feathers.
   d. a pointed beak.

7. What part of a bird's digestive tract grinds up food?
   a. crop
   b. teeth
   c. gizzard
   d. intestine

8. Which of the following is NOT characteristic of primates?
   a. forward-facing eyes
   b. flat fingernails instead of claws
   c. very intelligent
   d. development of embryos in pouches

9. Which of the following is NOT an adaptation for sustained flight in birds?
   a. excellent eyesight
   b. hollow bones
   c. rapid metabolic rate
   d. strong flight muscles

10. Which of the following birds is accurately described?
   a. parrot: is a songbird
   b. owl: is a bird of prey
   c. emu: has a large keel
   d. falcon: has webbed feet

11. Both birds and reptiles
    a. lay eggs.
    b. brood their young.
    c. have crops.
    d. All of the above

12. Birds that primarily eat meat and have good vision are known as
    a. flightless birds.
    b. perching birds.
    c. waterfowl.
    d. birds of prey.

Short Answer

13. Why do scientists think that birds evolved from dinosaurs?

____

____

____

____

____

____

____

____

14. How does the shape of a bird's wing enable it to fly?

____

____

____

____

____

____

15. List three ways that marsupials and monotremes are similar.

____

____

____

____

CONCEPT MAPPING

16. Use the following terms to complete the concept map below: placental mammal, egg, marsupial, uterus, monotreme, embryo.

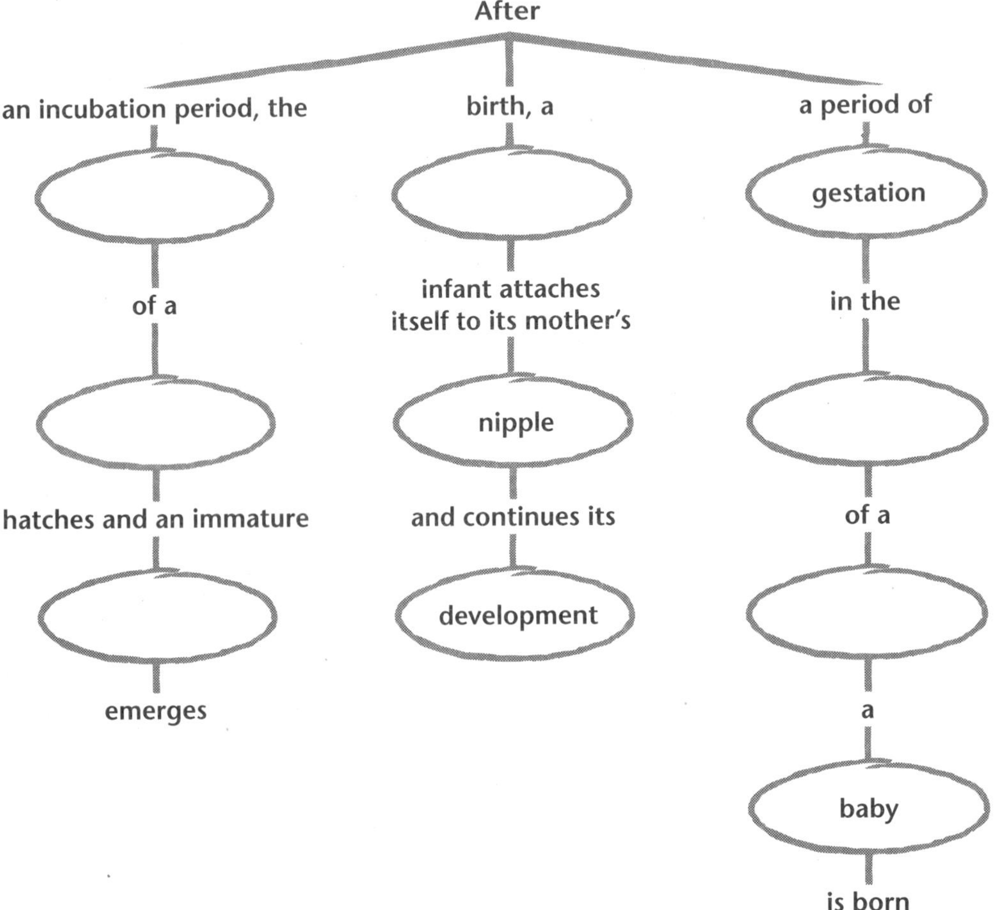

CRITICAL THINKING AND PROBLEM SOLVING

17. Suppose you find a baby bird in the schoolyard. Its eyes are closed, it has no feathers, and it is flopping around on the ground. How would you classify this chick? Explain your answer.

____

____

____

____

____

____

INTERPRETING GRAPHICS

The graph below shows the range of environmental temperatures over which various mammals can maintain a constant metabolic rate.

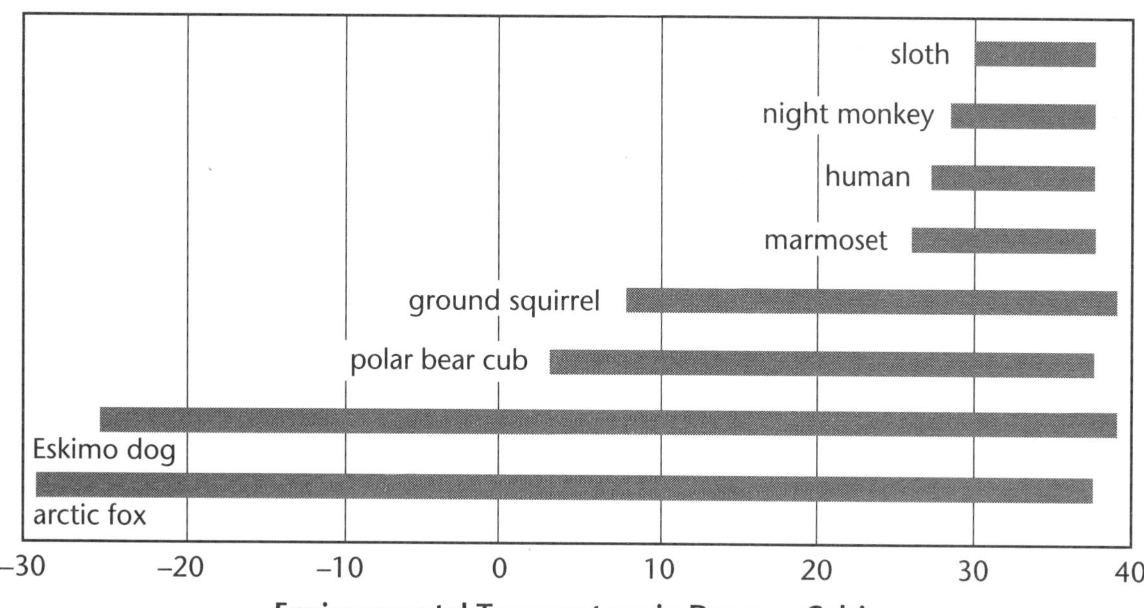

18. Which mammal can tolerate a wider range of temperatures before altering its metabolism: a human, a night monkey, or a marmoset?

____

____

____

MATH IN SCIENCE

19. One gram of fat yields about 9 kcal of energy. One gram of carbohydrate yields about 4 kcal. How many more calories are yielded by the breakdown of 50 g of fat than by the same amount of carbohydrate? (1 kcal = 1,000 cal) Show your work.

____

____

____

____

____

____

Name ______________________________ Date ______________ Class ______________

CHAPTER

BIRDS AND MAMMALS

Chapter 4 Performance-Based Assessment

TEACHER'S PREPARATORY GUIDE

Purpose

Students examine the differences between down and contour feathers and make a connection between structure and function.

Time Required

One 45-minute class period
Students will need 25 minutes to perform the procedure and 20 minutes to answer the analysis questions.

P. B. A. Ratings

EASY → HARD

TEACHER PREP

STUDENT SET-UP

CONCEPT LEVEL

CLEAN UP

Advance Preparation

Equip each student activity station with the necessary materials. If down pillows are not available, you may wish to substitute a down sleeping bag. Be sure the down is not cooler than room temperature—this will affect the results of the experiment.

Safety Information

Hot tap water is hot enough for this activity. Mop up all spills immediately. Ask students if anyone is allergic to feathers. Goggles should be worn while handling glassware.

Teaching Strategies

This activity works best in groups of 2–3 students. Students should know the names of the parts of a feather before starting the activity: shaft, barb, and barbule.

Evaluation Strategies

Use the following rubric to evaluate student performance.

Rubric for Chapter 4 Assessment

Possible points	Appropriate use of materials and equipment (10 points possible)
10–8	Successful completion of activity; safe and careful handling of materials and equipment; precise measurements; superior lab skills
7–5	Generally complete activity; acceptable handling of materials and equipment; somewhat precise measurements; average lab skills
4–1	Incomplete activity; unsafe handling of materials and equipment; imprecise measurements; apparent lack of skill
	Quality and clarity of observations (40 points possible)
40–28	Superior observations stated clearly and accurately; high level of detail
27–15	Accurate observations; moderate level of detail
14–1	Erroneous, incomplete, or unclear observations; little or no detail
	Explanation of observations (50 points possible)
50–35	Clear, detailed explanation; superior knowledge of the functions of different types of feathers; use of examples to support explanations
34–20	Somewhat unclear explanation; adequate understanding of the functions of different types of feathers; minor difficulty in expression
19–1	Unclear or irrelevant explanation; poor understanding of the functions of different types of feathers; substantial factual errors

Name ______________________ Date ____________ Class ____________

CHAPTER 4 BIRDS AND MAMMALS

Chapter 4 Performance-Based Assessment

Objective

All birds have two types of feathers that have different functions. In this activity you will examine these two feather types and demonstrate their differences.

Know the Score!

As you work through the activity, keep in mind that you will be earning a grade for the following:

- how well you work with materials and equipment (10%)
- how well you make observations about different types of feathers (40%)
- how well you explain your observations (50%)

MATERIALS

- graduated cylinder
- hot water
- 2 aluminum cans
- thermometer
- aluminum foil
- down pillow
- clock or watch

Procedure

1. Pour 250 mL of hot water into each aluminum can. Measure the temperature of the water in each can. Record the temperatures.

____

____

2. Cover the tops of the cans with aluminum foil. Put one can aside and cover the other one completely with the pillow, being careful not to spill the water. After 15 minutes, measure the temperature of the water in each can. What are the temperatures now?

____

____

____

____

____

Analysis

3. How did the down feathers affect the temperature of the water?

____

____

____

4. Examine the illustrations below. Label the parts of the feathers with these terms: shaft, barb, barbule.

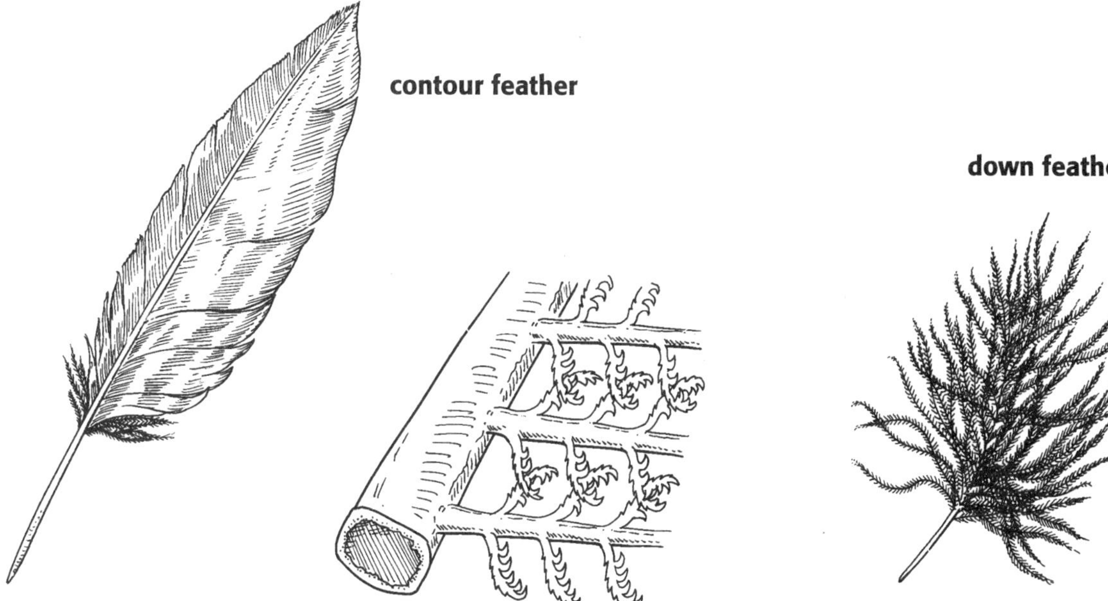

5. Describe how the structure of each feather part affects the feather's function.

____

____

____

____

____

____

____

____

____

Answer Key

Name ______________ Date ________ Class ________

CHAPTER 1 DIRECTED READING WORKSHEET

Animals and Behavior

Chapter Introduction

As you begin this chapter, answer the following.

1. Read the title of the chapter. List three things that you already know about this subject.

____

2. Write two questions about this subject that you would like answered by the time you finish this chapter.

____

3. How does the title of the Start-Up Activity relate to the subject of the chapter?

____

Section 1: What Is an Animal? (p. 4)

4. Natural bath sponges used to be living plants. True or (False)? (Circle one.)

5. Describe the smallest animal you've ever seen.

Accept any reasonable answer. Sample answer: The smallest animal I've ever seen was a fruit fly. It was black and had clear wings.

Name ______________ Date ________ Class ________

The Animal Kingdom (p. 4)

6. Which of the following lists contains types of organisms that are NOT animals?

a. corals, birds, kangaroos
(b.) dolphins, cactuses, whales
c. spiders, humans, sponges
d. sea anemones, fish, slugs

Use Figure 3 to determine whether each of the following types of animals is an invertebrate or a vertebrate. In the space provided, write *I* if it is an invertebrate and *V* if it is a vertebrate.

7. I beetles
8. V mammals
9. I worms
10. I spiders

That's an Animal? (p. 5)

Mark each of the following statements *True* or *False*.

11. True All animals are multicellular.
12. False Animal cells are prokaryotic.
13. True Some animals can reproduce asexually.

14. In the earliest stage of its development, an organism is called an embryo.

15. Which of the following specialized parts are organs? (Circle all that apply.)

a. muscles
(b.) kidneys
(c.) heart
d. nerves

16. Animals are the only organisms that can move. True or (False)? (Circle one.)

17. Plants can make their own food, but animals cannot. How do animals survive?

Animals are consumers. They survive by eating other organisms, parts of other organisms, or the products of other organisms.

Review (p. 7)

Now that you've finished Section 1, review what you learned by answering the Review questions in your ScienceLog.

Name ______________ Date ________ Class ________

Section 2: Animal Behavior (p. 8)

1. The activities that animals perform, such as building homes and stalking food, are called ___behaviors___.

Survival Behavior (p. 8)

2. Survival behaviors help animals find food, water, and a place to live, and help them avoid being eaten. (True) or False? (Circle one.)
3. Animals use different methods in order to obtain the most ___food___ for the least amount of ___energy___.
4. Predators hunt and eat other ___animals___, called prey.
5. Use the text to give one example of an animal that uses camouflage.

   Answers should include one of the following: Rabbits blend into shrubs and grass, walking sticks look like sticks, or a caterpillar can look like a twig.

6. How does the hooded pitohui bird defend itself from predators?
   - **a.** Its bite injects a powerful acid into its attacker.
   - **b.** It is covered in spines.
   - **c.** It can spray a chemical that smells very bad.
   - **(d.)** Its skin contains a toxin that can kill a predator.
7. Warning coloration is helpful to prey because it keeps prey from being eaten. Why is warning coloration sometimes helpful to predators?

   Warning coloration is sometimes helpful to predators because it helps them avoid animals that would cause them pain, make them sick, or kill them.

Why Do They Behave That Way? (p. 10)

8. Animals always know instinctively what to do. True or (False)? (Circle one.)
9. Innate behaviors are influenced by ___genes___ and do not depend on experience or ___learning___.
10. Innate behavior cannot be changed. True or (False)? (Circle one.)

Name ______________ Date ________ Class ________

11. The tendency of humans to speak is a(n) ___innate___ behavior but the language we speak is a(n) ___learned___ behavior.

Review (p. 10)

Now that you've finished the first part of Section 2, review what you learned by answering the Review questions in your ScienceLog.

Seasonal Behavior (p. 11)

12. What are two ways animals deal with winter?

    Student answers should include two of the following: traveling to warmer places, storing food, burrowing into the ground or mud, and hibernating.

13. The only reason animals travel from one place to another and back again is to find food and water. True or (False)? (Circle one.)
14. Which of the following does NOT happen during hibernation?
    - **a.** The animal's heart rate drops.
    - **b.** The animal survives on stored body fat.
    - **(c.)** The animal's temperature increases.
    - **d.** The animal does not wake for weeks at a time.
15. Sometimes desert animals experience an internal slowdown during the summer. (True) or False? (Circle one.)

The Rhythms of Life (p. 12)

16. To set their biological clock, animals use clues such as the ___length___ of the ___day___ and the ___temperature___.
17. Circadian rhythms are daily cycles. What is an example of a circadian rhythm?

    Sample answer: Getting up at about the same time each day and getting sleepy at about the same time each night are examples.

How Do Animals Find Their Way? (p. 12)

18. Arctic terns have to ___navigate___ to make their 38,000 km round trip.

Name ________ Date ________ Class ________

Chapter 1, continued

19. All of the landmarks that animals use to navigate are things that they can see, such as mountains and rivers. True or (False)? (Circle one.)

20. Look at the Physical Science Connection on the right hand side of page 13. Migratory birds have crystals of a mineral called magnetite above their nostrils. How do scientists think this mineral helps them?

Biologists think the mineral somehow moves or stimulates nerves so that the birds know where they are on Earth.

Review (p. 13)

Now that you've finished Section 2, review what you learned by answering the Review questions in your ScienceLog.

Section 3: Living Together (p. 14)

1. The ___interaction___ between animals of the same species requires communication.

Communication (p. 14)

2. What two things must happen for communication to occur between two animals?

For communication to exist between two animals, a signal must travel from one animal to another, and the receiver of the signal must respond in some way.

3. Why are the cranes in Figure 15 dancing?
- **a.** They are telling each other where to find food
- **(b.)** The dance leads to mating.
- **c.** They are frightening away predators.
- **d.** They are warning each other of danger.

4. The wolves in Figure 18 are howling to defend their living space from other wolves. (True) or False? (Circle one.)

How Do Animals Communicate? (p. 15)

5. Animals use their senses, such as sight and touch, to convey ___specific___ information.

Name ________ Date ________ Class ________

Chapter 1, continued

6. Which of the following messages do ants communicate using pheromones? (Circle all that apply.)
- **(a.)** Danger!
- **(b.)** I'm from your colony.
- **(c.)** Follow me!
- **(d.)** I'm your friend.

7. Insects use some of the same pheromones to attract mates that elephants use. (True) or False? (Circle one.)

Match the noise in Column B with the type of animal that uses that noise for communication in Column A, and write the corresponding letter in the space provided.

Column A	Column B
b **8.** elephants	**a.** songs
a **9.** male birds	**b.** low rumbles
d **10.** dolphins	**c.** howls
c **11.** wolves	**d.** complex clicks

12. Fireflies blinking and humans winking are both examples of communication. (True) or False? (Circle one.)

13. Look at the diagram "The Dance of the Bees" on page 16. If you were a honeybee, how would learning the waggle dance help you find food?

The waggle dance would tell me the direction of the nectar and the distance to the nectar from the hive if I were a honeybee.

Part of the Family (p. 17)

14. Look at the ground squirrel in Figure 23. What is one benefit and one downside to living in a group?

Benefits include the following: safety and help finding food.

Disadvantages include the following: attracting predators, needing more food, competing for food and mates, and spreading disease.

Answers should include one of each.

Review (p. 17)

Now that you've finished Section 3, review what you learned by answering the Review questions in your ScienceLog.

Name ______________ Date ________ Class ________

CHAPTER 1 VOCABULARY AND NOTES WORKSHEET

Animals and Behavior

By studying the Vocabulary and Notes listed for each section below, you can gain a better understanding of this chapter.

SECTION 1

Vocabulary

In your own words, write a definition for each of the following terms in the space provided.

1. vertebrate an animal with a skull and a backbone; examples include mammals, birds, reptiles, amphibians, and fish
2. invertebrate an animal without a backbone
3. embryo an organism in the earliest stage of development
4. tissue a group of similar cells that work together to perform a specific job in the body
5. organ a combination of two or more tissues that work together to perform a specific function in the body
6. consumer organisms that eat producers or other organisms for energy

Notes

Read the following section highlights. Then, in your own words, write the highlights in your ScienceLog.

- Animals with a skull and a backbone are vertebrates. Animals without a backbone are invertebrates.
- Animals are multicellular. Their cells are eukaryotic and lack a cell wall.
- Most animals reproduce sexually and develop from embryos.
- Most animals have tissues and organs.
- Most animals move.
- Animals are consumers.

Name ______________ Date ________ Class ________

SECTION 2

Vocabulary

In your own words, write a definition for each of the following terms in the space provided.

1. predator an animal that eats other animals
2. prey an organism that is eaten by another organism
3. innate behavior a behavior that is influenced by genes and does not depend on learning or experience
4. learned behavior a behavior that has been learned from experience or observation
5. hibernation a period of inactivity that some animals experience in winter; allows them to survive on stored body fat
6. estivation a period of reduced activity that some animals experience in the summer
7. biological clock an internal control of natural cycles
8. circadian rhythm daily cycle

Copyright © by Holt, Rinehart and Winston. All rights reserved.

Copyright © by Holt, Rinehart and Winston. All rights reserved.

Name ______________ Date ________ Class ________

Notes

Read the following section highlights. Then, in your own words, write the highlights in your ScienceLog.

- Many animals use camouflage, chemicals, or both to defend themselves against predators.
- Behavior may be classified as innate or learned. The potential for innate behavior is inherited. Learned behavior depends on experience.
- Some animals migrate to find food, water, or safe nesting grounds.
- Some animals hibernate in the winter, and some estivate in the summer.
- Animals have internal biological clocks to control natural cycles.
- Daily cycles are called circadian rhythms.
- Some biological clocks are regulated by cues from an animal's environment.
- Animals navigate close to home using landmarks and a mental image of their home area.
- Some animals use the positions of the sun and stars or Earth's magnetic field to navigate.

SECTION 3

Vocabulary

In your own words, write a definition for each of the following terms in the space provided.

1. social behavior the interaction between animals of the same species
2. communication a transfer of a signal from one animal to another that results in some type of response
3. territory an area occupied by one animal or a group of animals from which other members of the species are excluded
4. pheromone a chemical produced by animals for communication

Notes

Read the following section highlights. Then, in your own words, write the highlights in your ScienceLog.

- Communication must include both a signal and a response.
- Two important kinds of communication are courtship and territorial displays.
- Animals communicate through sight, sound, touch, and smell.
- Group living allows animals to spot both prey and predators more easily.
- Groups of animals are more visible to predators than are individuals, and animals in groups must compete with one another for food and mates.

Name ______________ Date ________ Class ________

CHAPTER 1 CHAPTER REVIEW WORKSHEET

Animals and Behavior

USING VOCABULARY

To complete the following sentences, choose the correct term from each pair of terms listed below, and write the term on the space provided.

1. An animal with a skull and a backbone is a vertebrate. An animal with no backbone is an invertebrate. (an invertebrate or a vertebrate)
2. A behavior that does not depend on experience is innate. (innate or learned)
3. In the summer, an animal enters a state of reduced activity. The animal is estivating. (estivating or hibernating)
4. Daily cycles are known as circadian rhythms. (biological clocks or circadian rhythms)
5. When an egg and a sperm come together, they form an embryo. (an embryo or an organ)

UNDERSTANDING CONCEPTS

Multiple Choice

6. Which characteristic is NOT true of animals?
   a. They are multicellular.
   b. They usually reproduce sexually.
   (c.) They make their own food.
   d. They have tissues.
7. Living in groups
   a. attracts predators.
   b. helps prey spot predators.
   c. helps animals find food.
   (d.) All of the above
8. Warning coloration is
   a. a kind of camouflage.
   (b.) a way to warn predators away.
   c. always black and white.
   d. always a sign that an animal is poisonous to eat.
9. Some birds use Earth's magnetic field
   a. to attract mates.
   (b.) to navigate.
   c. to set their biological clocks.
   d. to defend their territory.
10. To defend against predators, an animal might use
    a. camouflage.
    b. warning coloration.
    c. toxins.
    (d.) All of the above

Name ______________ Date ________ Class ________

Short Answer

11. How are pheromones used in communication?

Pheromones are released by one animal to send a message to another animal.

12. What is a territory? Give an example of a territory from your own environment.

A territory is an area occupied by one animal or a group of animals from which other members of the species are excluded. Examples will vary but may include a bedroom, a family house, or a school.

13. What landmarks help you navigate your way home from school?

Answers will vary but should be unchanging objects, such as buildings or roads.

14. What do migration and hibernation have in common?

Both are seasonal behaviors that are controlled by biological clocks.

Name ______________ Date ________ Class ________

Animals and Behavior, continued

CONCEPT MAPPING

15. Use the following terms to create a concept map: *estivation, circadian rhythms, seasonal behaviors, hibernation, migration, biological clocks.*

Biological clocks
control
circadian rhythms
seasonal behaviors
including
hibernation
migration
estivation

Name ____________ Date ________ Class ________

Animals and Behavior, continued

CRITICAL THINKING AND PROBLEM SOLVING

Write one or two sentences to answer each of the following questions:

16. If you smell a skunk while riding in a car and you shut the car window, has the skunk communicated with you? Explain.

Yes; even though you were not the intended recipient of the message, the skunk communicated with you. The skunk has sent a signal (its smell), and you have responded (by shutting the window).

17. Flying is an innate behavior in birds. Is it an innate behavior or a learned behavior in humans? Why?

It is a learned behavior. Humans are not born with the ability to fly, but we have learned to fly using airplanes.

18. Ants depend on pheromones and touch for communication, but birds depend more on sight and sound. Why might these two types of animals communicate differently?

Ants are much smaller and cannot see or hear over great distances, so they must depend on pheromones and touch for communication. Birds have better eyesight, and they can hear well and sing, so they can communicate by sound and sight.

Name ____________ Date ________ Class ________

Animals and Behavior, continued

INTERPRETING GRAPHICS

The pie chart below shows the major phyla of the animal species on Earth. Use the chart to answer the questions that follow.

19. What group of animals has the most species?

Beetles have the greatest number of species. Students may also list the group arthropods, which includes beetles, bugs, insects, and spiders.

20. How many species of beetles are on Earth? How does that compare with the number of mammal species?

There are 290,000 species of beetles. There are only 4,000 species of mammals.

21. How many species of vertebrates are known?

There are 42,300 vertebrate species (4,000 mammals + 38,300 other vertebrates).

Name ______ Date ______ Class ______

22. Scientists are still discovering new species. Which pie wedges are most likely to increase? Why do you think so?

Answers will vary, but students may suggest that new species of insects and beetles will be found. Because there are so many species in these groups, there is a greater chance that they have not all been found.

MATH IN SCIENCE

Use the data from the pie chart to answer the following questions:

23. What is the total number of animal species on Earth?

There are 1,032,300 animal species on Earth.

24. How many different species of moths and butterflies are on Earth?

There are 112,000 species of moths and butterflies on Earth.

25. What percentage of all animal species are moths and butterflies?

Moths and butterflies are 10.9 percent of all of the animal species on Earth.

26. What percentage of all animal species are vertebrates?

Vertebrates are 4.1 percent of all animal species.

READING CHECK-UP

Take a minute to review your answers to the ScienceLog questions at the beginning of the chapter. Have your answers changed? If necessary, revise your answers based on what you have learned since you began this chapter. Record your revisions in your ScienceLog.

Name ______ Date ______ Class ______

CHAPTER 1 SCIENCE PUZZLERS, TWISTERS & TEASERS

Animals and Behavior

Complements

1. Unscramble the words in the wheel below. Words opposite each other on the wheel are complementary terms.

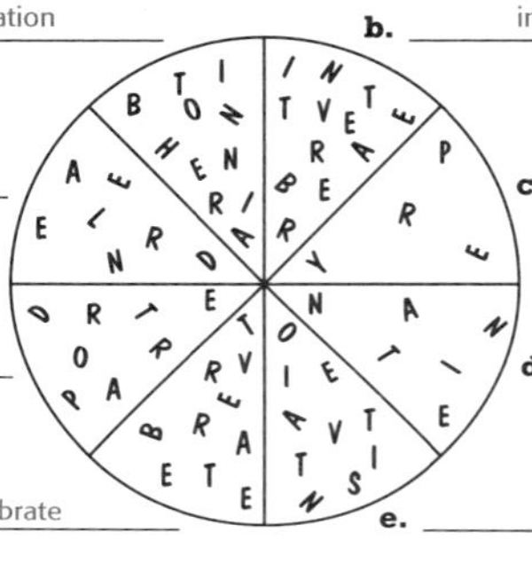

a. hibernation
b. invertebrate
c. prey
d. innate
e. estivation
f. vertebrate
g. predator
h. learned

Analogies

2. Give the animal-world equivalent to the human items below.

a. perfume — pheromones

b. wearing a suit to the office or the team colors to a football game — camouflage

c. house or bedroom — territory

d. compass — sun/stars

e. the big red house on the corner or the oak tree across town — landmark

f. winking, frowning, or nodding your head — body language

Name ______ Date ______ Class ______

Crazy 8's

3. Below are vocabulary words from the chapter that all end with the sound *eight.* Use the following clues to help you figure out each word.

a. "Country lodging" ______ innate

b. Not *low* but ______ + ______ hibernate

c. French for *green* + ______ vertebrate

d. Not *yeah,* but ______ + ______ navigate

e. Not *your,* but ______ + tiger sound ______ migrate

Strange Birds

4. Almost all rules have exceptions. If the rule has any exceptions, list them in the blanks. If there are no exceptions, write "no exceptions."

a. All animals start life as an embryo. ______ sponge

b. No animals have cell walls. ______ no exception

c. No plants are consumers. ______ Venus' flytrap

d. All animals are active. ______ sample answer: clam

e. All animals have nuclei. ______ no exception

Name ______ Date ______ Class ______

What Makes an Animal an Animal?

Complete this worksheet after reading Chapter 1, Section 1.

Whales, armadillos, hummingbirds, spiders… animals come in all shapes and sizes. Not all animals have backbones, and not all animals have hair. So what makes an animal an animal?

Complete the chart below by using the words and phrases at the bottom of the page.

Animal Characteristics

Animal Characteristics
- move
- are consumers
- have specialized parts
  - **tissues**
    - **organs**
- **reproduce**
  - sexually
    - **fertilized egg cell**
      - develop from embryos
  - asexually
    - budding
    - division
- multicellular
  - **cells are eukaryotic**
  - cells have no cell walls

Words and Phrases

- move
- budding
- develop from embryos
- have specialized parts
- sexually
- asexually
- multicellular
- cells have no cell walls
- division
- are consumers

Name ______________________ Date __________ Class __________

CHAPTER 1 REINFORCEMENT WORKSHEET

Animal Interviews

Complete this worksheet after reading Chapter 1, Section 2.

Imagine that you work with Dr. Phishtof Finz, a researcher who can really talk to the animals. Below are some sections of his taped animal interviews. Your job is to decide what animal behavior or characteristic is being described and to write it in the space provided. Possible answers are *warning coloration, migration, hibernation, estivation,* and *camouflage.*

Interviewed animal		Behavior or characteristic
Canada goose:	During the summer, we stay up in Canada. It's really a nice place in summer, with lots of food and lots of sun. But before the snow starts to fly, we high-tail it south!	migration
Arctic ground squirrel:	What's the winter like in Alaska? Strange, I really don't know. I spend all summer eating and getting my nest ready, but then during the fall I get so sleepy! I go to bed and—*poof!*—when I wake up it's spring!	hibernation
Desert mouse:	Oh, living in the desert is wonderful! I love sunshine. During the really hot part of the summer, of course, I stay inside my nest, and I nap a lot. It's so much cooler inside.	estivation
Ladybug:	Thank you! I am a lovely shade of red, aren't I? But just between you and me, did you know that this beautiful color tells birds that I am, well, rather nasty tasting?	warning coloration
Chameleon:	Yoo-hoo! I'm over here! See? In the potted plant. Well, yes, I am rather proud of being able to turn that particular shade of green. Not all animals can do that, you know.	camouflage

Name ______________________ Date __________ Class __________

CHAPTER 1 VOCABULARY REVIEW WORKSHEET

Puzzling Animal Behavior

After you finish reading Chapter 1, give this crossword puzzle a try!

Solve the clues below, and write the answers in the appropriate spaces in the crossword puzzle.

ACROSS

3. to find one's way from one place to another
4. an organism that eats other organisms
6. this type of behavior can change item 17 down
7. an organism in the earliest stage of development
8. to travel from one place to another in response to the seasons or environmental conditions
10. an internal control of natural cycles
16. an area occupied by an animal or a group of animals from which other members of the species are excluded
18. this type of behavior is the interaction between animals of the same species
19. an animal that eats other animals
20. made of many cells
21. a period of inactivity that some animals experience in winter

DOWN

1. chemicals animals produce for communication
2. an animal without a backbone
5. coloration and/or texture that enables an animal to blend in with its surroundings
7. a period of reduced activity that some animals experience in summer
9. a collection of similar cells that work together to perform a specific job in the body
11. a combination of two or more of item 9 down
12. takes place when a signal travels from one animal to another and the receiver of the signal responds
13. fixed object an animal uses to find its way
14. ________ rhythms are daily cycles.
15. any animal with a skull and a backbone
17. behavior that is influenced by genes and does not depend on learning or experience
22. an animal that is eaten by another animal

Name ______________________ Date ____________ Class ____________

Puzzling Animal Behavior, continued

3 NAVIGATE
4 CONSUMER
6 LEARNED
7 EMBRYO
8 MIGRATE
10 BIOLOGICAL CLOCK
16 TERRITORY
18 SOCIAL
19 PREDATOR
20 MULTICELLULAR
21 HIBERNATION

1 PHEROMONES
2 INVERTEBRATE
5 CAMOUFLAGE
7 ESTIVATION
9 TISSUE
11 ORGAN
12 COMMUNICATION
13 LANDMARK
14 CIRCADIAN
15 VERTEBRATE
17 INNATE
22 PREY

Name ______________________ Date ____________ Class ____________

CHAPTER 1 CRITICAL THINKING WORKSHEET

Masters of Navigation

FOR MANY PEOPLE, THE MOST INTRIGUING aspects of bird biology and behavior are associated with homing and migration. Several years ago, for example, a friend and I were nest-trapping Blue-winged Teal in Iowa. We captured a female that had been banded the previous year at a nest only thirty-five feet from the present one. I remember stroking her plumage and wondering if she spent the winter in Louisiana, Texas, or Mexico. It didn't make any difference as she certainly hit the bulls-eye on her return. While I found the accuracy of this hen teal to be remarkable, it is not extraordinary by avian standards. . . .

A very dramatic migration is seen in the New Zealand Bronzed Cuckoo. These birds are parasitic, laying their eggs in the nests of host species that hatch and rear the young cuckoos. In the fall, about a month after their parents migrate, the young cuckoos get together and begin migrating to their wintering ground. The birds fly almost 1,200 miles west to Australia and then nearly 1,000 miles north to the Solomon and Bismarck Islands where they join their parents.

USEFUL TERMS

intriguing
exciting interest or curiosity

homing
going home

nest-trapping
trapping birds in their nests for observation

plumage
feathers

avian
of or having to do with birds

parasitic
describes an organism that is dependent upon a host organism for survival, usually without killing its host

Observing for Detail

1. a. Do you think the migration of the Blue-winged Teal is more likely innate or learned behavior? Explain.

Sample answer: The migration of the Blue-winged Teal is probably a combination. The female Teal returned close to her original location by using previous knowledge. Her ability to navigate was probably innate.

b. Do you think the migration of the New Zealand Bronzed Cuckoo is more likely innate or learned behavior? Explain.

The migration of the New Zealand Cuckoo is probably innate behavior because the offspring migrated without knowledge of migration patterns.

Name ______ Date ______ Class ______

Demonstrating Reasoned Judgment

2. In order to navigate, birds often use a combination of visual clues, their sense of smell, the Earth's magnetic field, and the sun. Which of these would be more useful in an unfamiliar area? Explain your answer.

   The sun and the Earth's magnetic field would be more useful because they are consistent from place to place and because previous knowledge is not required to use them.

Making Comparisons

3. a. How is the navigation of migratory birds similar to the navigation of an airplane pilot?

   Both use the Earth's magnetic field, the sun, and visual clues to navigate.

   b. How is the navigation of migratory birds different from the navigation of an airplane pilot?

   Pilots do not use their sense of smell, and they must rely on a compass to use the Earth's magnetic field.

Making Inferences

4. Migration patterns vary among different species of birds. List three factors that might cause migration patterns to vary.

   Accept all reasonable answers. Sample answer: Migration patterns might vary because of changes in temperature, shortages of food and water, or differences in breeding patterns.

Name ______ Date ______ Class ______

Percentages, Fractions, and Decimals

Imagine that your science class is doing a school survey to determine which eye colors are most common. The report from the sixth-grade class says that $\frac{3}{5}$ of the students have black or brown eyes, while $\frac{2}{5}$ have blue or green eyes. The seventh-grade class reports that 45 percent have black or brown eyes, and 55 percent have blue or green eyes. The eighth-grade class reports that 0.8 have black or brown eyes, and 0.2 have blue or green eyes. Yikes! Each class has a different way of showing its data! So how do you compare the reports? Well, it's not as complicated as it might look. You see, percentages, fractions, and decimals are just different ways of expressing the same information. Each one tells you *how much* or *how many* of a certain amount. As you learned on the last page, a percentage can be changed to a decimal. For example, 45 percent is equal to 0.45. Percentages can also be changed into fractions. Likewise, every fraction can be expressed as a decimal or percentage, and so on. When comparing numbers or doing operations with numbers, it is often easier to have all of your numbers in the same form before doing calculations.

PROCEDURE 1: To change a fraction to a decimal or percentage, divide the numerator of the fraction by the denominator to make a decimal. To change the decimal number into a percentage, move the decimal point two places to the *right*.

SAMPLE PROBLEM: Change $\frac{3}{5}$ into a decimal number and a percentage.

Step 1: Divide the numerator by the denominator.	**Step 2:** To change the decimal into a percentage, move the decimal point two places to the right.
$3 \div 5 = 0.6$	$0.6 \rightarrow 0.60 \rightarrow$ **60%**

PROCEDURE 2: To change a decimal number into a fraction or percentage, place the decimal over its place value and reduce. To change a decimal into a percentage, see Step 2 of Procedure 1.

SAMPLE PROBLEM: Express 0.56 as a fraction and a percentage.

Step 1: Because 0.56 is in the *hundredths* place, put the whole number over 100 and reduce.	**Step 2:** To change a decimal into a percentage, move the decimal point two places to the right, as in step 2 of procedure 1.
$\frac{56}{100} = \frac{14}{25}$	$0.56 \rightarrow 0.56 \rightarrow 56\%$

Practice What You've Learned

1. Express the following percentages as decimal numbers:

   a. 52% $52 \rightarrow 0.52$ **b.** 99% $99 \rightarrow 0.99$

   c. 7.8% $07.8 \rightarrow 0.078$ **d.** 0.57% $00.57 \rightarrow 0.0057$

Name ______________ Date ______ Class ______

Percentages, Fractions, and Decimals, continued

2. Express the following fractions as both a decimal number and a percentage.

a. $\frac{75}{100}$ = 75 ÷ 100 = 0.75; 75%

b. $\frac{1}{8}$ = 1 ÷ 8 = 0.125; 12.5%

c. $\frac{9}{20}$ = 9 ÷ 20 = 0.45; 45%

d. $\frac{12}{4}$ = 12 ÷ 4 = 3; 300%

e. $\frac{26}{13}$ = 26 ÷ 13 = 2; 200%

f. $\frac{8}{32}$ = 8 ÷ 32 = 0.25; 25%

3. Change the following decimal numbers into both a fraction and a percentage:

a. 0.3 = $\frac{3}{10}$; 30%

b. 0.12 = $\frac{12}{100}$; 12%

c. 0.99 = $\frac{99}{100}$; 99%

d. 1.5 = $\frac{3}{2}$; 150%

e. 0.505 = $\frac{505}{1000}$; 50.5%

f. 0.01 = $\frac{1}{100}$; 1%

4. Write True or False next to each equation.

a. $2\frac{2}{5} = 2.4 = 24\%$ False

b. $0.03 = 3\% = \frac{3}{100}$ True

c. $0.45\% = \frac{90}{200} = 0.0045$ False

d. $5.25 = 5\frac{14}{28} = 525\%$ False

5. Convert the following equations into the same form and calculate. Hint: Do the calculation inside the parentheses before adding or subtracting.

a. $\frac{2}{5} + 0.12 =$ $\frac{2}{5} + \frac{12}{100} = \frac{52}{100} = \frac{13}{25}$

b. $(75\% \text{ of } 60) - 3\frac{3}{5} =$ $\frac{45}{1} - 3\frac{3}{5} = 41\frac{2}{5}$

c. $\frac{32}{8} - (15\% \text{ of } 20) =$ $\frac{32}{8} - \frac{3}{1} = 1$

Name ______________ Date ______ Class ______

CHAPTER 1 MATH SKILLS

Average, Mode, and Median

Although an average, or mean, is the most common way to simplify a list of numbers, there are other mathematical tools that can help you work with lists of numbers. **Mode** is the number or value that appears most often in a particular set of numbers. **Median** is the number that falls in the *numerical center* of a list of numbers. Read on to find out how to find mode and median.

PROCEDURE: *To find the mode,* list your numbers in numerical order. Then determine which number appears most often in the set. That number is the mode. **Note:** A list of numbers may have more than one mode. If no number appears more often than the others, that series of numbers does not have a mode.

SAMPLE PROBLEM: Find the mode of 4, 3, 6, 10, and 3.

Step 1: List the numbers in numerical order.

3, 3, 4, 6, 10

Step 2: Determine the number that appears most often in the set.

3, 3, 4, 6, 10

The mode of 4, 3, 6, 10, and 3 is **3.**

PROCEDURE: *To find the median,* list the numbers in numerical order. Next determine the number that appears in the middle of the set. **Note:** If more than one number falls in the middle, the median is the average of those numbers.

SAMPLE PROBLEM: Find the median of 25, 22, 24, 19, 25, 14, 26, and 15.

Step 1: List the numbers in numerical order.

14, 15, 19, 22, 24, 25, 25, 26

Step 2: Determine which number falls in the middle of the set.

14, 15, 19, 22, 24, 25, 25, 26

Because two numbers fall in the middle (22 and 24), the median is their average.

Median = (22 + 24) ÷ 2 = **23**

Get in the Mode!

1. Find the mode and median for the following sets of numbers:

a. 37, 30, 35, 37, 32, 40, 34
Mode 37 Median 35

b. 19, 29, 9, 12, 10
Mode none Median 12

c. 109, 84, 88, 107, 84, 94
Mode 84 Median 91

d. 26, 53, 39, 53, 49, 56, 35, 26
Mode 26; 53 Median 44

e. 25 m, 24 m, 27 m, 27 m, 49 m, 47 m, 45 m
Mode 27 m Median 27 m

f. 98 L, 99 L, 101 L, 111 L, 132 L, 103 L
Mode none Median 102 L

Name ______________ Date ________ Class ________

Average, Mode, and Median, continued

Peregrine Falcons—How Fast Can They Fly?

The peregrine falcon is the fastest bird in the world. It can reach speeds of almost 300 km/h when hunting. An ornithologist, a scientist who studies birds, has gathered the data in the chart below to try to learn exactly how fast the falcons can fly. Use what you have learned about averages, modes, and medians to analyze some of the birds' top speeds.

Falcon Flight Speeds*

Day	Falcon A	Falcon B	Falcon C	Falcon D	Falcon E
1	189	199	211	253	199
2	275	261	241	235	279
3	262	225	271	190	271
4	203	199	223	185	265
5	241	227	209	199	253
6	222	240	265	253	232
7	203	203	240	260	279

*All flight speeds are in km/h.

2. What was the average top speed of Falcon B for the entire week?

   199 + 261 + 225 + 199 + 227 + 240 + 203 = 1554; 1554 ÷ 7 = 222 km/h

3. What were the modes for Falcon D and Falcon E for the entire week?

   Falcon D: 185, 190, 199, 235, 253, 253, 260. The mode was 253 km/h.

   Falcon E: 199, 232, 253, 265, 271, 279, 279. The mode was 279 km/h.

4. Which had a faster median speed for the week, Falcon A or Falcon B?

   Falcon A: 189, 203, 203, 222, 241, 262, 275; The median was 222.

   Falcon B: 199, 199, 203, 225, 227, 240, 261; The median was 225.

   Falcon B had the faster median speed.

5. What were the median speeds for Falcon B and Falcon D for days 1–6?

   Falcon B: 199, 199, 225, 227, 240, 261; (225 + 227) ÷ 2 = 226 km/h

   Falcon D: 185, 190, 199, 235, 253, 253; (199 + 235) ÷ 2 = 217 km/h

Name ______________ Date ________ Class ________

CHAPTER 1 COMMUNICATING SKILLS

Introduction to Graphs

Examine the following table and graph:

Grade Distribution for Students Enrolled in Science Class

Grade	Number of students
A	22
B	79
C	50
D	9
F	2

Grade Distribution of Students Enrolled in Science Class

Number of students: 0, 10, 20, 30, 40, 50, 60, 70, 80

Grade: A, B, C, D, F

1. Both of these figures display the same information but in different ways. Which figure is easier to understand? Explain why you think so.

   The graph is easier to interpret because it visually organizes the data.

2. If you need to get specific data, such as the exact number of students who earned a B, which figure would you use? Explain your answer.

   The table provides more specific data than the graph.

Name ______________ Date ________ Class ________

Choose the Graph

What graph type do you think best presents each set of data? Explain.

1. The percentage of rabbits preferring various foods

Food	Percentage preferring that food
Skippy's Rabbit Chow	32
Homemade rabbit food	13
Happy Rabbit	10
Joe's Special Food for Rabbits	44
Premium Rabbit Nutrition Diet	1

a pie graph, because this data reflects percentages

2. Albert's grades for each month of the school year

Month	Grade in science class
September	98
October	94
November	88
December	78
January	82

Month	Grade in science class
February	83
March	86
April	81
May	97

a line graph, because the data reflects changes over time

3. The pH of solutions in experimental test tubes

Test-tube number	pH
1	6.7
2	7.1
3	7.4
4	7.1
5	7.0

a bar graph, because this graph type is best used for comparing data

Name ______________ Date ________ Class ________

CHAPTER 1 LAB DATASHEET — DISCOVERY LAB

Wet, Wiggly Worms!

Earthworms have been digging in the Earth for more than 100 million years! Earthworms fertilize the soil with their waste and loosen the soil when they tunnel through the moist dirt of a garden or lawn. Worms are food for many animals, such as birds, frogs, snakes, rodents, and fish. Some say they are good food for people, too!

In this activity, you will observe the behavior of a live earthworm. Remember that earthworms are living animals that deserve to be handled gently and with respect. Be sure to keep your earthworm moist during this activity. The skin of the earthworm must stay moist so that the worm can get oxygen. If the earthworm's skin dries out, the worm will suffocate and die. Use a spray bottle to moisten the earthworm with water.

MATERIALS

- spray bottle
- dissecting pan
- paper towels
- water
- live earthworm
- probe
- celery leaves
- flashlight
- shoe box with lid
- clock
- soil
- metric ruler

Procedure

1. Place a wet paper towel in the bottom of a dissecting pan. Put a live earthworm on the paper towel, and observe how the earthworm moves. Record your observations.

2. Use the probe to carefully touch the anterior end (head) of the worm. Gently touch other areas of the worm's body with the probe. Record the kinds of responses you observe.

3. Shine a flashlight on the anterior end of the earthworm. Record the earthworm's reaction to the light.

4. Place celery leaves at one end of the pan. Record how the earthworm responds to the presence of food.

5. Line the bottom of the shoe box with a damp paper towel. Cover half of the shoe box with the box top.

Name ______________ Date ______________ Class ______________

6. Place the worm on the uncovered side of the shoe box in the light. Record your observations of the worm's behavior for 3 minutes.

7. Place the worm on the covered side of the box. Record your observations of the worm's behavior for 3 minutes.

8. Repeat steps 6–7 three times.

9. Spread some loose soil evenly in the bottom of the shoe box so that it is about 4 cm deep. Place the earthworm on top of the soil. Observe and record the earthworm's behavior for 3 minutes.

10. Dampen the soil on one side of the box, and leave the other side dry. Place the earthworm in the center of the box between the wet and dry soil. Cover the box, and wait 3 minutes. Uncover the box, and record your observations. Repeat this procedure 3 times. (You may need to search for the worm!)

Name ______________ Date ______________ Class ______________

Analysis

11. How did the earthworm respond to being touched?

Students' answers will vary according to their own observations. They will probably observe that the worm squirms when touched.

Were some areas more sensitive than others?

Students will probably observe that some areas, such as the clitellum, are more sensitive than others.

12. How is the earthworm's behavior influenced by light?

Students will probably observe that earthworms avoid light.

Based on your observations, describe how an animal's response to a stimulus might provide protection for the animal.

Students should describe the worm's behavior as self-protective.

13. How did the earthworm respond to the presence of food?

Answers will vary according to student observations.

14. When the worm was given a choice of wet or dry soil, which did it choose? Explain this result.

Answers will vary according to student observations.

Name ______________ Date ________ Class ________

CHAPTER 1 LAB DATASHEET

DESIGN YOUR OWN

Aunt Flossie and the Bumblebee

Last week Aunt Flossie came to watch the soccer game, and she was chased by a big yellow-and-black bumblebee. Everyone tried not to laugh, but Aunt Flossie did look pretty funny. She was running and screaming, all perfumed and dressed in a bright floral dress, shiny jewelry, and a huge hat with a big purple bow. No one could understand why the bumblebee tormented Aunt Flossie and left everyone else alone. She said that she would not come to another game until you determine why the bee chased her.

Your job is to design an experiment that will determine why the bee was attracted to Aunt Flossie. You may simulate the situation by using objects that contain the same sensory clues that Aunt Flossie wore that day—bright, shiny colors and strong scents.

MATERIALS

- to be determined by each experimental design and approved by the teacher

Please review the Safety Caution on page 606 of the Annotated Teacher's Edition before introducing this lab to students.

SCIENTIFIC METHOD

Ask a Question

1. Use the information in the story above to help you form questions. Make a list of Aunt Flossie's characteristics on the day of the soccer game. What was Aunt Flossie wearing? What do you think she looked like to a bumblebee? What scent was she wearing? Which of those characteristics may have affected the bee's behavior? What was it about Aunt Flossie that affected the bee's behavior?

Aunt Flossie was wearing a bright floral dress and hat. She might have looked like a garden of flowers to the bumblebee. She was wearing perfume, probably with a floral scent. All of those characteristics probably attracted the bumblebee. Because Aunt Flossie had the characteristics of a flower garden, it might have sought after her to feed on the nectar of the flowers.

Form a Hypothesis

2. Write a hypothesis about insect behavior based on your observations of Aunt Flossie and the bumblebee at the soccer game. A possible hypothesis is, "Insects are attracted to strong floral scents." Write your own hypothesis.

Accept all reasonable hypotheses.

Name ______________ Date ________ Class ________

Test the Hypothesis

3. Outline a procedure for your experiment. Be sure to follow the steps in the scientific method. Design your procedure to answer specific questions. For example, if you want to know if insects are attracted to different colors, you might want to display cutouts of several colors of paper.

Answers will vary but should include the steps of the scientific method. In addition, the procedure should be designed to answer specific questions.

4. Make a list of materials for your experiment. You may want to include colored paper, pictures in magazines, or strong perfumes as bait. **You may not** use living things as bait in your experiment. Your teacher must approve your experimental design before you begin.

Answers will vary but should not include living things.

5. Determine a place to conduct your experiment. For example, you may want to place your materials in a box on the ground, or you may want to hang items from a tree branch. **Caution:** Be sure to remain at a safe distance from your experimental setup containing the bait. Do not touch any insects. Have an adult help you release any insects that are trapped or collected.

Name ______________ Date ________ Class ________

Effects of Color

Color	Number of bees	Number of ants	Number of wasps
Red			
Blue			
Yellow			

6. Develop data tables for recording the results of your trials. For example, a data table similar to the one at left may be used to record the results of testing different colors to see which insects are attracted to them. Design your data tables to fit your investigation.

Data charts will vary but should be tailored to the specifics of the students' procedures. Data should be clearly and carefully recorded.

Name ______________ Date ________ Class ________

Analyze the Results

7. Describe your experimental procedure. Did your results support your hypothesis? Explain.

Students should describe their experimental procedure and include as many steps of the scientific method as possible. All answers will depend on student observations.

8. Compare your results with those of your classmates. Which hypotheses were supported?

Answers will vary.

What conclusions can you draw from the class results?

Answers will vary.

Communicate Results

9. On the back of this page or on a separate piece of paper, write a letter to Aunt Flossie telling her what you have learned. Tell her what caused the bee attack. Invite her to attend another soccer game, and advise her about what she should or should not wear!

Letters will vary, but should demonstrate what the students have learned about insect behavior.

Name ______________ Date ________ Class ________

CHAPTER 1 STUDENT WORKSHEET

DISCOVERY LAB

Follow the Leader

How do you find your way around in an unfamiliar place? You probably use a variety of tools; you might use a map, a compass, verbal directions, or even hire a guide. How do other animals navigate in unfamiliar territory? Birds respond to a variety of calls, dolphins and bats use sonar, and bees use visual cues and communicate directions in an elaborate, buzzing dance.

But how do ants find their way around? In this lab, you will discover that ants have an unusual way of finding their way to and from their anthill.

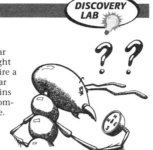

MATERIALS

- ant colony
- large, empty aquarium
- 15 mL of sugar
- jar lid
- tap water
- plastic transparency sheets
- sheet of paper
- 3–6 magnifying glasses
- can of compressed air
- damp sponge
- paper towels

SAFETY ALERT!

Do not touch the ants. Some ants bite.

SCIENTIFIC METHOD

Ask a Question

How do ants navigate?

Make Observations

1. Observe the ants traveling to and from the food dish for 2–3 minutes. Record all of your observations.

   Sample answer: The ants follow the leader with their eyes.

Make a Prediction

2. How do you think ants find their way to and from food and water?

   Sample answer: I think ants find their way around by watching what other ants do.

Conduct an Experiment

3. Slide a sheet of paper beneath the plastic that lines the bottom of the box. How does the paper affect the behavior of the ants? Record your observations.

   The ants seem to be unaffected by the white paper. The ants travel along the same path.

Name ______________ Date ________ Class ________

4. While the ants are still on the plastic sheet, rotate the sheet 90° so that it is perpendicular to the original orientation. Record your observations.

   The ants walk at a 90° angle to the original path, stop at the edge, and look around.

5. Continue to observe the ants. Do the ants find their original destination?

   Yes, the ants seem to find their original destination.

6. Carefully rotate the plastic sheet back to its original position. How do the ants respond?

   The ants continue on the path the same way as they did before.

7. Describe the signal you think the ants are using to navigate.

   Sample answer: I think the ants are waving their antennae to each other.

SAFETY ALERT!

Keep the compressed can of air away from heat and away from people's faces.

Remember the importance of humane treatment of lab animals.

8. Use the can of compressed air to GENTLY blow the ants from a section of the plastic sheet. Practice using the can first to avoid harming the ants. Observe whether the ants reestablish their path.
9. Now blow the ants from the plastic and quickly wipe a section of the ant path clean with a damp sponge, and dry the area with a paper towel. Observe the ants' behavior, and record your observations below.

   The ants seem confused. They wandered about on the cleaned section for a while, probably looking for the trail.

Name ______________________ Date ____________ Class ____________

Follow the Leader, continued

10. What do your observations tell you about the signal the ants follow?

The signal can be wiped off with a damp sponge—it could be some sort of chemical that the ants can detect.

11. Continue to observe the ants for several minutes. What change, if any, do you observe from their behavior in step 9?

They seem to start following one another after a few minutes of wandering around.

Analyze the Results

12. Look over your answers in steps 3–11. List every method that ants might use to navigate. Which method do you think is the most important and why?

Ants seem to use their eyes, their memories, and some kind of chemical signal to navigate. The chemical signal seems to be the most important. When we wiped the signal from the plastic, the ants were confused.

13. So, was your prediction in step 2 correct? Explain your answer.

Sample answer: It was partially correct. Ants seem to use some visual clues, but mostly rely on a chemical signal to find their way.

Name ______________________ Date ____________ Class ____________

CHAPTER 1 ANIMALS AND BEHAVIOR

Chapter 1 Test

USING VOCABULARY *(Recommended 3 pts. each)*

To complete the following sentences, choose the correct term from each pair of terms listed, and write the term in the blank.

1. All animals are ___multicellular___ and have eukaryotic cells. (vertebrates or multicellular)
2. A collection of similar cells is known as a(n) ___tissue___. (organ or tissue)
3. ___The biological clock___ is an animal's internal control of natural cycles. (Hibernation or The biological clock)
4. All animals are ___consumers___. (predators or consumers)
5. Some animals use the Earth's magnetic field to ___navigate___. (communicate or navigate)

UNDERSTANDING CONCEPTS

Multiple Choice *(Recommended 4 pts. each)*
Circle the correct answer.

6. ________ is NOT an example of how animals might deal with a food shortage.
   a. Migration
   b. Estivation
   (c.) Social behavior
   d. Hibernation
7. Reading is an example of
   a. an innate behavior.
   b. a behavior controlled by genes.
   (c.) a learned behavior.
   d. an inherited behavior.
8. All ________ lack a skull and backbone.
   a. vertebrates
   b. eukaryotes
   c. multicellular organisms
   (d.) invertebrates
9. Which statement about communication between animals is false?
   a. Animals use it to find mates.
   b. It helps animals find their food.
   c. It helps animals avoid enemies.
   (d.) It occurs only between members of the same species
10. The relationship between a worm and a robin can be expressed as
    a. vertebrate : invertebrate.
    (b.) prey : predator.
    c. producer : consumer.
    d. prokaryote : eukaryote.
11. The use of ________ is an example of chemical communication.
    a. camouflage
    (b.) pheromones
    c. hibernation
    d. estivation

Name ______ Date ______ Class ______

Chapter 1 Test, continued

12. Any animal with a skull and a backbone is classified as
   (a.) a vertebrate. c. a mammal.
   b. a consumer. d. multicellular.

Short Answer *(Recommended 7 pts. each)*

13. Humans are able to navigate short distances in the dark if they are in a familiar area. Explain how this is done.

Humans navigate in the dark by forming a mental image of the familiar area. By seeing the location of objects in their mind, they can travel short distances without seeing.

14. A male hanging fly will dangle a dead moth as a present for a future mate. The female hanging fly will choose as her mate the fly offering the largest dead moth. What form of communication is the male hanging fly using?

The male hanging fly is using visual communication. This kind of communication is called "showing off", because the fly is using body language to communicate.

CRITICAL THINKING AND PROBLEM SOLVING *(Recommended 11 pts.)*

15. Describe four types of communication that dogs use.

Sample answer: Dogs communicate with sounds, such as barks and whines. They use body language, such as wagging their tail when they are happy. Dogs use touch to communicate. For example, they may lick one another or their owner. They also use chemical scent to mark their territory.

Name ______ Date ______ Class ______

Chapter 1 Test, continued

MATH IN SCIENCE *(Recommended 10 pts.)*

16. There are approximately 21,000 known species of fish, 3,900 known species of amphibians, 7,000 known species of reptiles, 8,600 known species of birds, and 4,500 known species of mammals. What percentage of known vertebrate species are fish? Show your work.

$21,000 + 3,900 + 7,000 + 8,600 + 4,500 = 45,000$

$21,000 \div 45,000 = 46.7\%$

About 47 percent of vertebrate species are fish.

CONCEPT MAPPING *(Recommended 2 pts. each)*

17. Use the following terms to complete the concept map below: animals, multicellular, consumers, predators, prey.

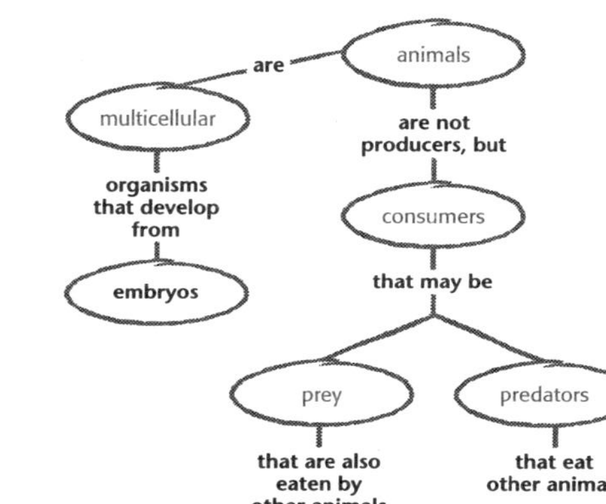

Name ______________________ Date __________ Class __________

INTERPRETING GRAPHICS *(Recommended 10 pts.)*

The graph below shows the relationship between the life span of primates and their dependence on parents and family. Examine the graph, and answer the questions that follow.

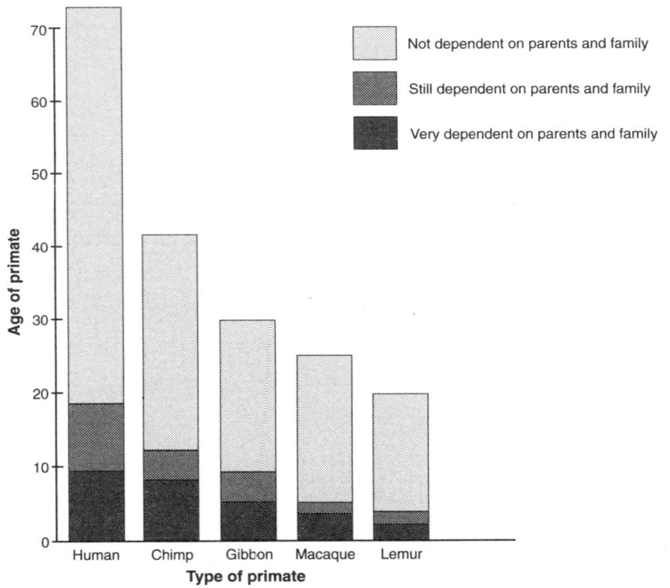

Age of primate
70
60
50
40
30
20
10
0
Human Chimp Gibbon Macaque Lemur
Type of primate
Not dependent on parents and family
Still dependent on parents and family
Very dependent on parents and family

18. a. According to the graph, how does a primate's dependence on its parents and family relate to its life span?

Generally, primates with longer life spans depend on their parents and family for a longer period of time.

b. Why do you think this relationship exists?

Sample answer: The longer the life span of a primate is, the longer each stage of its development.

Name ______________________ Date __________ Class __________

CHAPTER 1 ANIMALS AND BEHAVIOR — DISCOVERY LAB

Chapter 1 Performance-Based Assessment

Objective

Animals use pheromones and body language to communicate. In this activity, you will use scents (as pheromones) and body language to communicate something to your partner.

Know the Score!

As you work through the activity, keep in mind that you will be earning a grade for the following:

- how you work with the materials and equipment (30%)
- how you work out a code for communication (50%)
- how you analyze animal communication (20%)

MATERIALS

- various scents

Procedure

1. Examine the scents you have been given. With your partner, decide on a "code" for each scent. For example, vanilla could be used to show feelings of happiness. Describe the meaning of each scent below.

Scent	Meaning

2. Without discussing it with your partner, think of an idea you would like to communicate to him or her. You will be allowed to use only physical movements and the scents you were given. What will you communicate?

Answers will vary. Sample answer: I am happy that it is raining.

Name ______________________ Date ____________ Class ____________

Chapter 1 Performance-Based Assessment, continued

3. Communicate your idea to your partner using only movements and scents. Was the idea made clear? If not, why not?

   Answers will vary. Sample answer: No; the idea was not clearly understood because my partner had a stuffy nose.

4. Switch roles and repeat steps 2 and 3. Did you understand the idea your partner tried to communicate to you? If not, why not?

   Answers will vary. Sample answer: Yes; I understood perfectly.

5. What senses do humans use to communicate with other humans?

   Humans mainly use vision and hearing to communicate.

6. How close did you need to be to your partner to smell each scent he or she used for his or her idea?

   Answers may vary. Sample answer: I had to be 20 cm from my partner.

7. What kinds of movements do animals use to communicate with other animals? For example, a dog shows his teeth to show aggression.

   Answers may vary. Sample answer: An animal may lower its head to show submission.

Name ______________________ Date ____________ Class ____________

CHAPTER 2 **DIRECTED READING WORKSHEET**

Invertebrates

Chapter Introduction

As you begin this chapter, answer the following.

1. Read the title of the chapter. List three things that you already know about this subject.

2. Write two questions about this subject that you would like answered by the time you finish this chapter.

3. How does the title of the Start-Up Activity relate to the subject of the chapter?

Section 1: Simple Invertebrates (p. 28)

4. There are ___more than___ 1 million species of invertebrates on Earth. (more than or less than)

No Backbones Here! (p. 28)

5. List three features scientists use to compare different animals.

   Sample answers should include three of the following: body plan, presence of a head, and how they digest and absorb food.

Copyright © by Holt, Rinehart and Winston. All rights reserved.

Name ______ Date ______ Class ______

Chapter 2, continued

In the space provided, write *B* if the animal has bilateral symmetry, *R* if the animal has radial symmetry, or *A* if the animal is asymmetrical. To see an example of each body plan, look at page 29 in your text.

6. R sea anemone

7. B ant

8. A sponge

9. B butterfly

10. A brain controls many nerves in different parts of the body, while a ganglion controls only the functions near its location. (ganglion or brain, ganglion or brain)

11. The coelom and the gut are both digestive organs.
True or (False)? (Circle one.)

12. In animals without a coelom, moving from one place to another can aid or hinder digestion. (True) or False? (Circle one.)

Sponges (p. 30)

13. Is a sponge considered an animal? Explain.

Plants are producers, and animals are consumers. Sponges are consumers. Therefore, sponges are animals.

14. Sponge spicules are made of silicate or calcium carbonate.

15. Can you kill a sponge by breaking it into pieces? Explain.

No; if you break a sponge into pieces it will either re-form or grow as several smaller sponges. Either way, it will survive.

16. What physical characteristic of a sponge does the name Porifera suggest?

The name suggests the fact that sponges have thousands of pores.

Name ______ Date ______ Class ______

Chapter 2, continued

17. Why doesn't the sponge need to have a gut?

It has millions of collar cells that digest particles of food.

Review (p. 31)

Now that you've finished the first part of Section 1, review what you learned by answering the Review questions in your ScienceLog.

Cnidarians (p. 32)

18. Which of the following are true about cnidarians? (Circle all that apply.)

- (**a.**) They have stinging cells.
- **b.** They can regenerate lost body parts.
- **c.** They live only in fresh water.
- **d.** They include sponges, corals, and hydras.

19. Cnidarians are either in medusa form or in polyp form. Both body types have radial symmetry.

20. The sea anemone is a polyp. (True) or False? (Circle one.)

21. A cnidarian will always have the same body form for its entire life. True or (False)? (Circle one.)

22. All cnidarians have a nerve net, which controls movement of the body and tentacles.

23. Jellyfish have a nerve ring, which coordinates swimming.

Flatworms (p. 34)

24. Which of the following does NOT describe flatworms?

- **a.** They have a head.
- (**b.**) They are radially symmetric.
- **c.** They have eyespots.
- **d.** They have sensory lobes.

25. Flukes and tapeworms can live inside or outside a host.
True or (False)? (Circle one.)

26. Like all tapeworms, the tapeworm on page 35 has no ___gut___, ___eyespots___, or ___sensory lobes___.

Roundworms (p. 35)

27. Name two roundworm parasites that infect humans.

Pinworms and hookworms infect humans.

28. Which of the following meats could give you trichinosis if it is infected and you don't cook it thoroughly?

a. chicken
(b.) pork
c. steak
d. fish

Review (p. 35)

Now that you've finished Section 1, review what you learned by answering the Review questions in your ScienceLog.

Section 2: Mollusks and Annelid Worms (p. 36)

1. What features of mollusks make them more sophisticated organisms than roundworms, flatworms, and corals?

Mollusks and annelid worms have a coelom and a circulatory system as well as a more complex nervous system.

Mollusks (p. 36)

2. Which of the three main classes of mollusks are you most likely to encounter on land?

You are most likely to encounter gastropods on land.

3. Which of the following are true of the phylum Mollusca? (Circle all that apply.)

(a.) Some mollusks are 1 mm in length.
(b.) Some mollusks are 18 m in length.
c. Some land mollusks can move 40 km/h.
(d.) Some marine mollusks can swim 40 km/h.

Choose the part of the mollusk in Column B that best matches the definition in Column A, and write the corresponding letter in the space provided.

	Column A	Column B
b	4. a layer of tissue that protects mollusks that do not have a shell	a. shell
d	5. this contains the gills, gut, and other organs	b. mantle
a	6. this keeps land mollusks from drying out	c. foot
c	7. mollusks use this to move	d. visceral mass

8. Snails and slugs have a ___radula___ to scrape food off rocks.

9. How are open and closed circulatory systems different?

(a.) Open circulatory systems have sinuses.
b. Closed circulatory systems have sinuses.
c. Only open circulatory systems have blood vessels.
d. Only closed circulatory systems have blood vessels.

10. Octopuses have advanced nervous systems. Name two examples of difficult tasks that some octopuses can do.

Sample answers: Octopuses can navigate in a maze, distinguish between different colors and shapes, and build hiding places out of bricks or stones.

Review (p. 38)

Now that you've finished the first part of Section 2, review what you learned by answering the Review questions in your ScienceLog.

Annelid Worms (p. 39)

11. An earthworm has a brain. (True) or False? (Circle one.)

12. All the segments of an annelid worm are identical.

True or (False)? (Circle one.)

13. How do earthworms increase soil fertility? (Circle all that apply.)

a. They eat bugs that poison the soil.
(b.) Their excreted wastes provide nutrients to plants.
(c.) They burrow tunnels that allow water and air to reach deep into the soil.
d. They have bristles that protect plant roots.

Name ______________________ Date ____________ Class ____________

Chapter 2, continued

14. What does the bristle worm in Figure 19 use its bristles to do?

a. burrow　　**c.** deter predators

(b.) filter food out of water　　**d.** protect itself from drying out

15. How can leeches help sick people?

Leeches are used to drain blood and prevent swelling. Leeches also make a chemical that keeps blood from clotting.

Review (p. 40)

Now that you've finished Section 2, review what you learned by answering the Review questions in your ScienceLog.

Section 3: Arthropods (p. 41)

1. Which of the following invertebrates is NOT an arthropod?

a. a crab　　**c.** a centipede

b. a spider　　**(d.)** a sea urchin

Characteristics of Arthropods (p. 41)

2. Why are jointed limbs important to an arthropod?

Sample answer: Jointed limbs allow an arthropod to move easily.

3. The "suit of armor" that arthropods wear is called a(n) ___exoskeleton___, which is made of ___chitin___.

Kinds of Arthropods (p. 42)

4. The difference between a centipede and a millipede is that a millipede has ___two___ pairs of legs per segment, while a centipede has ___one___ pair(s). (two or three, one or two)

5. All crustaceans have ___mandibles___ and two pairs of ___antennae___. (legs or mandibles, antennae or eyes)

6. Ticks and mites are types of insects. True or (False)? (Circle one.)

Name ______________________ Date ____________ Class ____________

Chapter 2, continued

7. Why are insects important to us?

Sample answer: Insects pollinate most food-producing plants. Therefore, we would not have fruits to eat without insects.

Read pages 43–46 before answering questions 8–15. Match each type of arthropod in Column B to the correct statement in Column A, and write the corresponding letter in the appropriate space. Arthropod types can be used more than once.

Column A	Column B
___a___ **8.** has eight eyes	**a.** arachnid
___a___ **9.** has simple eyes	**b.** insect
___b___ **10.** has compound eyes	
___a___ **11.** has two main body parts	
___b___ **12.** has three main body parts	
___b___ **13.** has antennae	
___b___ **14.** has mandibles	
___a___ **15.** has chelicerae	

Look at the diagram on page 46. Place the following stages of complete metamorphosis in order by writing the appropriate number in the space provided.

16. ___3___ pupa

17. ___2___ larva

18. ___1___ egg

19. ___4___ adult

Review (p. 46)

Now that you've finished Section 3, review what you learned by answering the Review questions in your ScienceLog.

Section 4: Echinoderms (p. 47)

1. If you went snorkeling in a freshwater lake, would you see any echinoderms? Why or why not?

No; you wouldn't see any in a freshwater lake because echinoderms live only in the ocean.

Name ______ Date ______ Class ______

Spiny Skinned (p. 47)

2. How do echinoderms use their endoskeleton like an exoskeleton?
The endoskeleton of an echinoderm has spikes and spines that echinoderms can use to defend themselves.

3. An endoskeleton is covered by an outer skin, while a true exoskeleton has no covering. (True) or False? (Circle one.)

Bilateral or Radial? (p. 47)

4. Most echinoderms begin their life with bilateral symmetry and later have radial symmetry.

The Nervous System (p. 48)

5. Which sense does a sea star have?
   a. smell
   (b.) sight
   c. hearing
   d. taste

6. A sea star has a circle of nerve fibers around its mouth called a nerve ring. (mouth or arms)

Water Vascular System (p. 48)

7. Which of the following is NOT part of the water vascular system?
   a. ampulla
   b. radial canals
   c. sieve plate
   (d.) radial nerve

8. Tube feet help a starfish to capture food and hang onto rocks. (True) or False? (Circle one.)

Kinds of Echinoderms (p. 49)

9. Besides using their tube feet how else do some sea urchins get around?
Some sea urchins use their spines to walk.

Review (p. 49)

Now that you've finished Section 4, review what you learned by answering the Review questions in your ScienceLog.

Name ______ Date ______ Class ______

CHAPTER 2 VOCABULARY & NOTES WORKSHEET

Invertebrates

By studying the Vocabulary and Notes listed for each section below, you can gain a better understanding of this chapter.

SECTION 1

Vocabulary

In your own words, write a definition for each of the following terms in the space provided.

1. invertebrate an animal without a backbone

2. bilateral symmetry a body plan in which two halves of an organism's body are mirror images of each other

3. radial symmetry a body plan in which the parts of a body are arranged in a circle around a central point

4. asymmetrical without symmetry

5. ganglia groups of nerve cells

6. gut the pouch where food is digested in animals

Name ______________ Date ______ Class ______

7. coelom a cavity in the body of some animals where the gut and organs are located

Notes

Read the following section highlights. Then, in your own words, write the highlights in your ScienceLog.

- Invertebrates are animals without a backbone.
- Most animals have radial symmetry or bilateral symmetry.
- Unlike other animals, sponges have no symmetry.
- A coelom is a space inside the body. The gut hangs inside the coelom.
- Ganglia are clumps of nerves that help control the parts of the body.
- Sponges have special cells called collar cells to digest their food.
- Cnidarians have special stinging cells to catch their prey.
- Cnidarians have two body forms, the polyp and the medusa.
- Tapeworms and flukes are parasitic flatworms.

SECTION 2

Vocabulary

In your own words, write a definition for each of the following terms in the space provided.

1. open circulatory system a circulatory system consisting of a heart that pumps blood through spaces called sinuses

2. closed circulatory system a circulatory system in which a heart circulates blood through a network of vessels that form a closed loop

3. segment one of many identical or almost identical repeating body parts

Name ______________ Date ______ Class ______

Notes

Read the following section highlights. Then, in your own words, write the highlights in your ScienceLog.

- All mollusks have a foot, a visceral mass, and a mantle. Most mollusks also have a shell.
- Mollusks and annelid worms have both a coelom and a circulatory system.
- In an open circulatory system, the heart pumps blood through vessels into spaces called sinuses. In a closed circulatory system, the blood is pumped through a closed network of vessels.
- Segments are identical or nearly identical repeating body parts.

SECTION 3

Vocabulary

In your own words, write a definition for each of the following terms in the space provided.

1. exoskeleton an external skeleton made of protein and chitin found on arthropods

2. compound eye an eye that is made of many identical units, or eyes, that work together

3. antennae feelers on an arthropod's head that respond to touch or taste

4. mandible a jaw found on some arthropods

5. metamorphosis a process in which an insect or other animal changes form as it develops from an embryo or larva to an adult

Name ______________ Date ________ Class ________

Notes

Read the following section highlights. Then, in your own words, write the highlights in your ScienceLog.

- Seventy-five percent of all animals are arthropods.
- The four main characteristics of arthropods are jointed limbs, an exoskeleton, segments, and a well-developed nervous system.
- Arthropods are classified by the type of body parts they have.
- The four kinds of arthropods are centipedes and millipedes, crustaceans, arachnids, and insects.
- Insects can undergo complete or simple metamorphosis.

SECTION 4

Vocabulary

In your own words, write a definition for each of the following terms in the space provided.

1. endoskeleton an internal skeleton

2. water vascular system a system of water pumps and canals found in all echinoderms that allows them to move, eat, and breathe

Notes

Read the following section highlights. Then, in your own words, write the highlights in your ScienceLog.

- Echinoderms are marine animals that have an endoskeleton and a water vascular system.
- Most echinoderms have bilateral symmetry as larvae and radial symmetry as adults.
- The water vascular system allows echinoderms to move around by means of tube feet, which act like suction cups.
- Echinoderms have a simple nervous system consisting of a nerve ring and radial nerves.

Name ______________ Date ________ Class ________

CHAPTER 2 **CHAPTER REVIEW WORKSHEET**

Invertebrates

USING VOCABULARY

To complete the following sentences, choose the correct term from each pair of terms listed below, and write the term in the space provided.

1. Animals without a backbone are called invertebrates. (invertebrates or vertebrates)
2. A sponge uses pores to pull water in and releases water out through an osculum. (an osculum or pores)
3. Cnidarians have radial symmetry and flatworms have bilateral symmetry. (radial or bilateral)
4. The shell of a snail is secreted by the mantle. (radula or mantle)
5. Annelid worms have segments. (jointed limbs or segments)
6. An ampulla regulates water pressure in a tube foot. (water pressure in a tube foot or blood pressure in a closed circulatory system)

UNDERSTANDING CONCEPTS

Multiple Choice

7. Invertebrates make up what percentage of all animals?
   - a. 4 percent
   - b. 50 percent
   - c. 85 percent
   - (d.) 97 percent
8. Which of the following describes the body plan of a sponge:
   - a. radial symmetry
   - b. bilateral symmetry
   - (c.) asymmetry
   - d. partial symmetry
9. What cells do sponges have that no other animal has?
   - a. blood cells
   - b. nerve cells
   - (c.) collar cells
   - d. None of the above
10. Which of the following animals do not have ganglia?
    - a. annelid worms
    - (b.) cnidarians
    - c. flatworms
    - d. mollusks
11. Which of the following animals has a coelom?
    - a. sponge
    - b. cnidarian
    - c. flatworm
    - (d.) mollusk
12. Both tapeworms and leeches are
    - a. annelid worms.
    - (b.) parasites.
    - c. flatworms.
    - d. predators.

Name ____________________ Date __________ Class __________

Invertebrates, continued

13. Some arthropods do NOT have
- **a.** jointed limbs.
- **b.** an exoskeleton.
- **(c.)** antennae.
- **d.** segments.

14. Echinoderms live
- **a.** on land.
- **b.** in fresh water.
- **(c.)** in salt water.
- **d.** All of the above

15. *Echinoderm* means
- **a.** "jointed limbs."
- **(b.)** "spiny skinned."
- **c.** "endoskeleton."
- **d.** "shiny tube foot."

16. Echinoderm larvae have
- **a.** radial symmetry.
- **(b.)** bilateral symmetry.
- **c.** no symmetry.
- **d.** radial and bilateral symmetry.

Short Answer

17. What is a gut?

A gut is a pouch lined with cells that release enzymes to digest food.

18. How are arachnids different from insects?

Arachnids have two body parts—a cephalothorax and abdomen—and eight legs. Insects have three body parts—a head, a thorax, an abdomen—and six legs. Arachnids have chelicerae. Insects have antennae.

19. Which animal phylum contains the most species?

Anthropods have the most species.

Name ____________________ Date __________ Class __________

Invertebrates, continued

20. How does an echinoderm move?

An echinoderm moves by using its tube feet and its water vascular system.

CONCEPT MAPPING

21. Use the following terms to create a concept map: *insect, sponges, sea anemone, invertebrates, arachnid, sea cucumber, crustacean, centipede, cnidarians, arthropods, echinoderms.*

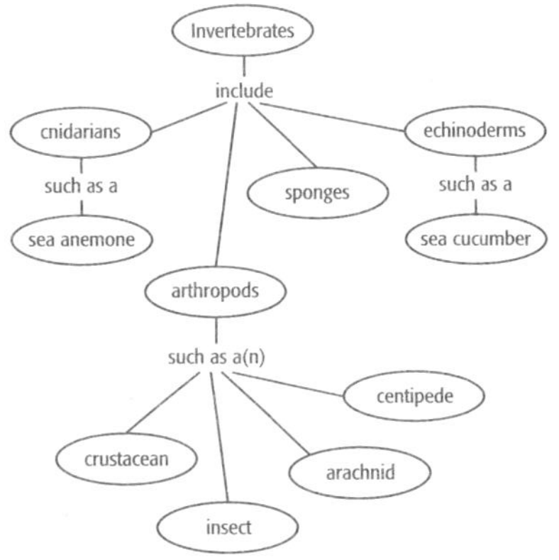

Invertebrates
include
cnidarians
such as a
sea anemone
sponges
echinoderms
such as a
sea cucumber
arthropods
such as a(n)
crustacean
insect
arachnid
centipede

Name ______________ Date ________ Class ________

CRITICAL THINKING AND PROBLEM SOLVING

Write one or two sentences to answer each of the following questions:

22. You have discovered a strange new animal that has bilateral symmetry, a coelom, and nerves. Will this animal be classified in the Cnidaria phylum? Why or why not?

No; cnidarians have radial symmetry and do not have coeloms.

23. Unlike other mollusks, cephalopods can move rapidly. Based on what you know about the body parts of mollusks, why do you think cephalopods have this ability?

Because cephalopods do not have a shell, they need to move rapidly to avoid predators. They can move rapidly because they have a large brain.

24. Roundworms, flatworms, and annelid worms belong to different phyla. Why aren't all the worms grouped in the same phyla?

All of the worms are not grouped in the same phylum because they have different characteristics. Annelid worms are segmented; the others are not. Annelid worms also have a coelom and a closed circulatory system. Roundworms have a round cross section, and flatworms do not. Roundworms have a more complex digestive system than flatworms. Flatworms are the only worms with eyespots and sensory lobes.

Name ______________ Date ________ Class ________

MATH IN SCIENCE

25. If 75 percent of all animals are arthropods and 40 percent of all arthropods are beetles, what percentage of all animals are beetles?

Thirty percent of all animals are beetles.

INTERPRETING GRAPHICS

Below is an evolutionary tree showing how the different phyla of animals may be related to one another. The "trunk" of the tree is on the left. Use the tree to answer the questions on the next page.

Sponges
Cnidarians
Roundworms
Echinoderms
Vertebrates
Annelid worms
Arthropods
Mollusks
Flatworms

Name ______________ Date ________ Class ________

26. Which phylum is the oldest?

The sponges are the oldest.

27. Are mollusks more closely related to roundworms or flatworms?

Mollusks are more closely related to flatworms.

28. What phylum is most closely related to the vertebrates?

The echinoderms are most closely related to the vertebrates.

READING CHECK-UP

Take a minute to review your answers to the ScienceLog questions at the beginning of the chapter. Have your answers changed? If necessary, revise your answers based on what you have learned since you began this chapter. Record your revisions in your ScienceLog.

Name ______________ Date ________ Class ________

CHAPTER 2 SCIENCE PUZZLERS, TWISTERS & TEASERS

Invertebrates

Odd One Out

1. For each group of terms, circle the one that doesn't belong and explain why not.

a. earthworm, bristle worm, roundworm, leech

All but roundworms are annelid worms.

b. dog, sponge, planarian, human

All but sponges have bilateral symmetry.

c. lobster, squid, crab, pillbug

All but squids are specific types of crustaceans.

d. hydra, clam, sea urchin, centipede

All but centipedes live in water.

e. spineless, asymmetrical, invertebrate, without backbone

All but asymmetrical describe lack of a backbone.

Analogies

2. In the analogies below, the first word is related to the second word in the same way that the third word is related to a fourth. For instance, the example below can be read, "Lemon is to yellow as lime is to green." Lemons are yellow in color, while limes are green. Fill in the blanks to complete the following analogies.

Example: lemon : yellow :: lime : green

a. blood vessels : cats :: sinuses : mollusks

b. skin : echinoderm :: foot : arthropod

c. ladybug : 6 :: tarantula : 8

d. ganglia : nervous :: coelom : digestive

Name ______________ Date ______________ Class ______________

Crack the Code

BRAIN BUSTER!

3. Use the clues to help you decode the secret message. By substituting the correct word for the coded word in each clue, you will find what each code letter stands for in the secret message. Each letter represents a different letter in the code. Each coded letter represents the same letter throughout the message. You may want to write each word below the code to help you break the code.
   - **a.** Sponges have no LNZZFCWN and no MFKI. symmetry, head
   - **b.** Slugs and snails eat with a WKIYOK. radula
   - **c.** Centipedes and millipedes have a single pair of KBCFBBKF, jaws called ZKBIAEOFL, and a hard MFKI RKVLYOF. antennae, mandibles, head capsule
   - **d.** Roundworms are also called BFZKCSIFL. nematodes
   - **e.** Annelid worms and arthropods have LFJZFBCFI bodies. segmented message: Insects are everywhere (almost).

   Secret message: Don't be alarmed, but . . .

   ABLFRCL KWF FTFWNHMFWF (KOZSLC)

Wordy Numbers

4. Vanity phone numbers are phone numbers that can be spelled out in easy-to-remember words. For example, a car dealer might choose the number 289-2277, which can be spelled as BUY CARS. What word from the chapter could each of these phone numbers represent? The words in parentheses are clues.

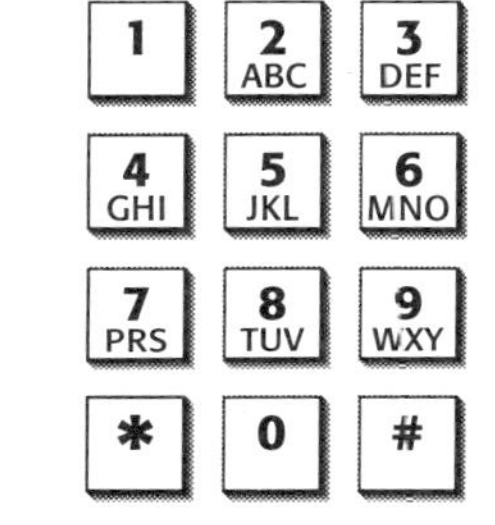

- **a.** 467-3287 (Creepy!) insects
- **b.** 665-5875 (Slimy!) mollusk
- **c.** 776-6437 (Bath buddies.) sponges

Name ______________ Date ______________ Class ______________

CHAPTER 2 REINFORCEMENT WORKSHEET

Life Without a Backbone

Complete this worksheet after you finish reading Chapter 2, Section 1.

What do a butterfly, a spider, a jellyfish, a worm, a snail, an octopus, and a lobster have in common? All of these animals are invertebrates. Clearly, there are many differences between these animals. Yet the most important characteristic these animals share is something none of them have—a backbone!

Despite their obvious differences, all invertebrates share some basic characteristics. Using the list of words provided, fill in the boxes with the correct answers. There will be some words that you will not use at all.

Characteristics

spicules
asymmetry
ganglia
gut
nerve cords
bilateral symmetry
collar cells
neutron
uniform
nerve networks
radial symmetry

All About Invertebrates

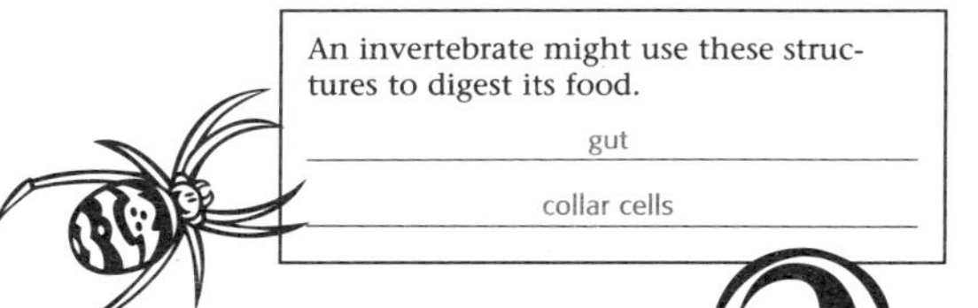

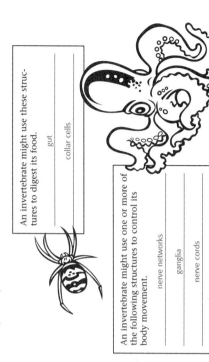

An invertebrate has a body plan that can have
- asymmetry
- bilateral symmetry
- radial symmetry

An invertebrate might use these structures to digest its food.
- gut
- collar cells

An invertebrate might use one or more of the following structures to control its body movement.
- nerve networks
- ganglia
- nerve cords

Name ______________ Date ________ Class ________

CHAPTER 2 REINFORCEMENT WORKSHEET

Spineless Variety

Complete this worksheet after you finish reading Chapter 2, Section 4.

In each of the four completed lists, seven phrases were accidentally placed in the wrong list. Those seven phrases describe Annelid Worms. Circle the phrases that were placed incorrectly in the complete lists, and use those phrases to complete the list for Annelid Worms.

Echinoderms

live only in the ocean
(have a brain)
have an endoskeleton
have a nerve ring
are covered with spines or bumps
some have a radial nerve
have a water vascular system
sand dollar
sea urchin
(a bristle worm)

Annelid Worms

have a closed circulatory system
have a brain
have a nerve cord
have segments
a leech
an earthworm
a bristle worm

Arthropods

have a well-developed brain
have jointed limbs
have a head
have an exoskeleton
have a well-developed nervous system
a tick
(an earthworm)
a dragonfly

Mollusks

live in the ocean, fresh water, or land
have open or closed circulatory system
have a foot and a mantle
usually have a shell
have a visceral mass
have complex ganglia
(a leech)
a clam
a snail
(have segments)

Cnidarians

live in the ocean or fresh water
(have a nerve cord)
have a gut
have a nerve net
are in polyp or medusa form
have stinging cells
a jellyfish
a sea anemone
coral
(have a closed circulatory system)

CHAPTER 2

Name ______________ Date ________ Class ________

CHAPTER 2 VOCABULARY REVIEW WORKSHEET

Searching for a Backbone

After you finish Chapter 2, give this puzzle a try!

Identify the word described by each clue, and write the word in the space provided. Then circle the word in the puzzle on the next page.

1. external body-support structure made of protein and chitin — exoskeleton
2. combination of head and thorax — cephalothorax
3. type of circulatory system in which blood is pumped through a network of vessels that form a closed loop — closed
4. symmetry in which an organism's body has two halves that are mirror images of each other — bilateral
5. groups of nerve cells — ganglia
6. identical or almost identical repeating body parts — segments
7. form of cnidarian that looks like a mushroom with tentacles — medusa
8. an animal without a backbone — invertebrate
9. vase-shaped form of cnidarian — polyp
10. type of circulatory system in which blood is pumped through spaces called sinuses — open
11. the process through which an insect develops from an egg to an adult while changing form — metamorphosis
12. without symmetry — asymmetrical
13. three specialized parts of arthropods formed when two or three segments grow together
    a. head
    b. thorax
    c. abdomen
14. symmetry in which an organism's body parts are arranged in a circle around a central point — radial
15. eye made of many identical light-sensitive cells — compound
16. pouch where almost all animals digest food — gut
17. jaws found on some arthropods — mandibles

Name ______________________ Date ____________ Class ____________

Searching for a Backbone, continued

18. the space in the body where the gut is located — coelom

19. an organism that feeds on another organism, usually without killing it — parasite

20. feelers that respond to touch or taste — antennae

21. internal body-support structure — endoskeleton

22. organism on which the organism in item 19 lives — host

23. system that allows echinoderms to move, eat, and breathe — water vascular

M	K	D	J	P	F	B	I	L	A	T	E	R	A	L	T	A
X	E	N	D	O	S	K	E	L	E	T	O	N	P	S	K	N
F	B	T	C	O	E	L	O	M	Y	E	P	V	O	E	X	T
P	A	G	A	A	S	U	D	E	M	L	E	H	F	T	M	E
I	Q	S	H	M	Z	O	W	A	Q	V	N	X	E	I	R	N
N	V	E	Y	K	O	D	A	N	I	P	A	X	J	S	A	N
V	G	L	L	M	P	R	E	A	G	R	O	N	S	A	L	A
E	X	B	N	X	M	M	P	M	O	S	Q	L	O	R	U	E
R	D	I	A	V	O	E	D	H	K	A	W	R	Y	A	C	F
T	L	D	W	D	B	N	T	E	O	B	P	X	G	P	S	S
E	A	N	B	A	P	O	L	R	D	S	A	R	A	M	A	E
B	S	A	O	C	L	E	J	E	I	R	I	W	N	S	V	G
R	E	M	P	A	T	G	S	G	O	C	P	S	G	U	R	M
A	D	E	H	O	B	O	X	H	U	K	A	X	L	N	E	E
T	A	P	N	X	L	Q	T	N	Z	T	S	L	I	V	T	N
E	E	J	P	C	O	M	P	O	U	N	D	O	A	Z	A	T
C	H	Z	G	F	R	I	L	A	I	D	A	R	T	U	W	S

Name ______________________ Date ____________ Class ____________

CHAPTER 2 **CRITICAL THINKING WORKSHEET**

A New Form of Danger in the Deep

This selection is from the magazine *Amazing Adaptations:*

A shrimp swims through the cool, still waters of a dark cave. There are fewer nutrients in the cave than in the open sea, and the shrimp is extremely hungry.

In its search for food, the shrimp swims too close to the floor of the cave. Suddenly, it is caught by a tentacle with spiky, hook-shaped filaments. The shrimp struggles to free itself, but it is no use. Slowly, tentacles wrap around the shrimp until it can no longer move.

Within a day, the shrimp is buried alive by the tentacles. New filaments on the tentacles begin to grow directly over the shrimp's body. Then the shrimp is slowly digested. Once digestion is complete, the organism returns to its normal shape. Slowly moving along the sea cave floor, it awaits its next victim.

Scientists were shocked to discover that this organism is a type of sponge! This cave sponge was found in the Mediterranean Sea about 20 m below the surface of the water.

Making Comparisons

1. How is this sponge different from other sponges?

This sponge does not filter food particles and microorganisms from the water. Instead, it uses hook-shaped filaments to capture small organisms as they swim by.

HELPFUL HINTS

Think about the conditions that exist in the cave.

Demonstrating Reasoned Judgment

2. Why do you think the cave sponge has developed a different method of feeding?

The cave sponge would have trouble filter-feeding because of the still water and the lack of nutrients. This sponge uses hook-shaped filaments to trap its food so it does not have to rely on nutrients floating in the water.

Name ______________ Date ______ Class ______

3. The closest relative to the cave sponge lives 8,840 m below the sea surface. How is the cave environment similar to an environment 8,840 m below the sea surface?

The cave is cool, has few nutrients, and receives no direct sunlight. All of these conditions are similar to the conditions that exist far below the sea surface.

Evaluating Information

4. Biologists have disagreed about how to classify the cave sponge. Do you think this organism should be classified in the phylum Porifera? Explain your answer.

Sample answer: Yes, it should be classified in the phylum Porifera because it still has most of the characteristics of a sponge. It is slow moving, can grow new body parts, and lives on the sea floor. It has adapted to its environment by developing specialized tentacles to capture food.

Thinking Logically

5. Why would this article appear in a magazine called *Amazing Adaptations*?

The sponge adapted to a cave environment by developing a new method of feeding. This is amazing because sponges do not usually eat other animals.

Name ______________ Date ______ Class ______

CHAPTER 2 MATH SKILLS

Dividing Whole Numbers with Long Division

Long division, which is used to divide numbers of more than one digit, is really just a series of simple division, multiplication, and subtraction problems. The number that you divide is called the *dividend*. The number you divide the dividend by is the *divisor*. The answer to a division problem is called a *quotient*.

SAMPLE PROBLEM: Divide 564 by 12, or 12)564.

Step 1: Because you cannot divide 12 into 5, you must start by dividing 12 into 56. To do this, ask yourself, "What number multiplied by 12 comes closest to 56 without going over?" 4 × 12 = 48, so place a 4 in the quotient.

```
   4
12)564
```

Step 2: Multiply the 4 by the divisor and place the product under the 56. Then subtract that product from 56.

```
   4
12)564
  -48
    8
```

Step 3: Bring the next digit down from the dividend (4), and divide this new number (84) by the divisor, as you did in Step 1. Because 12 divides into 84 seven times, write 7 in the quotient.

```
   47
12)564
  -48↓
    84
   -84
     0
```

The quotient is **47.**

Divide It Up!

1. Fill in the blanks in the following long-division problems:

a.
```
   [5]1
13)663
  [6]5
   [1]3
    1[3]
     [0]
```

b.
```
  1[0][2]
9)918
  [9]
  01
   [0]
   1[8]
   18
    [0]
```

c.
```
   2[4]
17)408
  [3][4]
    68
   [6]8
    [0]
```

2. Complete the following long-division problems on a separate sheet of paper:

a. 3575 ÷ 11 = 325

b. 52)1664 = 32

c. 3)2940 = 980

d. 4630 ÷ 5 = 926

Name ______________ Date ______ Class ______

CHAPTER 2 MATH SKILLS

Checking Division with Multiplication

Multiplication and division "undo" one another. This means that when you ask yourself, "What is 12 divided by 3?" it is the same as asking, "What number *multiplied* by 3 gives 12?" You can use this method to catch mistakes in your division.

PROCEDURE: To check your division with multiplication, multiply the quotient of your division problem by the divisor and compare the result with the dividend. If they are equal, your division was correct.

SAMPLE PROBLEM 1: Divide 564 by 47, and check your result with multiplication.

Step 1: Divide to find your quotient.	Step 2: Multiply the quotient by the divisor.	Step 3: Compare the product with your dividend.
$$\begin{array}{r} 12 \\ 47\overline{)564} \\ -47 \\ \hline 94 \\ -94 \\ \hline 0 \end{array}$$	$$\begin{array}{r} 12 \\ \times\ 47 \\ \hline 84 \\ 48 \\ \hline 564 \end{array}$$	**564** = **564** Correct!

Check It Out!

Complete the following divisions, and check your math by multiplying the quotient by your divisor. Are the product and the dividend equal?

1. $$\begin{array}{r} 27 \\ 15\overline{)405} \\ 30 \\ \hline 105 \\ 105 \\ \hline 0 \end{array} \qquad \begin{array}{r} \textit{quotient} \\ \times\ \textit{divisor} \\ \hline \end{array} \qquad \begin{array}{r} 27 \\ \times\ 15 \\ \hline \end{array}$$

   quotient = 27   product = 405

2. $$\begin{array}{r} 121 \\ 14\overline{)1694} \\ 14 \\ \hline 29 \\ 28 \\ \hline 14 \\ 14 \\ \hline 0 \end{array} \qquad \begin{array}{r} \textit{quotient} \\ \times\ \textit{divisor} \\ \hline \end{array} \qquad \begin{array}{r} 121 \\ \times\ 14 \\ \hline \end{array}$$

   quotient = 121   product = 1694

3. $$\begin{array}{r} 21 \\ 12\overline{)252} \\ 24 \\ \hline 12 \\ 12 \\ \hline 0 \end{array} \qquad \begin{array}{r} \textit{quotient} \\ \times\ \textit{divisor} \\ \hline \end{array} \qquad \begin{array}{r} 21 \\ \times\ 12 \\ \hline \end{array}$$

   quotient = 21   product = 252

Name ______________ Date ______ Class ______

CHAPTER 2 LAB DATASHEET — SKILL BUILDER

Porifera's Porosity

Early biologists thought that sponges were plants because sponges are like plants in some ways. In many species, the adults stick to a surface and stay there. They cannot chase their food. Sponges absorb and filter a lot of water to get food.

In this activity, you will observe the structure of a sponge. You will also think about how a sponge's structure affects its ability to hold water and collect food. You will think about how the size of the sponge's holes affects the amount of water the sponge can hold.

MATERIALS

- natural sponge
- kitchen sponge
- paper towel
- balance
- water
- bowl (large enough for sponge and water)
- graduated cylinder
- funnel
- calculator (optional)

Make Observations

1. Put on your safety goggles and lab apron. Observe the natural sponge. Identify the pores on the outside of the sponge. See if you can find the central cavity and oscula. Record your data.

2. Notice the size and shape of the sponge's holes. Look at the holes in the kitchen sponge and the holes in the paper towel. How do their holes compare with the sponge's holes?

   Answers will vary, but the holes in the natural sponge are much larger than holes in the kitchen sponge. The holes in the paper towel are the smallest.

Form a Hypothesis

3. Which item do you think can hold the most water per gram of dry mass? Formulate a testable hypothesis and record it below.

   Students may be inclined to believe that the natural sponge would hold the most water.

Test the Hypothesis

4. Read steps 5–9. Design a data table and draw it below. Remember, you will collect data for the natural sponge, the kitchen sponge, and the paper towel.

Name ______________ Date ______ Class ______

5. Use the balance to measure the mass of your sponge. Record the mass.

____

6. Place the sponge in the bowl. Use the graduated cylinder to add water to the sponge. Add 10 mL at a time, until the sponge is completely soaked. Record the amount of water added.

Answers will vary depending on the size of the sponges and the commercial brands used for the kitchen sponge and paper towel.

7. Gently remove the sponge from the bowl. Use the funnel and graduated cylinder to measure the amount of water left in the bowl. How much water did the sponge absorb? Record your data.

Answers will vary depending on the size of the sponges and the commercial brands used for the kitchen sponge and paper towel.

8. Calculate how many milliliters of water your sponge holds per gram of dry sponge. For example, let's say your sponge's dry mass is 12 g and your sponge holds 59.1 mL of water. Your sponge holds 4.9 mL of water per gram. (59.1 mL ÷ 12 g = 4.9 mL/g)

Answers will vary. Students should subtract the mass of the dry sponge from the mass of the wet sponge.

Name ______________ Date ______ Class ______

9. Repeat steps 5–8 using the kitchen sponge and the paper towel.

Analyze the Results

10. Which item held the most water per gram of dry mass?

Answers will vary depending on the size of the sponges and the commercial brands used for the kitchen sponge and paper towel.

11. Did your results support your hypothesis?

Answers will vary depending on the initial hypothesis.

12. Do you see a connection between the size of an item's holes and the item's ability to hold water?

Check student data to see if it supports a correlation.

Draw Conclusions

13. What can you conclude about how the size and shape of a sponge's holes affects the feeding ability of a sponge?

Check student data to see if it supports a conclusion. The idea to emphasize is that the correct answer is the one supported by student data.

Going Further

You have just studied how a sponge's body structure complements its feeding function. Now collect a few different types of insects. Observe how they eat, and examine the structure of their mouthparts. How does the structure of their mouthparts complement the mouthparts' function? Record your answers.

____

____

____

____

Name ______________ Date ______ Class ______

CHAPTER 2 LAB DATASHEET — DISCOVERY LAB

The Cricket Caper

Insects are a special class of invertebrates with more than 750,000 known species. Insects may be the most successful group of animals on Earth. In this activity you will observe a cricket's structure and the simple adaptive behaviors that help make it so successful. Remember, you will be handling a living animal that deserves to be treated with care.

MATERIALS

- 2 crickets
- 600 mL beakers (2)
- plastic wrap
- apple
- hand lens (optional)
- masking tape
- aluminum foil
- lamp
- sealable plastic bags (2)
- crushed ice
- hot tap water

Procedure

1. Place a cricket in a clean 600 mL beaker, and quickly cover the beaker with plastic wrap. The supply of oxygen in the container is enough for the cricket to breathe while you complete your work.
2. Without much movement, observe the cricket's structure. Record your observations.
3. Place a small piece of apple in the beaker. Set the beaker on a table. Sit quietly still for several minutes and observe the cricket. (Any movement may cause the cricket to stop what it is doing.) Record your observations.
4. Remove the plastic wrap and the apple from the beaker, and quickly attach a second beaker. Join the two beakers together at the mouths with masking tape. Handle the beakers carefully. Remember a living thing is inside.

Name ______________ Date ______ Class ______

5. Wrap one of the joined beakers with aluminum foil. Lay the joined beakers on their sides. If the cricket is not visible, gently tap the sides of the beaker until it is exposed.
6. Record the cricket's location. Shine a bright lamp on the uncovered side of the beaker. Record the cricket's location after 5 minutes.
7. Without disturbing the cricket, move the aluminum foil to the other beaker. Repeat step 6 to see if you get the same result.
8. Fill a sealable plastic bag halfway with crushed ice and seal it. Fill the other bag with hot tap water and seal it. Lay the bags side by side. Remove the aluminum foil from the beakers.
9. Gently rock the beakers until the cricket is in the center. Place the beakers on the plastic bags, so that one beaker is over the hot bag and the other beaker is over the cold one. Observe the cricket's behavior for 5 minutes. Record your observations.

Name ______________________ Date __________ Class __________

The Cricket Caper, continued

Cricket (alone)

15 s	
30 s	
45 s	
60 s	
75 s	
90 s	
105 s	
120 s	
135 s	
150 s	
165 s	
180 s	

Cricket A and Cricket B

	A	B
15 s		
30 s		
45 s		
60 s		
75 s		
90 s		
105 s		
120 s		
135 s		
150 s		
165 s		
180 s		

10. Set the beakers on one end. Carefully remove the masking tape and separate the beakers. Quickly replace the plastic wrap over the beaker with the cricket.

11. Observe the cricket's movement in the beaker every 15 seconds for 3 minutes. Fill in the Cricket (alone) data table using the following codes: 0= no movement, 1= slight movement, and 2 = rapid movement.

12. Place a second cricket (Cricket B) into the beaker with the first cricket (Cricket A). Observe both crickets' behavior every 15 seconds. Record data using the codes given in step 12.

Analysis

13. Describe crickets' feeding behavior. Are they lappers, suckers, or chewers?

Crickets are chewers.

14. Do crickets prefer light or dark? Explain.

Crickets generally prefer darkness.

15. From your observations, what can you infer about a cricket's temperature preferences?

Crickets will prefer the warmer location.

16. Based on your observations of Cricket A and Cricket B, what general statements can you make about the social behavior of crickets?

If well fed, crickets generally tolerate each other very well. They will fight and even eat each other if they are not fed properly.

Name ______________________ Date __________ Class __________

Here's Looking at You, Squid! continued

2. Use the magnifying glass to examine the suckers. How do you think the structure of the suckers helps the squid?

Sample answer: The toothed suckers help the squid hold its meal.

3. The squid's arms and tentacles both have suckers, but the suckers serve different functions. Describe what functions you think the different suckers might serve.

Sample answer: There are suckers at the ends of the tentacles. One possible reason for this is that the tentacles are used to grab passing prey. There are three long rows of suckers on the arms, so the arms might be used by the squid to hold its prey in place while eating.

4. Spread apart the arms, and look in the center of the squid. You will see a small black structure. Rub your finger over it, and describe what you observe.

This structure is sharp, and it seems to have parts that open.

5. What do you think the function of this structure is?

It appears to be the mouth of the squid.

6. Using the dissection knife, carefully remove the mantle from the head. Make a cut down the side of the mantle, and spread the mantle open on the plate. Use the diagram on page 116 to help you identify as many internal structures as you can.

Name ______________ Date ________ Class ________

Here's Looking at You, Squid! continued

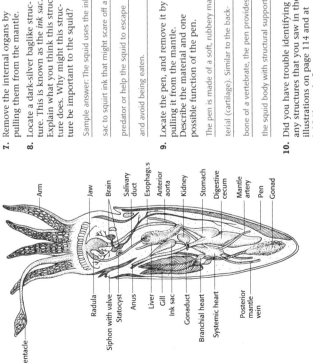

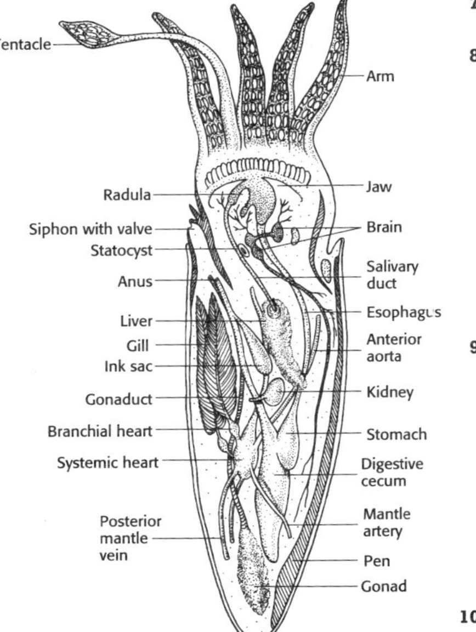

7. Remove the internal organs by pulling them from the mantle.
8. Locate a dark-silver baglike structure. This is known as the *ink sac.* Explain what you think this structure does. Why might this structure be important to the squid?

   Sample answer: The squid uses the ink sac to squirt ink that might scare off a predator or help the squid to escape and avoid being eaten.

9. Locate the pen, and remove it by pulling it from the mantle. Describe the material and one possible function of the pen.

   The pen is made of a soft, rubbery material (cartilage). Similar to the backbone of a vertebrate, the pen provides the squid body with structural support.

10. Did you have trouble identifying any structures that you saw in the illustrations on page 114 and at left? If so, why?

    Sample answer: Yes. The squid parts in the illustration don't look exactly like the real parts.

11. Explain two ways squid and human anatomies are similar and two ways they are different.

    Sample answer: Both squid and humans have arms and a body. Squids' heads are much bigger in relation to their bodies than humans' heads are. Squids have ten limbs and humans have four.

Name ______________ Date ________ Class ________

CHAPTER 2 STUDENT WORKSHEET

At a Snail's Pace

Dear Professor Sloe:

We would like to send a group of snails to outer space on the next shuttle mission. During a month-long study, these snails will be subject to fluctuations in gravity, light, and temperature. To ensure the safety of the snails while in space, we will need you to conduct a study in advance to learn about the snails' performance under various conditions. If the results conclude that a space mission with snails is possible, a representative will visit you to collect the most responsive of your snail candidates. Please report your results to me as soon as possible. Thank you for your cooperation.

Sincerely,

Dr. C. Stars
Director of Zoological Studies
AstroPet Project

MATERIALS

- 20 × 20 cm picture frame
- masking tape
- live snail
- watch or clock that indicates seconds
- washable marker
- metric ruler
- paper towels
- books
- protractor
- magnifying glass
- tub of warm water
- tub of ice water
- cardboard
- table lamp

SCIENTIFIC METHOD

Ask a Question

How do snails respond to different stimuli?

Make a Prediction

1. How will the slope of the glass affect the distance a snail travels?

Conduct an Experiment

2. Tape one side of a picture frame to a table. Place the frame flat on the table, as shown below. Label the tape "Start."

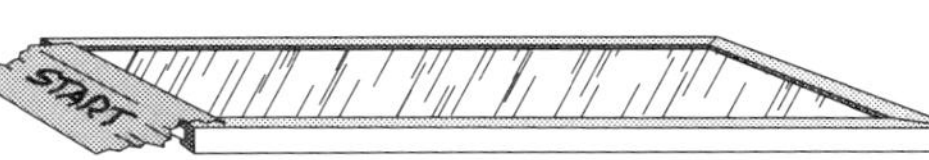

Name ______________ Date ______ Class ______

SNAIL SAFETY

Wash your hands before and after handling the snails. Treat snails gently and with respect. To pick up a snail, wet your fingers and carefully roll the snail from the front to the back. Touch only the shell of the snail. Touching the soft tissues could injure the snail.

3. Gently place the snail on the starting spot. Start timing when the snail comes out of its shell and begins to move.
4. After two minutes, mark the snail's position on the glass with a washable marker. Measure the distance traveled, and record it in the table below. Gently remove the snail. Clean the glass with water, and dry it thoroughly.
5. Use a book to raise the picture frame to a 30° angle. Check the angle with a protractor. Repeat steps 3–4.
6. Repeat step 3–4 for 45°, 60°, and 90° angles. You should either hold the frame or wedge it between two solid, sturdy objects at the 90° angle.

Snail Response Data: Angle of Incline

Angles	Distance traveled	Observations
0°	3 cm	Observations will vary but should be clear and reasonable.
30°	4.5 cm	
45°	6 cm	
60°	7 cm	
90°	10 cm	

Analyze the Results

7. Was your prediction correct? Explain your answer.

Sample answer: No; as the angle increased, the snail traveled farther.

8. Why do you think the snail responded as it did?

Sample answer: The snail might have moved toward the highest point as a survival mechanism. It might be safer for the snail to be at a higher position.

Name ______________ Date ______ Class ______

Communicate Results

9. Graph your results below. What is the shape of the graph?

The graph resembles a straight line.

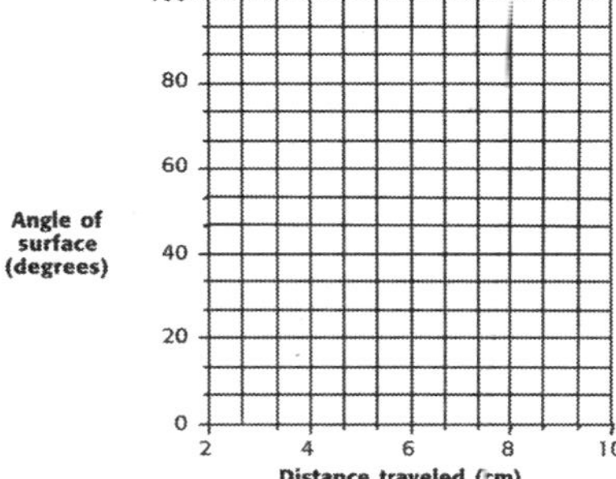

Make a Prediction

10. How will your snail respond to temperature?

Sample answer: The snail will recoil into its shell when it touches the cold glass.

Conduct an Experiment

11. Label a 20 cm length of tape "Start." Place a picture frame in ice water. After one minute, remove and dry the glass.
12. Place the picture frame flat on the table, and use the tape to anchor one edge of the frame to the table. Use books to raise the frame to a 60° angle. Verify the angle with a protractor.
13. Gently place the snail on the starting point. Start timing when the snail comes out of its shell and moves.
14. After two minutes, mark the snail's position on the glass with a washable marker. Measure the distance traveled, and record it in the table on the next page. Repeat steps 11–13 using warm water.

Name ______________ Date ______ Class ______

Snail Response Data: Temperature

Temperature	Distance traveled	Observations
Cool	5 cm	
Warm	1 cm	

Analyze the Results

15. Was your prediction correct? Explain your answer.

Sample answer: My prediction was not correct. The snail traveled farther on the cool glass. The snail withdrew into its shell on the warm glass. Warm surfaces might dehydrate the snail.

Make a Prediction

16. How will your snail respond to light or darkness?

Sample answer: The snail will move away from light and toward darkness.

Conduct an Experiment

17. Create a 60° ramp as you did in step 12. Focus the light from a lamp onto the ramp. Position the lamp far enough from the glass so it doesn't heat up the glass or the snail. Fold the cardboard in half, and place it over the ramp like a tent. The snail should be able to travel up the ramp by passing under the cardboard tent.

18. Gently place the snail on the starting point. Start timing when the snail begins to move.

19. After two minutes, mark the snail's position on the glass with a washable marker. Measure and record the distance traveled in the table below.

20. Repeat steps 18–19 without the cardboard tent.

Snail Response Data: Light

Conditions	Distance traveled	Observations
Light	1 cm	
Dark	4 cm	

Name ______________ Date ______ Class ______

Analyze the Results

21. Was your prediction correct? Explain your answer.

Sample answer: Yes, the snail moved toward the dark area.

22. What general conclusions can you make about the movement of the snail in light compared with its movement in darkness?

Snails tend to move farther in darkness. The light causes snails to withdraw into their shell.

23. Based on your results, where are you more likely to find snails—in cool, dark areas or warm, bright areas? Explain your answer.

Snails are more likely to be found in cool, dark areas. The snails moved away from light. Since light is associated with warmer temperatures, this may indicate why the snails were more active in cool, dark areas.

24. Snails that move toward a stimulus show a positive response. Snails that move away from a stimulus show a negative response. What type of responses did the snails exhibit in each experiment?

The snails exhibited negative responses as they moved up the glass sheet, or away from gravity. They also moved away from the light and recoiled into their shell on the warm glass. This is also a negative response. Snails, therefore, respond in a negative way to gravity, light, and warm temperatures.

Name ____________ Date ________ Class ________

Draw Conclusions

25. Were your snail's responses similar to those of your classmates' snails? Explain your answer.

Sample answer: My snail seemed to respond as the other snails did. As the angle of the surface increased, all of the snails traveled farther. All of the snails also responded negatively to heat and to light.

26. Why is it important to collect data on more than one test subject?

Sample answer: It is important to collect data on more than one test subject because they may not all respond in the same way. It is important to see how snails tend to behave as a group.

Answers to Going Further:

Snails usually recoil their antennae when tickled. A snail moves faster on wet and smooth surfaces than on dry and rough surfaces. Snails usually approach lettuce, probably to eat it. Soothing music or sounds often coax a hiding snail from its shell.

Critical Thinking

27. If you were going to test a moth's response to different stimuli, what type of stimulus might cause a positive response?

Sample answer: A light source would cause a positive response because the moth would move toward the light.

Going Further

Test the snail with other stimuli:

- Tickle the snail with a feather near its antennae.
- Place the snail on various surfaces.
- Place the snail near a piece of lettuce.
- Provide soothing music or sounds.

Name ____________ Date ________ Class ________

Chapter 2 Test

USING VOCABULARY *(Recommended 3 pts. each)*

To complete the following sentences, choose the correct term from each pair of terms listed, and write the term in the blank.

1. The body parts of some invertebrates are controlled by individual groupings of nerve cells called ___ganglia___. (ganglia or coelom)
2. The body form of a jellyfish is the ___medusa___, which looks like a bell with tentacles hanging underneath. (polyp or medusa)
3. In ___open___ circulatory systems, blood is pumped through vessels that empty into sinuses. (closed or open)
4. Insects have a rigid ___exoskeleton___ made of chitin. (endoskeleton or exoskeleton)
5. Many arthropods have feelers called ___antennae___ that respond to touch or taste. (mandibles or antennae)

UNDERSTANDING CONCEPTS

Multiple Choice *(Recommended 5 pts. each)*
Circle the correct answer.

6. The phylum Mollusca includes
   a. octopuses, nematodes, and snails.
   b. slugs, flukes, and clams.
   (c.) slugs, clams, and octopuses.
   d. squids, annelid worms, and oysters.
7. The word *arthropod* means
   a. "large brain."
   (b.) "jointed foot."
   c. "spiny skin."
   d. "paralyzing toxin."
8. The ________ of crustaceans make them different from all other arthropods.
   a. segmented bodies
   b. head capsules
   (c.) double antennae
   d. chitinous skeletons
9. The organs of more-complex invertebrates such as the earthworm are contained in a body cavity called the
   a. gut.
   (b.) coelom.
   c. abdominal hollow.
   d. visceral mass.
10. Digestion of food particles in a sponge takes place in its
   a. gut.
   b. ampulla.
   c. osculum.
   (d.) collar cells.

Name ______________ Date ________ Class ________

Chapter 2 Test, continued

Short Answer *(Recommended 10 pts. each)*

11. Name three of the four distinguishing characteristics of arthropods.

Arthropods are distinguished by (1) jointed limbs; (2) segmented body with specialized structures (divided into cephalothorax and abdomen in arachnids, and into head, thorax, and abdomen in insects); (3) an exoskeleton made of protein and chitin; and (4) a well-developed nervous system that is coordinated by a brain.

12. Sponges move too slowly to escape predators. What adaptation do some sponges have that protects them from being eaten by predators?

The spicules of some sponges are made of silicate or calcium carbonate. The spicules are hard and sharp and therefore discourage predators.

CRITICAL THINKING AND PROBLEM SOLVING *(Recommended 10 pts.)*

13. People who eat raw oysters or clams taken from polluted waters can develop mild to serious illnesses. Think about how oysters and other bivalves eat; then develop a hypothesis to explain why some people get sick from eating them.

Bivalves, such as oysters and clams, filter bacteria and other tiny particles from the water around them. If they live in polluted waters, they are likely to consume disease-causing bacteria and chemical pollutants, which could make people sick.

MATH IN SCIENCE *(Recommended 7 pts.)*

14. Wood ants, which are common in North America, work together to feed their colony. A typical colony can bring as many as 28 dead insects to their nest per minute. How many dead insects could a colony of wood ants bring to the nest if they worked for 24 hours without stopping? Show your work.

28 insects/min × 60 min/h × 24 h/day = 40,320 insects per day

Name ______________ Date ________ Class ________

Chapter 2 Test, continued

INTERPRETING GRAPHICS *(Recommended 8 pts. each)*

Tapeworm grows in dog.
Tapeworm segment full of eggs is expelled from the dog's digestive system.
tapeworm segment (enlarged)
Dog eats flea.
Egg
A.
Larva eats tapeworm segment.
B.
Pupa
Flea jumps on dog.
Adult flea carries tapeworm eggs.

15. Analyze the diagram above. Identify two main similarities between the flea and the tapeworm that set them apart from the dog.

Both the flea and tapeworm are invertebrates and parasites. The dog is a vertebrate and functions as a host for the parasites.

16. Does the diagram show the flea undergoing simple or complete metamorphosis? Use the diagram to support your conclusion. (Be sure to refer to stages *A* and *B* in your explanation.)

The flea undergoes complete metamorphosis because its life cycle has four distinct stages: egg (embryo), larva *(A)*, pupa *(B)*, and adult. Simple metamorphosis involves only three stages; there is no pupal stage. In simple metamorphosis, the immature form of the insect (nymph) looks like a tiny version of the adult.

Name ______________________ Date ____________ Class ____________

Chapter 2 Test, continued

CONCEPT MAPPING *(Recommended 1 pt. each)*

17. Use the following words to complete the concept map below: bilateral, nematocysts, endoskeleton, radial, exoskeleton, cnidarians, echinoderms.

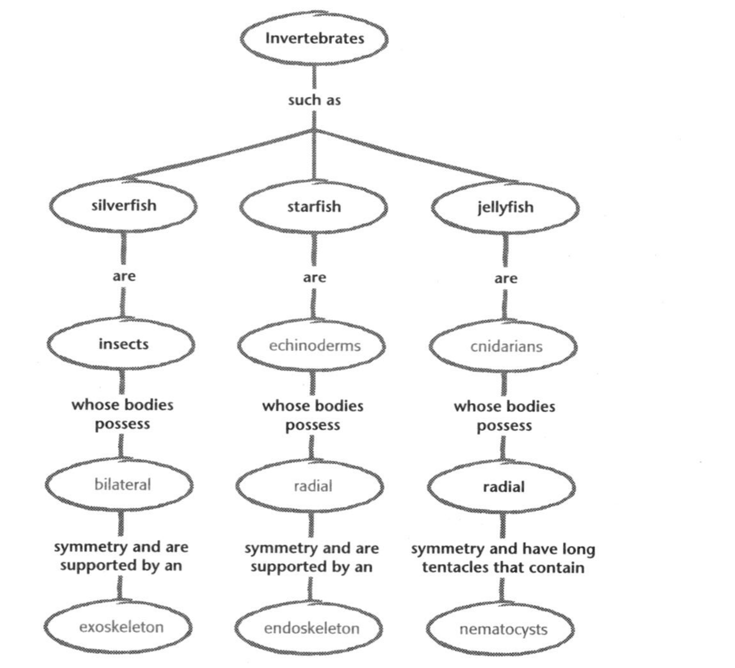

Name ______________________ Date ____________ Class ____________

CHAPTER 2 **INVERTEBRATES** DISCOVERY LAB

Chapter 2 Performance-Based Assessment

MATERIALS

- reference materials on invertebrates
- Internet access

Objective

You will use what you already know as well as what you learn by doing research to help an invertebrate get a job.

Know the Score!

As you work through the activity, keep in mind that you will be earning a grade for the following:

- how thoroughly you complete the activity (100%)

Procedure

1. What type of invertebrate has your teacher assigned you?

   Sample answer: a leech

2. Imagine that you work for an employment agency. The invertebrate that you have been assigned is your client. Read about your client using the reference materials that your teacher has provided. Write a paragraph about your client and his special traits, such as medicinal uses, agricultural uses, regenerative abilities, etc.

   Sample answer: Harold Hirudo is an olive green-colored leech that has adapted to living in warm, moist, land environments. Harold produces hirudin, which is used by doctors to prevent blood clots. He is interested in a position that would allow him to work in a hospital.

3. Think about what types of companies could use this invertebrate. Make up a name for such a company and describe it below. How will your client "fit in" there?

   Sample answer: "Retro Medicine" is a company that revives forgotten forms of medical treatment. These treatments include the use of leeches for bloodletting.

Name ____________ Date ________ Class ________

CHAPTER 3 DIRECTED READING WORKSHEET

Fishes, Amphibians, and Reptiles

Chapter Introduction

As you begin this chapter, answer the following.

1. Read the title of the chapter. List three things that you already know about this subject.

____

____

____

____

____

2. Write two questions about this subject that you would like answered by the time you finish this chapter.

____

____

____

Section 1: What Are Vertebrates? (p. 60)

3. What does a dinosaur skeleton have in common with your skeleton?

Both the dinosaur skeleton and my skeleton have backbones and many other similar bones.

Chordates (p. 60)

Mark each of the following statements *True* or *False*.

4. True Animals with a backbone belong to the phylum Chordata.

5. True The largest group of chordates are vertebrates.

6. False Lancelets do not have a backbone and therefore are not true chordates.

7. False An organism must have all four of the special chordate body parts as an adult in order to belong to the phylum Chordata.

Name ____________ Date ________ Class ________

Use Figure 3 on page 61 to choose the term in Column B that best matches the definition in Column A. Then write the corresponding letter in the space provided.

Column A	Column B
d **8.** In vertebrates this structure is filled with spinal fluid.	**a.** notochord
c **9.** This structure is located behind the anus.	**b.** pharyngeal pouch
a **10.** In most vertebrates this structure disappears and a backbone grows in its place.	**c.** tail
b **11.** This structure develops into a gill or other body part as an embryo matures.	**d.** hollow nerve cord

Getting a Backbone (p. 61)

12. Vertebrates are different from other chordates because

a. tunicates and lancelets have pharyngeal pouches.
b. they have a notochord.
c. they do not have a postanal tail.
(d.) they have a backbone and a skull.

13. A segmented column of bones called vertebrae protects the nerve cord, and a skull protects the head.

14. The name of the tough material in the flexible parts of your nose and ears is called cartilage. (True) or False? (Circle one.)

15. Why do you think we know more about the evolution of vertebrates than any other group of organisms?

Sample answer: The bones of vertebrates are so hard that they become fossilized. Scientists study the fossils and learn more about the evolution of the vertebrates.

Are Vertebrates Warm or Cold? (p. 62)

16. There is an ideal temperature range for the chemical reactions that take place inside an animal's body cells. (True) or False? (Circle one.)

Name ______________ Date ________ Class ________

17. How does an endotherm stay warm when it's cold outside?

An endotherm uses the heat released by the chemical reactions in its cells to stay warm.

18. An endotherm's body temperature stays about the same when the temperature of the environment changes. (changes a lot or stays about the same)

19. Which of the following statements is NOT true?
   - a. Ectotherms include most fish, amphibians, and reptiles.
   - (b.) Ectotherms' body temperature does not fluctuate.
   - c. Ectotherms' body temperature depends on their environment.
   - d. Ectotherms are sometimes called "coldblooded."

Review (p. 62)

Now that you've finished Section 1, review what you learned by answering the Review questions in your ScienceLog.

Section 2: Fishes (p. 63)

1. Which of the following statements is NOT true?
   - (a.) Fish can live almost anywhere except in cold arctic waters.
   - b. The first vertebrates appeared about 500 million years ago.
   - c. There are more species of fishes today than all other vertebrates combined.
   - d. More than 25,000 species of fishes exist.

2. Take a look at the fishes in Figure 6. Why do you think a seahorse is considered a fish?

Accept any reasonable answer. Sample answer: The seahorse has fins and gills, just like other species of fishes.

Fish Characteristics (p. 63)

3. What parts of a fish's body help the fish move, steer, stop, and balance?

Fins help the fish move, steer, stop, and balance.

4. The lateral line system in fish enables them to keep track of information. True or (False)? (Circle one.)

Name ______________ Date ________ Class ________

5. How do fish use their gills to breathe?

Gills remove oxygen from water, and the oxygen passes into the bloodstream. Gills also remove carbon dioxide from the blood.

6. In external fertilization, the male fish drops sperm onto the unfertilized eggs in the water. (True) or False? (Circle one.)

7. After internal fertilization takes place, fish always give birth to live young. True or (False)? (Circle one.)

Types of Fishes (p. 65)

8. There are three different classes of fishes alive today. Two other classes of fishes are now extinct.

9. Which is NOT true of jawless fishes?
   - a. They are eel-like.
   - (b.) They have backbones.
   - c. They have round mouths.
   - d. They were the first fishes.

10. The skeleton of a cartilaginous fish, such as a ray, never changes from cartilage to bone. (True) or False? (Circle one.)

11. A cartilaginous fish has a jaw and is an expert predator.

12. How can a shark's skin hurt you?

A shark's skin is covered with denticles that can cut you if you rub the shark from tail to head.

13. In order to stay afloat, a cartilaginous fish stores oil in its liver and keeps swimming.

14. How does a cartilaginous fish keep from suffocating? (Circle all that apply.)
   - (a.) It keeps swimming.
   - b. It goes to the surface for air.
   - (c.) It pumps water across its gills.
   - d. It swims at certain depths.

Name ______________ Date ________ Class ________

15. All bony fishes have a ___skeleton___ made of bone instead of cartilage.
16. Bony fishes have a body covered by scales. (True) or False? (Circle one.)
17. Which is NOT true of a swim bladder?
    a. It's found in bony fishes.
    b. It's filled with gases from the bloodstream.
    c. It gives the fish buoyancy.
    (d.) It helps fishes steer against wave action.
18. Most bony fishes are ___ray___-finned fishes.
19. ___Lobe___-finned fishes, such as coelacanths, have thick, muscular fins.
20. Lungfishes, like the one shown in Figure 15 at the bottom of page 381, can gulp air. (True) or False? (Circle one.)

Review (p. 67)

Now that you've finished Section 2, review what you learned by answering the Review questions in your ScienceLog.

Section 3: Amphibians (p. 68)

1. 350 million years ago, what made the land such a wonderful place for vertebrates?

   The land had lush green forests, many insects, and few predators.

Moving to Land (p. 68)

2. The lungs of lungfishes became an adaptation for walking. True or (False)? (Circle one.)
3. What did the first amphibians look like?

   They looked like a cross between a fish and a salamander.

4. Early amphibians needed to return to the water from time to time. (True) or False? (Circle one.)

Name ______________ Date ________ Class ________

Characteristics of Amphibians (p. 69)

5. How do amphibians lead a "double-life"?

   Sample answer: When amphibians hatch, they live in the water like fish. Later they develop into animals that can live on land, but they must always be near the water.

Mark each of the following statements *True* or *False*.

6. ___True___ Amphibians do not drink water.
7. ___True___ An amphibian's skin makes it easy for the animal to become dehydrated.
8. ___True___ Some amphibians breathe only through their skin.
9. ___False___ All amphibians with brightly colored skin are deadly.
10. Amphibian embryos must develop in a wet environment because
    (a.) their eggs lack shells.
    b. they begin life as fish.
    c. they are ectotherms.
    d. the water is less polluted than the air.
11. When an amphibian goes through ___metamorphosis___, it changes from its larval form, a tadpole, into its adult form.
12. Where does the embryo of the Darwin frog finish developing?

    The embryo finishes developing in the male frog's vocal sacs.

Kinds of Amphibians (p. 71)

13. Frogs and toads belong to the same group of amphibians. (True) or False? (Circle one.)
14. How are caecilians different from most other amphibians? (Circle all that apply.)
    (a.) They don't have legs.
    (b.) Some have bony scales.
    (c.) They are shaped like snakes.
    d. They have thin, moist skin.

Name ______________ Date ________ Class ________

Chapter 3, continued

15. How are salamanders similar to their prehistoric amphibian ancestors?

They have a similar body shape, four strong legs, and a long tail.

16. A good place to look for a salamander in North America is under a stone or a log.

17. All salamanders go through metamorphosis. True or (False)? (Circle one.)

18. Frogs and toads are found only in temperate parts of the world. True or (False)? (Circle one.)

Use the information on page 72 to mark each of the following phrases *F* if it is characteristic of a frog, *T* if it is characteristic of a toad, or *B* if it is characteristic of both a frog and a toad.

19. B extendible, sticky tongue

20. T dry, bumpy skin

21. F spends more time in the water

22. B vocal chords

23. B powerful leg muscles

24. B well-developed ears

25. F moist skin

26. Frogs have a special structure called a vocal sac that humans don't have. What does this structure do?

The vocal sac inflates with air and vibrates. The vibrations of the sac increase the volume of the song so the song can be heard over long distances.

Review (p. 72)

Now that you've finished Section 3, review what you learned by answering the Review questions in your ScienceLog.

Name ______________ Date ________ Class ________

Chapter 3, continued

Section 4: Reptiles (p. 73)

1. After 35 million years, some amphibians evolved into animals that could live on dry land.

2. Which of the following traits allowed the first reptiles to live completely out of the water? (Circle all that apply.)

(a.) an egg that could be laid on dry land
(b.) stronger, more vertical legs
(c.) thick, dry skin
d. teeth

Reptile History (p. 73)

3. Some prehistoric reptiles could fly. (True) or False? (Circle one.)

4. Mammals had reptile ancestors called therapsids that are now extinct.

Characteristics of Reptiles (p. 74)

5. How is a reptile's skin an important adaptation for life on land?

A reptile's skin is an important adaptation for life on land because it is thick and dry, so it forms a water-tight layer that keeps cells from losing water due to evaporation.

6. Reptiles are less active when the environment is cool and more active when the environment is warm.

7. Most reptiles live in mild climates because they usually cannot maintain a constant body temperature. (True) or False? (Circle one.)

8. What are the advantages of an amniotic egg?

An amniotic egg has a hard shell and can be laid anywhere. The egg provides protection from predators, bacterial infections, and dehydration.

Name ______ Date ______ Class ______

Chapter 3, continued

Choose the part of the amniotic egg in Column B that best matches the definition in Column A, and write the corresponding letter in the space provided.

Column A	Column B
a **9.** supplies the embryo with food	**a.** yolk
d **10.** stores waste from the embryo and passes oxygen to the embryo	**b.** albumen
e **11.** keeps the egg from drying out	**c.** amniotic sac
c **12.** fluid-filled structure that protects the embryo from injury	**d.** allantois
b **13.** provides the embryo with protein and water	**e.** shell

14. Which of the following are true of reptiles? (Circle all that apply.)
- (**a.**) Reptiles don't undergo metamorphosis.
- (**b.**) Reptile embryos develop directly into tiny reptiles.
- **c.** All reptiles lay eggs.
- (**d.**) Reptiles don't have a larval stage.

Types of Reptiles (p. 75)

15. Most of the reptiles that have ever lived are now extinct.

16. List the three groups of modern reptiles.

The three groups are turtles and tortoises, crocodiles and alligators, and snakes and lizards.

17. Which of the following is NOT true of both turtles and tortoises?
- **a.** They are only distantly related to the other reptiles.
- (**b.**) They spend all of their lives on land.
- **c.** Their armorlike shells protect them from predators.
- **d.** They are slow and inflexible.

18. All crocodiles and alligators are carnivores. (carnivores or herbivores)

19. In Figure 32 at the bottom of page 76, how can you tell the difference between a crocodile and an alligator?

An alligator has a broad head and a rounded snout. A crocodile has a narrow head and a pointed snout.

Name ______ Date ______ Class ______

Chapter 3, continued

Mark each of the following statements *True* or *False*.

20. False Lizards include skinks, chameleons, alligators, and geckos.

21. True On rare occasions, the largest lizards, one of which is shown in Figure 33, have been known to eat humans.

22. False Snakes move on smooth surfaces by using suckers on their bellies to grip the surface and pull forward.

23. True Snakes are not herbivores.

24. True Snakes have special, five-jointed jaws that allow them to swallow their prey whole.

25. False Snakes have an acute sense of hearing.

26. How does a snake use its tongue to smell?

Sample answer: The snake samples tiny particles and molecules in the air with its tongue. When it pulls its tongue back inside its mouth, it puts the tips of its tongue into two openings in the roof of its mouth and senses the molecules.

Review (p. 77)

Now that you've finished Section 4, review what you've learned by answering the Review questions in your ScienceLog.

Name ______________________ Date __________ Class __________

CHAPTER 3 VOCABULARY & NOTES WORKSHEET

Fishes, Amphibians, and Reptiles

By studying the Vocabulary and Notes listed for each section below, you can gain a better understanding of this chapter.

SECTION 1

Vocabulary

In your own words, write a definition for each of the following terms in the space provided.

1. vertebrate an animal with a skull and a backbone; includes mammals, birds, reptiles, amphibians, and fish
2. vertebrae segments of bone or cartilage that interlock to form a backbone
3. endotherm an animal that maintains a constant body temperature despite temperature changes in its environment
4. ectotherm an animal whose body temperature fluctuates with the temperature of its environment

Notes

Read the following section highlights. Then, in your own words, write the highlights in your ScienceLog.

- At some point during their development, chordates have a notochord, a hollow nerve cord, pharyngeal pouches, and a tail.
- Chordates include lancelets, tunicates, and vertebrates. Most chordates are vertebrates.
- Vertebrates differ from the other chordates in that they have a backbone and skull made of bone or cartilage.
- The backbone is composed of units called vertebrae.
- Vertebrates may be ectotherms or endotherms.
- Endotherms control their body temperature through the chemical reactions of their cells. Ectotherms do not.

Name ______________________ Date __________ Class __________

SECTION 2

Vocabulary

In your own words, write a definition for each of the following terms in the space provided.

1. fins fanlike structures that help fish move, turn, stop, and balance
2. scales bony structures that cover the skin of bony fishes
3. lateral line system row of tiny sense organs along the sides of a fish's body
4. gills organs that remove oxygen from the water and carbon dioxide from the blood
5. denticles small, sharp toothlike structures on the skin of cartilaginous fishes
6. swim bladder balloonlike organ that is filled with oxygen and other gases; gives bony fishes their buoyancy

Notes

Read the following section highlights. Then, in your own words, write the highlights in your ScienceLog.

- There are three groups of living fishes: jawless fishes, cartilaginous fishes, and bony fishes.
- The cartilaginous fishes have an oily liver that helps them float.
- Most bony fishes have a swim bladder. The swim bladder is a balloonlike organ that gives bony fishes buoyancy.
- In external fertilization, eggs are fertilized outside the female's body. In internal fertilization, eggs are fertilized inside the female's body.

Name ______ Date ______ Class ______

SECTION 3

Vocabulary

In your own words, write a definition for each of the following terms in the space provided.

1. lung a saclike organ that takes oxygen from the air and delivers it to the blood
2. tadpole aquatic larvae of an amphibian
3. metamorphosis process in which an insect or other animal changes form as it develops from an embryo or larva to an adult

Notes

Read the following section highlights. Then, in your own words, write the highlights in your ScienceLog.

- Amphibians were the first vertebrates to live on land.
- Amphibians breathe by gulping air into their lungs and by absorbing oxygen through their skin.
- Amphibians start life in water, where they breathe through gills. During metamorphosis, they lose their gills and develop lungs and legs that allow them to live on land.
- Modern amphibians include caecilians, salamanders, and frogs and toads.

Name ______ Date ______ Class ______

SECTION 4

Vocabulary

In your own words, write a definition for each of the following terms in the space provided.

1. therapsid prehistoric reptile ancestor of mammals
2. amniotic egg egg containing amniotic fluid to protect the developing embryo; usually surrounded by a hard shell

Notes

Read the following section highlights. Then, in your own words, write the highlights in your ScienceLog.

- Reptiles evolved from amphibians by adapting to life on dry land.
- Reptiles have thick, scaly skin that protects them from drying out.
- A tough shell keeps the amniotic egg from drying out and protects the embryo.
- Amniotic fluid surrounds and protects the embryo in an amniotic egg.
- Vertebrates that evolved from early reptiles are reptiles, birds, and mammals.
- Modern reptiles include turtles and tortoises, lizards and snakes, and crocodiles and alligators.

Name ______________________ Date __________ Class __________

CHAPTER 3 **CHAPTER REVIEW WORKSHEET**

Fishes, Amphibians, and Reptiles

USING VOCABULARY

To complete the following sentences, choose the correct term from each pair of terms listed below, and write the term in the space provided.

1. At some point in their development, all chordates have a hollow nerve cord and a tail. (lungs and a notochord or a hollow nerve cord and a tail)
2. Mammals evolved from early ancestors called therapsids. (therapsids or dinosaurs)
3. Fish are ectotherms. (endotherms or ectotherms)
4. When a frog lays eggs that are later fertilized by sperm, it is an example of external fertilization. (internal or external)
5. The vertebrae wrap around and protect the hollow nerve cord of vertebrates. (notochord or hollow nerve cord)

UNDERSTANDING CONCEPTS

Multiple Choice

6. Which of the following is NOT a vertebrate?
   - **a.** tadpole
   - **b.** lizard
   - **c.** lamprey
   - **(d.)** tunicate
7. Tadpoles change into frogs by the process of
   - **a.** evolution.
   - **b.** internal fertilization.
   - **(c.)** metamorphosis.
   - **d.** temperature regulation.
8. The swim bladder is found in
   - **a.** jawless fishes.
   - **b.** cartilaginous fishes.
   - **(c.)** bony fishes.
   - **d.** lancelets.
9. The amniotic egg first evolved in
   - **a.** bony fishes.
   - **b.** birds.
   - **(c.)** reptiles.
   - **d.** mammals.

Name ______________________ Date __________ Class __________

10. The yolk holds
    - **(a.)** food for the embryo.
    - **b.** amniotic fluid.
    - **c.** wastes.
    - **d.** oxygen.
11. Both bony fishes and cartilaginous fishes have
    - **a.** denticles.
    - **(b.)** fins.
    - **c.** an oily liver.
    - **d.** a swim bladder.
12. Reptiles are adapted to a life on land because
    - **a.** they can breathe through their skin.
    - **b.** they are ectotherms.
    - **c.** they have thick, moist skin.
    - **(d.)** they have an amniotic egg.

Short Answer

13. How do amphibians breathe?

    Amphibians breathe through their skin, and some breathe with lungs.

14. What characteristics allow fish to live in the water?

    They have gills to get oxygen from the water and fins and tails that allow them to swim.

15. How does an embryo in an amniotic egg get oxygen?

    Air passes through pores in the shell.

Name ______________ Date ________ Class ________

CONCEPT MAPPING

16. Use the following terms to create a concept map: *dinosaur, turtle, reptiles, amphibians, fishes, shark, salamander, vertebrates.*

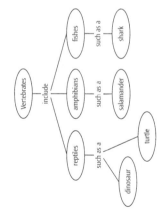

Vertebrates
include
reptiles — such as a — dinosaur, turtle
amphibians — such as a — salamander
fishes — such as a — shark

Name ______________ Date ________ Class ________

CRITICAL THINKING AND PROBLEM SOLVING

Write one or two sentences to answer each of the following questions:

17. Suppose you have found an animal that has a backbone and gills, but you can't find a notochord. Is it a chordate? How can you be sure?

Yes; animals with a backbone are vertebrates, and all vertebrates are chordates; the notochord is replaced by the backbone as a vertebrate develops.

18. Suppose you have found a shark that lacks the muscles needed to pump water over its gills. What does that tell you about the shark's lifestyle?

The shark must swim constantly to pass water over its gills.

19. A rattlesnake does not see very well, but it can detect a temperature change of as little as three-thousandths of a degree Celsius. How is this ability useful to a rattlesnake?

A snake could use such a skill to detect the warm body of a mouse or other prey.

20. It's 43°C outside, and the normal body temperature of a velociraptor is 38°C. Would you most likely find the raptor in the sun or in the shade? Explain.

The velociraptor would be in the shade. Because it is an ectotherm, its body temperature will respond to the environmental temperature. Since the outside temperature is already higher than the velociraptor's normal temperature, it will try to find a cool spot in the shade to cool its body down.

MATH IN SCIENCE

21. A Costa Rican viper can eat a mouse that has one-third more mass than the viper. How much can you eat? Write down your mass in kilograms. To find your mass in kilograms, divide your mass in pounds by 2.2. If you were to eat a meal with a mass one-third larger than your mass, what would the mass of the meal be in kilograms?

Answers will vary but can be determined by the following formula: mass of student (kg) + (mass of student (kg) $\times \frac{1}{3}$) = mass of meal (kg).

Name ______________________ Date ____________ Class ____________

INTERPRETING GRAPHICS

Examine the graph of body temperatures below, and answer the questions that follow.

Body Temperatures

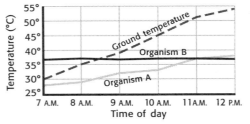

22. How do the body temperatures of organism A and organism B change with the ground temperature?

The body temperature of organism A increases as ground temperature increases. The body temperature of organism B does not change with ground temperature.

23. Which of these organisms is most likely an ectotherm? Why?

Organism A is probably an ectotherm. Its body temperature is dependent on the temperature of the environment.

Name ______________________ Date ____________ Class ____________

24. Which of these organisms is most likely an endotherm? Why?

Organism B is probably an endotherm. Its body temperature is constant even though the environmental temperature changes.

READING CHECK-UP

Take a minute to review your answers to the ScienceLog questions at the beginning of the chapter. Have your answers changed? If necessary, revise your answers based on what you have learned since you began this chapter. Record your revisions in your ScienceLog.

Name ______ Date ______ Class ______

CHAPTER 3 SCIENCE PUZZLERS, TWISTERS & TEASERS

Fishes, Amphibians, and Reptiles

Chordate Code

1. Use the clue that is given to help you find several terms found in this chapter. Write your answers in the spaces provided.

   If the phrase:

   V E R T E B R A T E S A R E C H O R D A T E S

   is represented as:

   3 8 1 6 8 10 1 5 6 8 4 5 1 8 2 20 9 1 7 5 6 8 4

   what are the following vertebrate-related terms?

   a. 18 9 6 9 2 20 9 1 7 notochord
   b. 6 5 12 14 tail
   c. 2 5 1 6 12 14 5 11 8 cartilage
   d. 8 2 6 9 6 20 8 1 15 ectotherm
   e. 10 5 2 22 10 9 18 8 backbone
   f. 4 19 12 18 5 14 2 9 1 7 spinal cord

Scrambled Eggs

2. Below you will find several different reptilian eggs. The reptiles have begun to hatch, so all of the eggs have cracked open. The same letter has been lost out of each one. Unscramble the letters found within each egg and combine them with the missing letter to find what type of reptile is hatching from each egg. Write the names of the reptiles in the spaces provided.

   The missing letter is: The missing letter is R.

   L U E T T — a. turtle

   O L T G L A A I — b. alligator

   O T I S O T E — c. tortoise

   A L D I Z — d. lizard

   L I D O C E O C — e. crocodile

Name ______ Date ______ Class ______

Who's Who

BRAIN BUSTER!

3. For each lettered statement below, decide if the statement best describes fishes, amphibians, or reptiles. If the statement describes fishes, place the capital letter in the box labeled *Fishes*. If the statement best describes amphibians, place the capital letter in the *Amphibians* box, and so on. Then unscramble the letters in each box to find the name of a reptile, fish, or amphibian. Write the name of the animal on the line beneath the box.

   a. first vertebrates on Earth (K) fishes
   b. have a thick dry skin which helps them live on land (E) reptiles
   c. obtain oxygen by gulping air into their lungs or by absorbing it through their skin (D) amphibians
   d. all use lungs to breathe air (U) reptiles
   e. most have a lateral line (A) fishes
   f. live part of their life in the water and part on land (O) amphibians
   g. thought to be the ancestors of modern birds and mammals (T) reptiles
   h. have three classes: jawless, cartilaginous, and bony (R) fishes
   i. undergo metamorphosis to change from larval to adult form (T) amphibians
   j. lay eggs surrounded by a shell to protect them from drying out (T) reptiles
   k. most use gills to breathe throughout their life (S) fishes
   l. live in almost every water environment (H) fishes
   m. often called ecological indicators due to their sensitivity to air and water pollution (A) amphibians
   n. have stronger, more vertical legs (R) reptiles
   o. eggs contain an amniotic sac filled with amniotic fluid (L) reptiles

Fishes	Amphibians	Reptiles
x. shark	y. toad	z. turtle

Name ______________________ Date ____________ Class ____________

Coldblooded Critters, continued

Coldblooded Critter Chart

Amphibians	metamorphosis eggs laid in water no scales vertebrates thin, moist skin ectotherms "double life" breathe through skin and lungs external or internal fertilization almost all adults have lungs many have bright colors to scare predators
Reptiles	ectotherms only internal fertilization amniotic egg most lay eggs on land thick, dry skin vertebrates breathe through lungs some have young born live many have scales
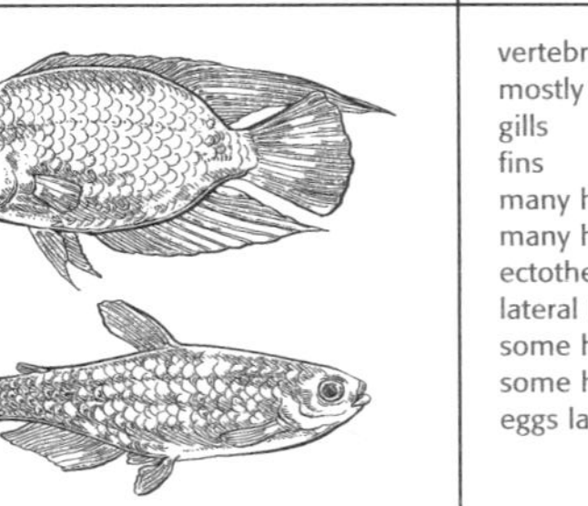 Fishes	vertebrates mostly external fertilization gills fins many have scales many have swim bladders ectotherms lateral line system some have skeletons of cartilage some have young born live eggs laid in water

Name ______________________ Date ____________ Class ____________

CHAPTER 3 VOCABULARY REVIEW WORKSHEET

Fishin' for Vertebrates

Complete this puzzle after you finish reading Chapter 3.

ACROSS

1. crocodiles, turtles, and snakes

6. system of tiny rows of sense organs along the sides of a fish's body

8. cartilaginous fishes store oil here to stay afloat

9. group of fishes with skeletons made of bone and swim bladders

10. aquatic larva of an amphibian

11. balloonlike organ that gives bony fish buoyancy

14. an animal that maintains a constant body temperature

16. bony structures covering the skin of bony fishes

21. body parts of a fish that remove oxygen from water and carbon dioxide from blood

22. prehistoric reptile ancestor of mammals

23. frogs use a vocal sac to do this

24. structures made of bone contained in the fins of perch, minnows, and eels

25. hard-shelled reptiles that live only on land

DOWN

2. fertilization of an egg that occurs inside the female's body

3. fertilization of an egg that occurs outside the female's body

4. the first fishes were this type of fish

5. an animal with a body temperature that fluctuates with the temperature of its environment

7. an egg that is usually surrounded by a hard shell

12. small, toothlike structures on the skin of cartilaginous fishes

13. a change from a larval form to an adult form

15. sharks and skates are this type of fish

17. saclike organs that take oxygen from the air and deliver it to the blood

18. an animal with a skull and a backbone

19. these fishes have air sacs and can gulp air

20. fanlike structures that help fish move, steer, stop, balance

Name ______________________ Date ____________ Class ____________

Across:
1. REPTILES
6. LATERAL LINE
8. LIVER
9. BONY
10. TADPOLE
11. SWIM BLADDER
14. ENDOTHERM
16. SCALES
21. GILLS
22. THERAPSID
23. SING
24. RAYS
25. TORTOISES

Down:
2. INTERNAL
3. EXTERNAL
4. JAWLESS
5. ECTOTHERM
7. AMNIOTIC
12. DENTICLES
13. METAMORPHOSIS
15. CARTILAGINOUS
17. LUNGS
18. VERTEBRATE
19. LUNGFISHES
20. FINS

Name ______________________ Date ____________ Class ____________

CHAPTER 3 CRITICAL THINKING WORKSHEET

Frogs Aren't Breathing Easy

Something is killing frogs all over the world. The list of suspects includes acid rain, pollution, and vanishing wetlands. But the real killer may be none of the above. A team of biologists suspects that a previously unknown fungus may be at least partly responsible for the global decline of frogs. . . .

To date the researchers have found the fungus in about 30 frog species from Australia, Central America, and the United States and have shown that it kills frogs in laboratory trials. The fungus attacks the frogs' skin . . .

The fungus, apparently a new species of aquatic chytrid fungi, has yet to be named.

From "The Frog Killer" by Lybi Ma from "Breakthroughs" from *Discover,* vol. 19, no. 11, November 1998. Copyright © 1999 by Lybi Ma. Reprinted by permission of ***Discover Magazine.***

USEFUL TERMS

fungus
a multicellular organism that gets food by breaking down other substances and absorbing the nutrients

chytrid
belonging to the phylum Chytridiomycota

Comprehending Ideas

1. Why would a fungus that affects skin be especially deadly to frogs?

Sample answer: Frogs absorb both water and oxygen through their skin. Frogs may not be able to breathe or drink if their skin is affected by this fungus.

Making Comparisons

2. Are fish or reptiles more likely to be affected by this fungus? Explain your answer.

Sample answer: The fungus is more likely to affect fish because they drink and breathe through their gills, which are directly exposed to water. Reptiles breathe with lungs, drink through their mouths, and typically live on land.

Name ______________ Date ________ Class ________

Predicting Consequences

3. Complete the chart below by stating how the factors in the left column could affect the frog population and lead to fungal infection. Sample answers are below.

Factors Contributing to Fungal Infection

Possible factors	Effect on frog population
increased pollution	could weaken the frogs and make them more sensitive to the fungus
a foreign material or species in the frogs' habitat	could bring the fungus into the frogs' habitat
vanishing wetlands	could force the frogs into areas where this deadly fungus lives

HELPFUL HINTS
Think about the effects of various treatments on other plants and animals.

Demonstrating Reasoned Judgment

4. If a substance were made that could rid the frogs of this killer fungus, how might it be given to the frogs?

Sample answer: The substance could be added to the water supply if it was harmless to other plants and animals. If it was harmful to other plants and animals, it could be applied directly to the frogs' skin.

HELPFUL HINTS
Because of their "double life," amphibians are easily affected by small environmental changes in water or on land.

Making Inferences

5. The Declining Amphibian Population Task Force was created in 1990. An estimated 500 environmental groups joined the force. Why do you think declining amphibian populations caused this much concern?

Sample answer: The health of amphibians may be directly related to general environmental health and could warn us of environmental changes.

Name ______________ Date ________ Class ________

CHAPTER 3 MATH IN SCIENCE: INTEGRATED SCIENCE

MATH SKILLS USED
Addition
Multiplication
Fractions
Decimals
Scientific Notation

Using Temperature Scales

Convert between degrees Fahrenheit and degrees Celsius.

Do you remember the last time you had your temperature taken? Your body temperature is usually about 98.6°F. This temperature is in degrees Fahrenheit (°F). The Fahrenheit temperature scale is a common temperature scale. In science class, however, a scale known as the Celsius (°C) scale is used. Temperatures in one scale can be mathematically converted to the other system using one of the equations below.

EQUATIONS: Conversion from Fahrenheit to Celsius: $\frac{5}{9} \times (°F - 32) = °C$

Conversion from Celsius to Fahrenheit: $\frac{9}{5} \times °C + 32 = °F$

SAMPLE PROBLEMS:

A. Convert 59°F to degrees Celcius.

$°C = \frac{5}{9} \times (°F - 32)$

$°C = \frac{5}{9} \times (59 - 32)$

$°C = \frac{5}{9} \times 27$

$°C = \mathbf{15°C}$

B. Convert 112°C to degrees Fahrenheit.

$°F = \frac{9}{5} \times °C + 32$

$°F = \frac{9}{5} \times 112 + 32$

$°F = 201\frac{3}{5} + 32$

$°F = \mathbf{233\frac{3}{5}°F}$

Turn Up the Temperature!

1. Convert the following temperatures from degrees Fahrenheit to degrees Celsius:
   a. 98.6°F $\frac{5}{9} \times (98.6 - 32) = 37°C$
   b. 482°F $\frac{5}{9} \times (482 - 32) = 250°C$
   c. −4°F $\frac{5}{9} \times (-4 - 32) = -20°C$
2. Convert the following temperatures from degrees Celsius to degrees Fahrenheit:
   a. 24°C $\frac{9}{5} \times 24 + 32 = 43\frac{1}{5} + 32 = 75\frac{1}{5}°F$
   b. 17°C $\frac{9}{5} \times 17 + 32 = 30\frac{3}{5} + 32 = 62\frac{3}{5}°F$
   c. 0°C $\frac{9}{5} \times 0 + 32 = 0 + 32 = 32°F$

Challenge Yourself!

3. Convert 2.7×10^4°C to degrees Fahrenheit. $\frac{9}{5} \times 27{,}000 + 32 = 48{,}600 + 32 = 48{,}632°F$

Name ______________________ Date ____________ Class ____________

CHAPTER 3 COMMUNICATING SKILLS

Grasping Graphing

When you bake cookies, you must use the right ingredients to make the cookies turn out right. Graphs are the same way. They require the correct ingredients, or components, to make them readable and understandable.

Bar and Line Graphs

- First, set up your graphs with an *x*-axis and a *y*-axis. The **x-axis** is horizontal, and the **y-axis** is vertical as shown in the example at right. The axes represent different variables in an experiment.
- The *x*-axis represents the independent variable. The **independent variable** is the variable whose values are chosen by the experimenter. For example, the range of grades is the independent variable.
- The *y*-axis represents the dependent variable. The values for the **dependent variable** are determined by the independent variable. If you are grouping students by grades, the number of students in each group **depends** on the grade they get.
- Next choose a **scale** for each of the axes. Select evenly spaced intervals that include all of your data, as shown on the grade-distribution bar graph. When you label the axes, be sure to write the appropriate units where they apply.
- Next, plot your data on the graph. Make sure you double-check your numbers to ensure accuracy.
- Finally, give your graph a title. A **title** tells the reader what he or she is studying. A good title should explain the relationship between the variables. Now your graph is complete!

y-axis / *x*-axis

Independent variable

Dependent variable

Grade Distribution of Students Enrolled in Science Class

Number of students: 0, 10, 20, 30, 40, 50, 60, 70, 80

Grade: A, B, C, D, F

Name ______________________ Date ____________ Class ____________

Pie Graphs

When you convert data to show percentages, you can use a pie graph. Pie graphs are shaped like a circle. The size of each "pie slice" is determined by the percentage it will represent. A full pie is equal to 100 percent, half a pie is equal to 50 percent, and so on.

Like bar and line graphs, pie graphs have independent and dependent variables. The independent variable is whatever the pie or slice of pie represents. The dependent variable is the size of the pie slice, the percentage of the whole it represents.

Percentage of Students Picking Various Lunch Entrees

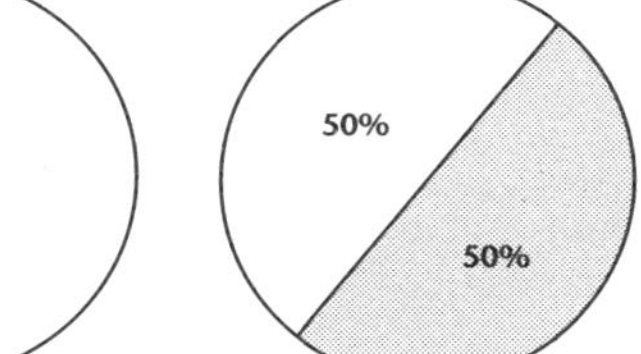

Percentage of Students Picking Various Lunch Entrees

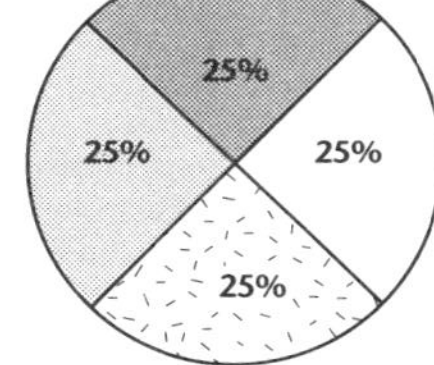

Your Turn

For each table (a) identify the independent and dependent variable, (b) determine the type of graph to use, and (c) provide a title.

1.

Amount of daily sunlight exposure (min)	Average height of plants (cm)
50	14.8
60	14.9
95	15.2
75	15.1
110	16.5
135	17.3
100	16.1
30	11.0

a. Dependent variable: Average height of plants; Independent variable: Amount of daily sunlight exposure

b. Line graph or bar graph is reasonable.

c. Sample answer: Heights of Plants Exposed to Various Amounts of Sunlight

Name ______________________ Date ____________ Class ____________

Grasping Graphing, continued

2.

Student	Number of jelly beans consumed
Anthony	15
Keiko	28
Leigh Ann	58
Adam	22
Katie	12
Juan	17

The Effect of Fertilizer on Plant Growth

Average height of plants (cm)

Amount of fertilizer added to soil (g)

a. Dependent variable: Number of jelly beans consumed; Independent variable: Student

b. Bar graph

c. Sample answer: Number of jelly beans consumed by student

Give It a Try

Graph the data below in your ScienceLog. Don't forget to do the following:

- Select the appropriate graph type.
- Identify the independent and the dependent variable.
- Choose an appropriate scale.
- Label the axes.
- Give your graph a title.

Amount of fertilizer added to soil (g)	Average height of plants (cm)
5	13.2
10	14.1
15	14.9
20	15.4
25	16.5
30	17.3
35	16.1
40	11.0

Name ______________________ Date ____________ Class ____________

CHAPTER 3 LAB DATASHEET — MAKING MODELS

Floating a Pipe Fish

Bony fishes control how deep or shallow they swim with a special structure called a swim bladder. As gases are absorbed and released by the swim bladder, the fish rises or sinks in the water. In this activity, you will make a model of a fish with a swim bladder. Your challenge will be to make the fish float halfway between the top of the water and the bottom of the container. It will probably take several tries and a lot of observing and analyzing along the way.

MATERIALS

- water
- container for water at least 15 cm deep
- slender balloon
- small cork
- 12 cm length of PVC pipe, 3/4 in. diameter
- rubber band

Procedure

1. Estimate how much air you will need in the balloon so that your pipe fish will float halfway between the top of the water and the bottom of the container. Will you need to inflate the balloon halfway, just a small amount, or all the way? (It will have to fit inside the pipe, but there will need to be enough air to make the pipe float.)

2. Inflate your balloon. Hold the neck of the balloon so that no air escapes, and push the cork into the end of the balloon. If the cork is properly placed, no air should leak out when the balloon is held underwater.

3. Place your swim bladder inside the pipe, and place a rubber band along the pipe as shown. The rubber band will keep the swim bladder from coming out of either end.

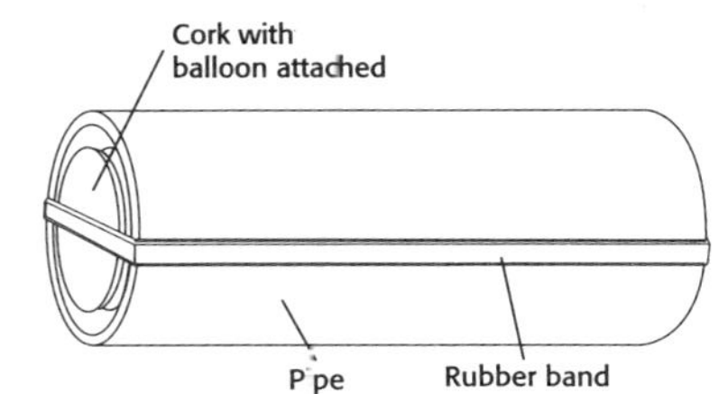

4. Place your pipe fish in the water, and note where the fish floats. Record your observations.

Name ______________________ Date ____________ Class ____________

5. If the pipe fish does not float where you want, take it out of the water, adjust the amount of air in the balloon, and try again.
6. You can release small amounts of air from the bladder by carefully lifting the neck of the balloon away from the cork. You can add more air by removing the cork and blowing more air into the balloon. Keep adjusting and testing until your fish floats halfway between the bottom of the container and the top of the water.

Analysis

7. Was the estimate you made in step 1 correct? Explain your answer.

8. In relation to the length and volume of the entire pipe fish, how much air was needed to make the fish float? State your answer as a percentage.

   Filling less than 10 percent of the internal volume of the pipe with air will make the pipe float in the middle of the water column.

9. Based on the amount of space the balloon took up inside the pipe in your model, how much space do you estimate is taken up by a swim bladder inside a living fish? Explain.

   Have students give this answer in a proportion or fraction. Less than one-third of the inside of the pipe is taken by the inflated balloon. Explain that the flesh of a fish is not as dense as PVC pipe and the swim bladder does not need to be very large to adjust the floating depth of the fish.

Going Further

Some fast-swimming fishes, such as sharks, and marine mammals, such as whales and dolphins, do not have a swim bladder. Find out from the library or the Internet how these animals keep from sinking to the bottom of the ocean. Create a poster, and explain your results on index cards. Include drawings of the fish or marine mammals you have researched.

Sharks and marine mammals, such as dolphins and whales, must swim almost constantly to keep from sinking to the bottom. Dolphins and whales must come to the surface to breathe. A shark must move constantly or lie in moving water in order to keep water moving past its gills. Sharks and marine mammals are able to dive to great depths because they don't have a swim bladder that would rupture under pressure.

Name ______________________ Date ____________ Class ____________

CHAPTER 3 LAB DATASHEET

A Prince of a Frog

Imagine that you are a scientist interested in amphibians. You have heard in the news about amphibians disappearing all over the world. What a great loss it will be to the environment if all amphibians become extinct! Your job is to learn as much as possible about how frogs normally behave so that you can act as a resource for other scientists who are studying the problem.

In this activity, you will observe a normal frog in a dry container and in water.

MATERIALS

- live frog in a dry container
- live crickets
- 600 mL beaker
- container half-filled with dechlorinated water
- large rock
- protective gloves

Procedure

1. Use the data table below to record your observations in steps 3–11.

Observations of a Live Frog

Characteristic	Observation
Breathing	
Eyes	
Legs	
Response to food	
Response to noise	
Skin texture	
Swimming behavior	
Skin coloration	

2. Observe a live frog in a dry container. Draw the frog in the space on the next page. Label the eyes, nostrils, front legs, and hind legs.

Name ______________________ Date ____________ Class ____________

A Prince of a Frog, continued

Illustrations should show the basic structural details of a frog. Those details should be clearly labeled.

3. Watch the frog's movements as it breathes air with its lungs. Write a description of the frog's breathing in the data table.
4. Look closely at the frog's eyes and note their location. Examine the upper and lower eyelids as well as the transparent third eyelid. Which of these three eyelids actually moves over the eye? Record your observation.
5. Study the frog's legs. Note in your data table the difference between the front and hind legs.
6. Place a live insect, such as a cricket, in the container. Observe and record how the frog reacts.
7. Carefully pick up the frog, and examine its skin. How does it feel? Record your observations. **Caution:** Remember that a frog is a living thing and deserves to be handled gently and with respect.
8. Place a 600 mL beaker in the container. Place the frog in the beaker. Cover the beaker with your hand and carry it to a container of dechlorinated water. Tilt the beaker and gently submerge it in the water until the frog swims out of the beaker.
9. Watch the frog float and swim in the water. How does the frog use its legs to swim? Notice the position of the frog's head. Record your observations.
10. As the frog swims, bend down and look up into the water so that you can see the underside of the frog. Then look down on the frog from above. Compare the color on the top and the underside of the frog. Record your observations.

Name ______________________ Date ____________ Class ____________

A Prince of a Frog, continued

Answers 11–15 are sample answers.

Analysis

11. From the position of the frog's eyes, what can you infer about the frog's field of vision?

    With a large eye on each side of its head, the frog likely has a wide field of vision.

    How might the position of the frog's eyes benefit the frog while it is swimming?

    The frog can see above the water when most of its body is below water.

12. How can a frog "breathe" while it is swimming in water?

    The frog "breathes" underwater through its skin.

13. How are the hind legs of a frog adapted for life on land and in water?

    The enlarged hind legs are an adaptation for swimming and jumping.

14. What differences did you notice in coloration on the frog's top side and its underneath side? What advantage might these color differences provide?

    Camouflage helps protect the frog. A darker top side helps the frog avoid being seen from above when all or portions of it are out of the water. A lighter bottom side helps protect the frog from predators swimming below.

15. How does the frog eat? What senses are involved in helping the frog catch its prey?

    The frog eats by flipping out its long, sticky tongue to quickly catch insects. Frogs use sight, smell, and hearing to locate a desirable meal.

Going Further

Observe another type of amphibian, such as a salamander. How do the adaptations of other types of amphibians compare with those of the frog you observed in this investigation?

Answers will vary, but students should notice several similar adaptations among amphibians.

Name ______ Date ______ Class ______

CHAPTER 3 FISHES, AMPHIBIANS, AND REPTILES

Chapter 3 Test

USING VOCABULARY *(Recommended 3 pts. each)*

To complete the following sentences, choose the correct term from each pair of terms listed, and write the term in the blank.

1. In some chordates, pharyngeal pouches develop into ___gills___ as the embryo matures. (vertebrae or gills)
2. ___Vertebrates___ make up the largest group of chordates. (Vertebrates or Invertebrates)
3. ___Fins___ help a fish move, steer, stop, and balance. (Fins or Denticles)
4. The ___lateral line system___ allows fish to detect vibrations in the surrounding water. (swim bladder or lateral line system)
5. ___Endotherms___ can regulate their internal temperature. (Ectotherms or Endotherms)

UNDERSTANDING CONCEPTS

Multiple Choice *(Recommended 5 pts. each)*
Circle the correct answer.

6. The flexible ______ is an embryonic structure that is usually replaced by a backbone.
   a. nerve cord
   (b.) notochord
   c. alimentary canal
   d. postanal tail
7. Which of the following is a member of the largest class of fishes?
   (a.) perch
   b. lamprey
   c. shark
   d. skate
8. Fish first appeared on Earth about
   a. 1 billion years ago.
   (b.) 500 million years ago.
   c. 65 million years ago.
   d. 400 billion years ago.
9. The life cycle of a salamander involves
   a. eggs with protective shells.
   b. a land-based larval stage.
   (c.) internal fertilization.
   d. All of the above
10. Which statement is false?
    a. All mammals are vertebrates.
    (b.) Most vertebrates have an open circulatory system.
    c. Vertebrates have a well-developed head with a skull.
    d. The skeletons of all vertebrate embryos are made of cartilage.

Name ______ Date ______ Class ______

Short Answer *(Recommended 9 pts. each)*

11. Identify and describe the stages in the metamorphosis of an ordinary frog.

    Amphibian eggs lack a shell or special membrane, so they are deposited in a very wet environment. The embryo in a fertilized egg develops into a tadpole, a larva that has gills and is aquatic. The tadpole undergoes metamorphosis into an adult form with lungs and limbs. Even though the adult frog takes oxygen from air and can live on land, it remains close to water. The adult lays eggs, and the cycle repeats.

12. Reptiles are entirely adapted for life on land. Describe these adaptations.

    Reptiles have thick, dry skin that forms a watertight layer, preventing moisture loss. They have lungs, and they reproduce by internal fertilization. Their embryos usually develop in a well-protected (fertilized) amniotic egg with a shell.

CRITICAL THINKING AND PROBLEM SOLVING *(Recommended 10 pts. each)*

13. At the zoo you see an unusual four-legged, hairless animal. It is smaller than your hand and lives in a hole in the ground in a darkened display case. One of the zoo assistants allows you to reach into the display and touch the animal. Although the ground and air in the display are cool, the animal feels warm to the touch. Is this strange animal likely to be an ectotherm or an endotherm? Why do you think so?

    Even though the air and ground are cool, the animal feels warm. It must be capable of controlling its body temperature internally. Thus, the animal is most likely an endotherm.

Name ______________ Date ________ Class ________

14. Suppose you put one goldfish in a relatively warm aquarium and another goldfish of equal size and age in a relatively cold aquarium. If you put equal amounts of food in each tank, which goldfish would eat the most food? Explain your choice.

The fish in the warm water would probably eat more. Fish are ectotherms, which means that their body temperature varies with the temperature of their environment. The fish in the cold aquarium would have a lower body temperature and would be less active, so it would eat less food.

INTERPRETING GRAPHICS *(Recommended 10 pts.)*

Examine the graph below and answer the questions that follow.

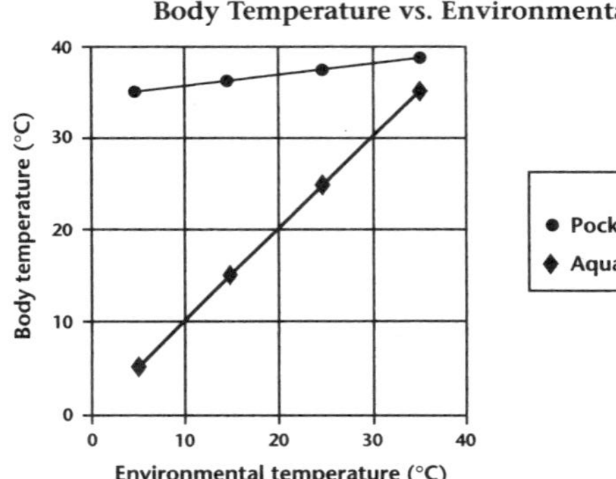

15. Compare the relationship of body temperature to environmental temperature in ectotherms with that of endotherms.

As environmental temperature increases, endotherms' body temperature changes only slightly, while ectotherms' body temperature changes dramatically.

Name ______________ Date ________ Class ________

CONCEPT MAPPING *(Recommended 2 pts. each)*

16. Use the following terms to complete the concept map below: skin with denticles, jawless fishes, hard scales, cartilaginous fishes, bony fishes, smooth and slimy skin.

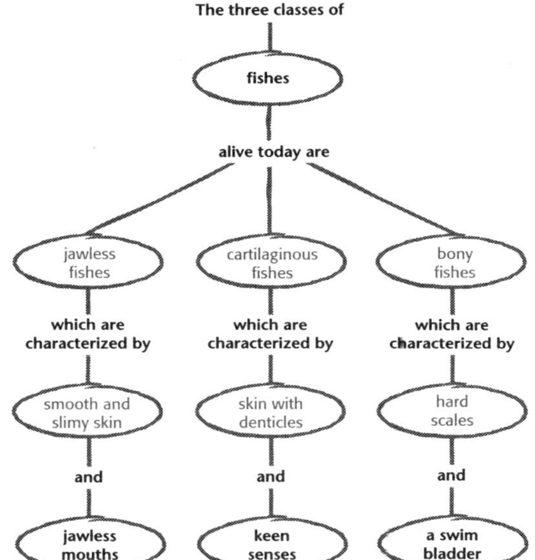

Name ______________ Date ______ Class ______

CHAPTER 3 FISHES, AMPHIBIANS, AND REPTILES — DISCOVERY LAB

Chapter 3 Performance-Based Assessment

MATERIALS
- goldfish in a fishbowl or other clear container
- ruler
- colored pencils or markers

Objective
You've read about bony fishes. Now you can use what you have learned—together with the observations you will make of your own fish—to identify anatomical structures of a bony fish.

Know the Score!
As you work through the activity, keep in mind that you will be earning a grade for the following:
- the quality and clarity of your observations (50%)
- your explanation of these observations (50%)

Procedure
1. Get at eye level with your fish. Remember not to tap the container because fish are particularly sensitive to vibrations. Observe your fish closely. Most aquarium goldfish are 5–10 cm long. Estimate the length of your fish from its mouth to the tip of its caudal fin, or tail. How long is your fish in centimeters?

   Sample answer: 6 cm

2. In the space provided, draw just the body of your goldfish, including the caudal fin, or tail.

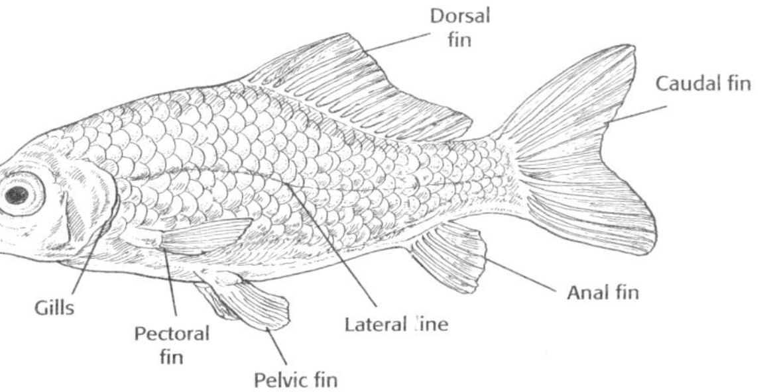

3. All bony fishes have paired fins, both pectoral and pelvic. Pectoral fins are located just behind the gills. Pelvic fins are located below the pectoral fins. Add fins to your fish and label them with the appropriate names. Observe closely how your fish uses its fins to move forward and maneuver.

Name ______________ Date ______ Class ______

4. Draw and label the median (dorsal and anal) fins. The dorsal fin is along the backbone, and the anal fin is near the tail, along the belly.
5. Locate the gills. The gills are covered by a structure called the operculum. Draw and label the gills on your fish. Observe the opening and closing of the mouth and relate this to the movement of the gills. Does this gill movement occur only when the fish is moving?

   Sample answer: No, the gills move all the time.

6. Look at the fish from above and from below as best you can. Color your fish drawing with colored pencils. Make note of the difference in color between the top and bottom of your fish.
7. Locate the lateral line system on your fish. It appears as a line of tiny dots. Draw and label this feature on your drawing. What is the function of the lateral line system?

   The lateral line system is a row of tiny sense organs that detect vibrations in the water, such as those caused by predators.

8. Draw eyes on your fish.

Analysis
9. How does the location of the eyes increase the field of vision?

   Sample answer: The eyes are located on either side of the fish. This enables it to see almost 360°.

10. Fish cannot swim backward. What about their body structure prevents them from doing this?

    Sample answer: A fish cannot swim backward because swinging its tail fin from side to side thrusts its body forward. The other fins can help the fish alter its forward direction, but those fins cannot completely reverse the fish's direction.

Name ______________ Date ______ Class ______

CHAPTER 4 DIRECTED READING WORKSHEET

Birds and Mammals

Chapter Introduction

As you begin this chapter, answer the following.

1. Read the title of the chapter. List three things that you already know about this subject.

____

____

____

____

2. Write two questions about this subject that you would like answered by the time you finish this chapter.

____

____

____

3. How does the title of the Start-Up Activity relate to the subject of the chapter?

____

____

____

Section 1: Birds (p. 88)

4. If a living animal has ___feathers___, it's a bird.

Bird Characteristics (p. 88)

5. Which of the following characteristics do birds share with modern-day reptiles? (Circle all that apply.)
   - **(a.)** They have thick, dry scales on their legs and feet.
   - **(b.)** They have vertebrae.
   - **(c.)** They have amniotic eggs.
   - **d.** They lay eggs with hard eggshells.
6. When bird feathers get old, they fall out, and new feathers grow in their place. (True) or False? (Circle one.)
7. Down feathers help keep birds from losing ___heat___.

Name ______________ Date ______ Class ______

Chapter 4, continued

8. The main function of contour feathers is to
   - **(a.)** form a streamlined flying surface.
   - **b.** attract a mate.
   - **c.** provide protection.
   - **d.** provide warmth.
9. How does preening make a bird's feathers water-repellent?

   During preening, birds use their beaks to spread oil on their feathers.

   ____
10. How do birds cool off on hot days?
    - **a.** They fly higher in the atmosphere, where the air is cooler.
    - **(b.)** They lay their feathers flat and pant like dogs.
    - **c.** They shed feathers.
    - **d.** They sweat.
11. Birds eat and digest their food quickly because their metabolisms require a lot of energy. (True) or False? (Circle one.)
12. How does a gizzard help a bird digest food?

    Sample answer: Birds don't have teeth, so they use stones in their gizzard to grind up their food and make it easier for the intestine to digest.

    ____

    ____

    ____

Up, Up, and Away (p. 90)

Choose the bird characteristic in Column B that best matches the use in Column A, and write the corresponding letter in the space provided.

Column A	Column B
e 13. ensuring flight muscles get as much oxygen as possible	a. keen eyesight
c 14. maneuvering rapidly	b. air sac
a 15. finding food from a distance	c. short wing
f 16. soaring	d. rigid skeleton
b 17. increasing the bird's oxygen intake	e. rapid heart rate
d 18. moving wings powerfully and efficiently	f. long, narrow wing

Name ______________ Date ________ Class ________

Chapter 4, continued

Getting off the Ground (p. 92)

19. The upward pressure on the wing that keeps a bird in the air is called ___lift___.

Mark each of the following statements *True* or *False*.

20. ___False___ The top of a bird's wing is curved so air flowing under the wing moves faster than the air flowing over the wing.

21. ___True___ The larger the wings, the greater the lift.

22. ___False___ Birds must flap their wings constantly to stay in the air.

Fly Away (p. 93)

23. Why do some birds migrate for the winter?

By migrating, birds can find better territories with more food.

Bringing Up Baby (p. 93)

24. Which of the following is NOT true about brooding?

a. It keeps a bird's eggs warm.
(b.) All birds share the responsibility between males and females.
c. A bird does this until its eggs hatch.
d. Birds sit on their eggs.

25. How do cuckoos and cowbirds make other birds work for them?

They lay their eggs in the nests of another species of bird and let the other birds raise their young.

26. Precocial chicks depend on their parents to feed and protect them. True or (False)? (Circle one.)

27. Altricial chicks hatch with their eyes closed. (True) or False? (Circle one.)

Review (p. 94)

Now that you've finished the first part of Section 1, review what you learned by answering the Review questions in your ScienceLog.

Copyright © by Holt, Rinehart and Winston. All rights reserved.

Name ______________ Date ________ Class ________

Chapter 4, continued

Kinds of Birds (p. 95)

28. One of the smallest birds is the 1.6 g bee ___hummingbird___.

29. Look at the description of Flightless Birds on page 95. Describe an adaptation that helps each of the following flightless birds get around.

a. Ostriches have hooflike feet that allow them to run fast.

b. Penguins have wings that they use as flippers that help them to swim underwater.

30. Look at the description of Water Birds on page 96. Water birds, also known as ___waterfowl___, usually have ___webbed___ feet.

31. What is the the blue-footed booby known for?

a. remaining underwater for long periods of time
b. attracting females with beautiful plumage
(c.) courting females by raising one foot at a time

32. Look at the description of Birds of Prey at the bottom of page 96. Which of the following is NOT helpful to birds of prey?

a. keen vision
b. sharp claws and beaks
c. strong muscles
(d.) webbed feet

33. Most birds of prey, such as eagles, falcons, and hawks, eat meat and hunt during the ___day___.

34. Look at the description of Perching Birds on page 97. Why don't perching birds fall off their perches when they fall asleep?

Perching birds don't fall off because their feet close around the branch.

35. Chickadees sometimes hunt while dangling upside down. (True) or False? (Circle one.)

Review (p. 97)

Now that you've finished Section 1, review what you learned by answering the Review questions in your ScienceLog.

Name ______________ Date ________ Class ________

Section 2: Mammals (p. 98)

1. There are more species of ___mollusks___ than there are species of ___mammals___. (mollusks or mammals, mollusks or mammals)
2. The largest animal that has ever lived is a mammal. (True) or False? (Circle one.)

The Origin of Mammals (p. 98)

3. Many scientists believe mammals are descended from reptiles called ___therapsids___.
4. Which of the following statements is NOT true about the first mammals?
   - **a.** They appear in the fossil record about 200 million years ago.
   - **b.** They foraged for food at night.
   - (**c.**) They existed only after dinosaurs became extinct.
   - **d.** They were endotherms.

Characteristics of Mammals (p. 99)

5. Mammary glands are special organs that only female mammals have. True or (False)? (Circle one.)
6. The milk of mammals is made up of fat, water, ___protein___, and ___sugar___.
7. A mammal's body temperature never changes, even when hibernating. True or (False)? (Circle one.)
8. Name two adaptations that help keep mammals warm.

   Sample answer: Mammals have varying amounts and types of body hair to keep them warm. Most also have a layer of fat.

Match the type of tooth in Column B to its use in Column A, and write the corresponding letter in the space provided.

Column A	Column B
b 9. cutting	a. canine
c 10. grinding	b. incisor
a 11. stabbing	c. molar

Name ______________ Date ________ Class ________

12. The shape of a mammal's teeth reflects the ___diet___ of the mammal. (size or diet)
13. Mammals have ___two___ sets of teeth.
14. The main purpose of the diaphragm muscle is to
    - (**a.**) bring air into the lungs.
    - **b.** separate blood with oxygen from blood without oxygen.
    - **c.** provide as much oxygen as possible to the heart.
    - **d.** help mammals make sounds necessary for communication.
15. Mammals use their well-developed senses and large brains to respond quickly to their environment. (True) or False? (Circle one.)
16. Which of the following statements are true of young mammals? (Circle all that apply.)
    - (**a.**) They result from sexual reproduction.
    - (**b.**) They are protected by their parent(s).
    - (**c.**) They have milk teeth.
    - (**d.**) They nurse.

Review (p. 101)

Now that you've finished the first part of Section 2, review what you learned by answering the Review questions in your ScienceLog.

Kinds of Mammals (p. 102)

17. Why are monotremes considered mammals even though they lay eggs?

    Monotremes are considered to be mammals because they have all the mammal traits—fur, mammary glands, and they are endotherms.

18. The duckbilled platypus and the ___echidnas___ are the only living monotremes. Monotremes are found only in Australia and ___New Guinea___.
19. A baby platypus gets milk from its mother by licking the milk from the skin and hair around its mother's nipples. True or (False)? (Circle one.)
20. Marsupials lay eggs just like monotremes do. True or (False)? (Circle one.)

Name ______________ Date ______ Class ______

21. Marsupials use their pouches for
- **a.** storing food in the winter.
- **b.** giving birth to their young.
- **(c.)** carrying and protecting young.
- **d.** digesting food for their young.

22. The ___opossum___ is the only marsupial living in North America north of Mexico.

23. Female placental mammals do NOT
- **a.** have a uterus.
- **b.** supply food and oxygen to their embryo through a placenta.
- **c.** have a gestation period lasting from a few weeks to many months.
- **(d.)** lay eggs.

Kinds of Placental Mammals (p. 104)

24. Look at the description of Toothless Mammals on page 104. All toothless mammals, such as armadillos, pangolins, and sloths, have no teeth. True or (False)? (Circle one.)

25. Most toothless mammals catch insects with a long, sticky tongue. (True) or False? (Circle one.)

26. Look at the description of Insect Eaters on page 105. Insectivores are tiny mammals that live on every continent except ___Australia___ and ___Antarctica___. Most of them dig in the soil with their long, pointed ___noses___.

27. Look at the description of Rodents on page 105. Rodents gnaw so much that they grow several sets of teeth. True or (False)? (Circle one.)

28. Look at the description of Lagomorphs on page 106. Which of the following is NOT a characteristic of a lagomorph?
- **a.** sensitive nose
- **b.** large ears
- **c.** two sets of incisors
- **(d.)** long tail

29. Look at the description of Flying Mammals on page 106. Explain how bats use sound to find their dinner.

Sample answer: Bats make clicking noises, which bounce off objects. They listen for the types of echoes that reflect off the things they eat.

Name ______________ Date ______ Class ______

30. Look at page 107. Animals that eat almost only meat are called ___carnivores___. Meat-eaters have large canines and special ___teeth___ for slicing meat.

31. Some carnivores eat ___plants___ as well as meat.

32. Look at page 108. Hoofed mammals are divided into groups based on the thickness of their hooves. True or (False)? (Circle one.)

33. Giraffes are the tallest living mammals. (True) or False? (Circle one.)

34. Look at page 109. Elephants use their trunk the same way we use our nose, ___hands___, and ___lips___.

35. Look at the description of Cetaceans on page 110. Sperm whales are cetaceans that use echolocation to stun their food as well as to find it. (True) or False? (Circle one.)

36. Look at the description of Sirenia on page 110. Which of the following characteristics does NOT describe Sirenia, such as manatees or dugongs?
- **a.** plant-eaters
- **b.** completely aquatic
- **c.** quiet
- **(d.)** make up the largest group of mammals

Look at the description of Primates on page 111. Then mark each of the following statements *True* or *False*.

37. ___True___ Monkeys, humans, and prosimians are all primates.

38. ___True___ Primates have large brains in proportion to their body size.

39. ___True___ In primates, the eyes face forward.

40. ___False___ All primates have five fingers on each hand and five toes on each foot.

41. ___False___ All primates live on the ground.

42. ___False___ Primates have claws.

Review (p. 111)

Now that you've finished Section 2, review what you learned by answering the Review questions in your ScienceLog.

Name ______________ Date ______ Class ______

CHAPTER 4 VOCABULARY & NOTES WORKSHEET

Birds and Mammals

By studying the Vocabulary and Notes listed for each section below, you can gain a better understanding of this chapter.

SECTION 1

Vocabulary

In your own words, write a definition for each of the following terms in the space provided.

1. down feather a fluffy insulating feather that lies next to a bird's body
2. contour feather a feather made of a stiff central shaft with many side branches called barbs
3. preening activity in which a bird uses its beak to spread oil on its feathers
4. lift an upward force on an object (such as a wing) caused by differences in pressure above and below the object; opposes the downward pull of gravity
5. brooding when a bird sits on its eggs until they hatch

Notes

Read the following section highlights. Then, in your own words, write the highlights in your ScienceLog.

- Like reptiles, birds lay amniotic eggs and have thick, dry scales.
- Unlike reptiles, birds are endotherms and are covered with feathers.
- Because flying requires a lot of energy, birds must eat a high-energy diet and breathe efficiently.
- Birds' wings are shaped so that they generate lift. Lift is air pressure beneath the wings that keeps a bird in the air.
- Birds are lightweight. Their feathers are strong but lightweight, and their skeleton is relatively rigid, compact, and hollow.
- Because birds can fly, they can migrate great distances. They can nest in one habitat and winter in another. Migrating birds can take advantage of food supplies and avoid predators.

Name ______________ Date ______ Class ______

SECTION 2

Vocabulary

In your own words, write a definition for each of the following terms in the space provided.

1. mammary glands glands that secrete a nutritious fluid called milk
2. diaphragm the sheet of muscle underneath the lungs of mammals that helps draw air into the lungs
3. monotreme a mammal that lays eggs
4. marsupial a mammal that gives birth to live, partially developed young that continue to develop inside the mother's pouch or skin fold
5. placental mammal a mammal that nourishes unborn offspring with a placenta inside the uterus
6. gestation period the time during which an embryo develops within the mother

Notes

Read the following section highlights. Then, in your own words, write the highlights in your ScienceLog.

- All mammals have mammary glands; in females, mammary glands produce milk. Milk is a highly nutritious fluid fed to the young.
- Like birds, mammals are endotherms.
- Mammals maintain their high metabolism by eating a lot of food and breathing efficiently.

Name ______________ Date ________ Class ________

Birds and Mammals, continued

- Mammals have a diaphragm that helps them draw air into their lungs.
- Mammals have highly specialized teeth for chewing different kinds of food. Mammals that eat plants have incisors and molars for cutting and grinding plants. Carnivores have canines for seizing and tearing their prey.
- Mammals are the only vertebrates that have mammary glands, fur, and two sets of teeth.
- Mammals are divided into three groups: monotremes, marsupials, and placental mammals.
- Monotremes lay eggs instead of bearing live young. Monotremes produce milk but do not have nipples or a placenta.
- Marsupials give birth to live young, but the young are born as embryos. The embryos climb into their mother's pouch, where they drink milk until they are more developed.
- Placental mammals develop inside of the mother for a period of time called a gestation period. Placental mothers nurse their young after birth.

Name ______________ Date ________ Class ________

CHAPTER 4 **CHAPTER REVIEW WORKSHEET**

Birds and Mammals

USING VOCABULARY

To complete the following sentences, choose the correct term from each pair of terms listed below, and write the term in the space provided.

1. ___Precocial___ chicks can run after their mother soon after they hatch. ___Altricial___ chicks can barely stretch their neck out to be fed when they first hatch. (Altricial or Precocial)

2. The ___diaphragm___ helps mammals breathe. (diaphragm or air sac)

3. The ___placenta___ allows some mammals to supply nutrients to young in the mother's uterus. (mammary gland or placenta)

4. Birds take care of their feathers by ___preening___. (brooding or preening)

5. A lion belongs to a group of mammals called ___carnivores___. (carnivores or primates)

6. ___Down feathers___ are fluffy feathers that help keep birds warm. (Contour feathers or Down feathers)

UNDERSTANDING CONCEPTS

Multiple Choice

7. Both birds and reptiles
- (**a.**) lay eggs.
- **b.** brood their young.
- **c.** have air sacs.
- **d.** have feathers.

8. Flight requires
- **a.** a lot of energy and oxygen.
- **b.** a lightweight body.
- **c.** strong flight muscles.
- (**d.**) All of the above

9. Only mammals
- **a.** have glands.
- (**b.**) nurse their young.
- **c.** lay eggs.
- **d.** have teeth.

10. Monotremes do NOT
- **a.** have mammary glands.
- **b.** care for their young.
- (**c.**) have pouches.
- **d.** have fur.

Name ______________ Date ________ Class ________

11. Lift

a. is air that travels over the top of a wing.
b. is provided by air sacs.
(c.) is the upward force on a wing that keeps a bird in the air.
d. is created by pressure from the diaphragm.

12. Which of the following is not a primate?

a. a lemur
b. a human
(c.) a pika
d. a chimpanzee

Short Answer

13. How are marsupials different from other mammals? How are they similar?

Marsupials bear live young that continue to develop in their mother's pouches. Like other mammals, they have fur, specialized teeth, and mammary glands.

14. Both birds and mammals are endotherms. How do they stay warm?

Birds and mammals stay warm by converting their food to energy for body heat. Mammals have fur, and birds have feathers, in part, to help retain body heat.

15. What is the Bernoulli effect?

The Bernoulli effect is the vacuum created by fast-moving air.

16. Why do some bats have large ears?

Bats need large ears to hear echoes they use in locating food and other objects.

Name ______________ Date ________ Class ________

CONCEPT MAPPING

17. Use the following terms to create a concept map: *monotremes, endotherms, birds, mammals, mammary glands, placental mammals, marsupials, feathers, hair.*

Name ______________ Date ________ Class ________

CRITICAL THINKING AND PROBLEM SOLVING

Write one or two sentences to answer each of the following questions:

18. Unlike bird and monotreme eggs, the eggs of placental mammals and marsupials do not have a yolk. How do developing embryos of marsupials and placental mammals get the nutrition they need?

Marsupials get their nutrition from their mother's milk. Placental mammals get their nutrition from their mother's body through the placenta.

19. Most bats and cetaceans use echolocation. Why don't these mammals rely solely on sight to find their prey and examine their surroundings?

Bats and cetaceans are both active in dark environments, where sound is more helpful than sight.

20. Suppose you are working at a museum and are making a display of bird skeletons. Unfortunately, the skeletons have lost their labels. How can you separate the skeletons of flightless birds from those of birds that fly? Will you be able to tell which birds flew rapidly and which birds could soar? Explain your answer.

Birds that fly will have a large keel and larger wings. The birds with longer wings probably soared because longer wings are necessary to provide enough surface area for greater lift.

MATH IN SCIENCE

21. A bird is flying at a speed of 35 km/h. At this speed, its body consumes 60 Calories per gram of body mass per hour. If the bird has a mass of 50 g, how many Calories will it use if it flies for 30 minutes at this speed?

The bird will use 1,500 Cal.

$\frac{60\ \text{Cal/g}}{\text{h}} \times 0.5\ \text{h} \times 50\ \text{g} = 1{,}500\ \text{Cal}$

Name ______________ Date ________ Class ________

INTERPRETING GRAPHICS

Endotherms use a lot of energy when they run or fly. The graph below shows how many Calories a small dog uses while running at different speeds. Use this graph to answer the questions below.

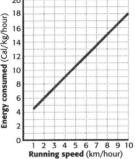

Energy consumed (Cal/kg/hour)
20
18
16
14
12
10
8
6
4
2
0
1 2 3 4 5 6 7 8 9 10
Running speed (km/hour)

22. As the dog runs faster, how does the amount of energy it consumes per hour change?

The faster the dog goes, the more energy it uses.

23. How much energy per hour will this dog consume if it is running at 4 km/h? at 9 km/h?

At 4 km/h, the dog consumes 9 Cal/kg/h. At 9 km/h, the dog consumes 16.5 Cal/kg/h.

24. Energy consumed is given in Calories per kilogram of body mass per hour. If the dog has a mass of 6 kg and is running at 7 km/h, how many Calories per hour will it use?

At 7 km/h, the dog consumes 13.5 Cal/kg/h.

13.5 Cal/kg/h × 6 kg = 81 Cal/h

READING CHECK-UP

Take a minute to review your answers to the ScienceLog questions at the beginning of the chapter. Have your answers changed? If necessary, revise your answers based on what you have learned since you began this chapter. Record your revisions in your ScienceLog.

Name ______________ Date ______________ Class ______________

CHAPTER 4 SCIENCE PUZZLERS, TWISTERS & TEASERS

Birds and Mammals

Flying Without a Spare

1. You've borrowed your next-door neighbor's space cruiser to visit a cousin who lives on Mars. But on the way there, one of your engines blows out. The contraption won't fly without all six engines, and now only five work. Your neighbor never keeps a spare and the escape pod appears to be out of whack. Being your resourceful self, you tinker about until you get the escape pod in semi-decent shape. Have you ever driven a rickety old escape pod? Well, it's difficult to steer. You land on various continents on Earth in your search for home. Looking out the porthole, determine—by what you see—where you've landed.

a. 1st landing: You see a large animal—a huge rodent. It must weigh over 70 kg! What is it, and where have you landed?

capybara, South America

b. 2nd landing: Immediately after landing, you spot a smaller furry animal. It seems to have small copies of itself hugging onto its belly. The mammal sees you too, and it stops moving. Perhaps it died of fright. What is this creature, and where are you?

opossum, North America

c. 3rd landing: This time you see a flat-nosed, large-eared mammal. You pry open your portal and stick your head out. This animal's breath smells of eucalyptus, like a cough drop. What is it? Where are you?

koala; Australia, New Guinea, or South America

d. 4th landing: Now something strikes at the glass of the porthole. It's the beak of a large (almost 125 kg!), bad-tempered bird. Its feet look like hooves! What is it?

ostrich, (Africa)

e. 5th landing: Another bird! This time it's a shy one with soft, hairy feathers and a long, pointed beak. It doesn't look like it does much flying. What bird is this? Where are you?

kiwi, New Zealand

Name ______________ Date ______________ Class ______________

The Wedding Reception

2. Many animals will attend Elephant's wedding reception. His mother is trying to arrange the guests so that each sits next to another animal with whom it shares something in common. In particular, there are four guests who are giving Elephant's mom a headache. Who will sit next to whom? The guests in question are:

Spider Monkey—Mrs. Elephant remembers how Spider Monkey embarrassed everyone at Ostrich's picnic last year by insisting on shaking hands. Really, *hands*! Good gracious!

Bat—With all his talk of moving around in the dark, and how those of us with good eyesight are supposedly "missing out," Bat can be such an awful bore!

Mole—He means well, Elephant's mom admits, but it is kind of creepy having Mole always smelling you and touching you with his nose.

Archaeopteryx—Frankly, everyone is tired of Archaeopteryx's talk of the "good old days."

Here are the guests that Elephant's mother can choose from: Swordfish, Manatee, Therapsids, Whale, Platypus, Orangutan. Match one of these guests up with each of our "problem" guests, and explain your choice.

a. Spider Monkey: orangutan, because they both have hands

b. Bat: whale, because they both use sonar to navigate

c. Mole: platypus, because it uses its sensitive nose to find food

d. Archaeopteryx: therapsids, because they are both extinct

Name ______________ Date ________ Class ________

CHAPTER 4 REINFORCEMENT WORKSHEET

Mammals Are Us

Complete this worksheet after you finish reading Chapter 4, Section 2.

Each of the following terms is either an order of animals or an example of a particular order. Use the characteristics and facts in the table below to identify the order and one example of each group of animals, and record the corresponding terms in the spaces provided.

dolphin	cetaceans	hoofed mammals	sirenia
rabbit	human	carnivores	rodents
porcupine	aardvark	cow	toothless mammals
primates	manatee	Siberian tiger	
insectivores	lagomorphs	hedgehog	

Order	Characteristic	Example	An interesting fact
toothless mammals	generally eat insects and have long, sticky tongues	aardvark	only one is truly "toothless"
insectivores	tend to have pointed noses for digging	hedgehog	live on all continents but Australia
rodents	small animals that have sharp front teeth for gnawing	porcupine	front teeth never stop growing
lagomorphs	have strong legs for jumping, sensitive noses, and big ears	rabbit	some gather plants and shape them in "haystacks" to dry
primates	have eyes that face forward and oppos-able thumbs	human	considered the most intelligent mammals
carnivores	eat mostly meat	Siberian tiger	most have special teeth for slicing meat
hoofed mammals	generally fast runners; they have flat teeth for chewing plants	cow	divided into groups according to the number of toes
cetaceans	water-dwelling mammals that resemble fish	dolphin	use echolocation like bats do
sirenia	eat seaweed and water plants	manatee	only four species in this order

Name ______________ Date ________ Class ________

CHAPTER 4 VOCABULARY REVIEW WORKSHEET

Is It a Bird or a Mammal?

Complete this worksheet after you finish reading Chapter 4.

Match each description in the second column with the correct term in the first column, and write the corresponding letter in the space provided.

d 1. primates
j 2. contour feathers
i 3. carnivores
k 4. down feathers
c 5. gestation period
n 6. preening
f 7. placenta
m 8. lift
b 9. placental mammals
p 10. brooding
q 11. marsupials
o 12. precocial chicks
g 13. monotremes
e 14. altricial chicks
h 15. therapsids
l 16. mammary glands
a 17. diaphragm

a. a large muscle at the bottom of the rib cage that helps bring air into the lungs
b. a mammal that nourishes its unborn offspring with a special organ inside the uterus
c. the time during which an embryo develops within the mother
d. a group of mammals that have opposable thumbs and binocular vision; includes humans, apes, and monkeys
e. chicks that hatch weak, naked, and helpless
f. a special organ of exchange that provides a developing fetus with nutrients and oxygen
g. mammals that lay eggs
h. prehistoric reptile ancestors of mammals
i. consumers that eat animals
j. feathers made of a stiff central shaft with many side branches called barbs
k. fluffy, insulating feathers that lie next to a bird's body
l. glands that secrete a nutritious fluid called milk
m. the upward pressure on the wing of a bird that keeps a bird in the air
n. when a bird uses its beak to spread oil on its feathers
o. chicks that hatch fully active
p. when a bird sits on its eggs until they hatch
q. a mammal that gives birth to partially developed, live young that develop inside the mother's pouch or skin fold

Name ____________ Date ________ Class ________

CHAPTER 4 CRITICAL THINKING WORKSHEET

A Puzzling Piece of Paleontology

In today's episode, we find Outback Jack and his trusty partner, Diego, on the exotic island of Madagascar, off the east coast of Africa. After a dozen dusty days of digging in the dirt, Diego declares with delight, "Jack, I've found something! It's part of a skeleton!"

Jack sprints to his partner's side to see the bounty of bones. "Great Scott!" exclaims Jack. "It's a bird! An ancient bird! Look at these wing bones, Diego. See these bumps? That's where the flight feathers were attached."

Diego, however, notices something nearby and nudges his partner. "But look over here, Jack," he says, pointing to a hole in the ground several centimeters away. "It's the rear half of the skeleton. And look at the second toe on the left foot!"

Jack examines the foot and jumps back. "Can they be sickle-shaped claws like those found on dromaeosaurs?" he wonders out loud. "It looks like a velociraptor claw!"

"But the first toe is pointing backward, like a bird's foot!" exclaims Diego. "I think we may have found an important piece of the puzzle! It must be from an animal that is closely related to both birds and dinosaurs."

Outback Jack and Diego quickly take their discovery to Professor Pronk at the university. "These are definitely bird wings," Professor Pronk proclaims, "and these look an awful lot like dinosaur feet. But, my fine friends, I'm still not convinced that you've found a meaningful piece of evidence."

USEFUL TERMS

dromaeosaurs
a group of dinosaurs that included the velociraptor

Establishing Connections

1. When Diego says, "I think we may have found an important piece of the puzzle," which puzzle is he referring to?

Sample answer: He is referring to the puzzle of birds' evolutionary descent from dinosaurs. Many scientists believe that birds are descendants of dinosaurs. Some even say that birds are dinosaurs. This piece of evidence could help prove that birds evolved from dinosaurs.

Name ____________ Date ________ Class ________

2. Why are toes that point backward useful to birds?

Sample answer: Toes that point backward help birds perch on branches.

Demonstrating Reasoned Judgment

3. Professor Pronk is not totally convinced that Jack and Diego have found a meaningful piece of evidence. Why do you think he is skeptical?

Sample answer: Professor Pronk might doubt that all the bones came from the same creature. Even though the bones were found at the same time and were near each other, they could be from two different animals—a bird and a dinosaur.

Identifying Relationships

4. If Jack and Diego's hypothesis is correct, which ancient animal could this creature be closely related to?

Sample answer: If Jack and Diego's hypothesis is correct, this animal may be related to the *Archaeopteryx*, the earliest known true bird, which had many dinosaurlike characteristics.

Name ______________________ Date __________ Class __________

CHAPTER 4 MATH SKILLS

The Unit Factor and Dimensional Analysis

The measurements you take in science class, whether for time, mass, weight, or distance, are more than just numbers—they are also units. To make comparisons between measurements, it is convenient to have your measurements in the same units. A mathematical tool called a **unit factor** is used to convert back and forth between different kinds of units. A unit factor is a ratio that is equal to 1. Because it is equal to 1, multiplying a measurement by a unit factor changes the measurement's units but does not change its value. The skill of converting with a unit factor is known as **dimensional analysis.** Read on to see how it works.

Part 1: Converting with a Unit Factor

PROCEDURE: To convert units with a unit factor, determine the conversion factor between the units you have and the units you want to convert to. Then create the unit factor by making a ratio, in the form of a fraction, between the units you want to convert to in the numerator and the units you already have in the denominator. Finally, multiply your measurement by this unit factor to convert to the new units.

SAMPLE PROBLEM A: Convert 3.5 km to millimeters.

Step 1: Determine the conversion factor between kilometers and millimeters.

$$1 \text{ km} = 1{,}000{,}000 \text{ mm}$$

Step 2: Create the unit factor. Put the units you want to convert to in the numerator and the units you already have in the denominator.

$$\frac{1{,}000{,}000 \text{ mm}}{1 \text{ km}} = 1$$

Step 3: Multiply the unit factor by the measurement. Notice that the original unit of the measurement cancels out with the unit in the denominator of the unit factor, leaving the units you are converting to.

$$3.5 \cancel{\text{km}} \times \frac{1{,}000{,}000 \text{ mm}}{1 \cancel{\text{km}}} = \mathbf{3{,}500{,}000 \text{ mm}}$$

On Your Own!

1. Convert the following measurements using a unit factor:

Conversion	Unit factor	Answer
a. 2.34 cm = ? mm	$\frac{10 \text{ mm}}{1 \text{ cm}}$	23.4 mm
b. 54.6 mL = ? L	$\frac{1 \text{ L}}{1000 \text{ mL}}$	0.0546 L
c. 12 kg = ? g	$\frac{1000 \text{ g}}{1 \text{ kg}}$	12,000 g

Name ______________________ Date __________ Class __________

Part 2: Working with Square Units

Many times in your science class, you will work with units of two dimensions, such as square centimeters (cm^2) or square kilometers (km^2). Dimensional analysis is especially useful when working with these types of units because it can help you to avoid confusing the different dimensions of your units. Carefully follow the steps in Sample Problem B to see how it works.

SAMPLE PROBLEM B: 1 km^2 is how many square meters?

Step 1: Simplify the units you are converting.

$$1 \text{ km}^2 = 1 \text{ km} \times 1 \text{ km}$$

Step 2: Create the unit factor for converting meters to kilometers. As in Sample Problem A, put the units you are converting *to* in the numerator.

$$\frac{1000 \text{ m}}{1 \text{ km}} = 1$$

Step 3: Multiply the measurement you are converting by the unit factor. Because 1 km^2 = 1 km × 1 km, you will need to multiply the measurement you are converting from by *two* unit factors. Notice that the original unit of measurement cancels the units in the denominator. This leaves the units you are converting *to.*

$$1 \cancel{\text{km}^2} \times \frac{1000 \text{ m}}{1 \cancel{\text{km}}} \times \frac{1000 \text{ m}}{1 \cancel{\text{km}}} = 1{,}000{,}000 \text{ m} \times \text{m}$$

$$1 \text{ km}^2 = \mathbf{1{,}000{,}000 \text{ m}^2}$$

Practice Your Skills!

2. Convert the following measurements:

Conversion	Unit factor	Answer
a. 3 cm^2 = ? m^2	$\frac{1 \text{ m}}{100 \text{ cm}}$	0.0003 m^2
b. 12,000 m^2 = ? km^2	$\frac{1 \text{ km}}{1000 \text{ m}}$	0.012 km^2
c. 980 cm^2 = ? mm^2	$\frac{10 \text{ mm}}{1 \text{ cm}}$	98,000 mm^2

3. An Olympic-sized soccer field has an area of 0.007776 km^2. How many square meters does a soccer field cover?

Unit factor: $\frac{1000 \text{ m}}{1 \text{ km}}$; $0.007776 \cancel{\text{km}^2} \times \frac{1000 \text{ m}}{1 \cancel{\text{km}}} \times \frac{1000 \text{ m}}{1 \cancel{\text{km}}} = 7776 \text{ m}^2$

Name ______________ Date ________ Class ________

Working with Cubic Dimensions

Because volume can be measured by multiplying length times height times width, volume is expressed in units of three dimensions, or cubic units. Volume is often expressed in cubic millimeters (mm^3) or cubic centimeters (cm^3), but larger volumes may be expressed in cubic meters (m^3) or cubic kilometers (km^3). A cubic centimeter (cm^3) is equal to one milliliter (mL), and a cubic decimeter (dm^3) is equal to one liter (L). Doing dimensional analysis with cubic units is much like doing dimensional analysis with square units, except that with cubic units you will multiply the measurement you are converting by three unit factors instead of two. Follow the steps in Sample Problem C to see how it is done.

SAMPLE PROBLEM C: A certain plant needs about 525 cm^3 of soil to grow properly. How many cubic meters of soil is this?

Step 1: Simplify the units you are converting.

$$cm^3 = cm \times cm \times cm$$

Step 2: Create the unit factor for converting centimeters to meters, putting the units you are converting *to* in the numerator.

$$\frac{1\ m}{100\ cm}$$

Step 3: Multiply the measurement you are converting by the unit factors. Because $cm^3 = cm \times cm \times cm$, you will need to multiply the measurement you are converting from by *three* unit factors.

$$525\ \cancel{cm^3} \times \frac{1\ m}{100\ \cancel{cm}} \times \frac{1\ m}{100\ \cancel{cm}} \times \frac{1\ m}{100\ \cancel{cm}} = 0.000525\ m \times m \times m$$

$$525\ cm^3 = \mathbf{0.000525\ m^3}$$

Try It Yourself!

4. Convert the following measurements:

Conversion	Unit factor	Answer
a. $30\ m^3 = ?\ cm^3$	$\frac{100\ cm}{1\ m}$	30,000,000 cm^3
b. $9000\ mm^3 = ?\ m^3$	$\frac{1\ m}{1000\ mm}$	0.000009 m^3
c. $4\ km^3 = ?\ m^3$	$\frac{1000\ m}{1\ km}$	4,000,000,000 m^3

Challenge Yourself!

5. The Mississippi River has an average water discharge of 17,000 m^3 per second. How many cubic kilometers of water does the river discharge in 1 hour? Show your work.

Unit factor: $\frac{1\ km}{1000\ m}$; $17{,}000\ \cancel{m^3}/s \times \frac{1\ km}{1000\ \cancel{m}} \times \frac{1\ km}{1000\ \cancel{m}} \times \frac{1\ km}{1000\ \cancel{m}} = 0.000017\ km^3/s$;

$0.000017\ km^3/\cancel{s} \times 60\ \cancel{s}/min = 0.00102\ km^3/min$; $0.00102\ km^3/\cancel{min} \times 60\ \cancel{min}/hr = 0.0612\ km^3/hr$

Name ______________ Date ________ Class ________

CHAPTER 4 LAB DATASHEET — MAKING MODELS

What? No Dentist Bills?

When you eat, you must chew your food well. Chewing food into small bits is the first part of digestion. But birds don't have teeth. How do birds make big chunks of food small enough to begin digestion? In this activity, you will develop a hypothesis about how birds digest their food. Then you will build a model of a bird's digestive system to test your hypothesis.

MATERIALS

- several sealable plastic bags of various sizes
- birdseed
- aquarium gravel
- water
- string
- drinking straw
- transparent tape
- scissors or other materials as needed

Ask a Question

1. How are birds able to begin digestion without having any teeth?

Form a Hypothesis

2. Look at the diagram below of a bird's digestive system. Form a hypothesis that answers the question above. Write your hypothesis below.

Answers will vary

Test the Hypothesis

3. Design a model of a bird's digestive system using the materials listed at left. Include in your design as many of these parts as possible: esophagus, crop, gizzard, intestine, cloaca.

4. Using the materials you selected, build your model.

5. Test your model with the birdseed. Record your observations.

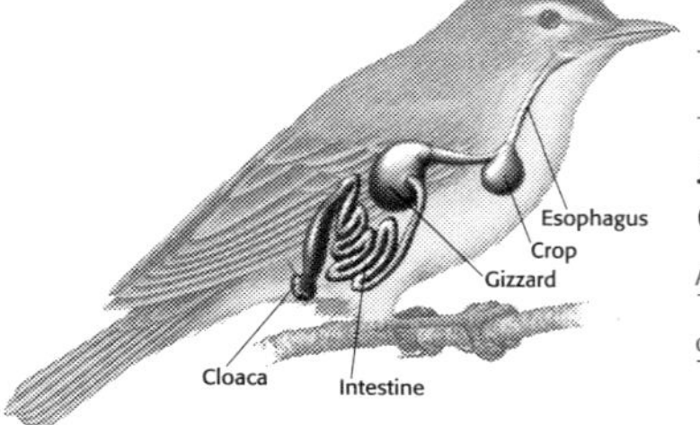

Analyze the Results

6. Did your "gizzard" grind the food?

Answers will vary, but most students should observe that the stones grind the food.

Name ______________ Date ________ Class ________

What? No Dentist Bills? continued

7. What do you think *gizzard stones* are? How do you think they help a bird?

Gizzard stones are small pebbles that birds sometimes swallow. They settle in the gizzard and aid in digestion.

8. Does the amount of material added to your model gizzard change its ability to work effectively? Explain your answer.

Model gizzards that are no more than three-fourths full will probably be most effective.

9. Birds can break down food particles without teeth. What conclusions can you draw about how they do this?

Hard particles in the bird's gizzard are able to grind up food particles.

Draw Conclusions

10. Analyze the strengths and weaknesses of your hypothesis based on your results. Was your hypothesis correct? Explain your answer.

Answers will vary. Look for arguments based on the original hypothesis.

11. What are some limitations of your model? How do you think you could improve it?

Answers will vary, but may include reducing the amount of food, adding gizzard stones, or adding more liquid to the food.

Going Further

Did you know that "gizzard stones" have been found at the sites of fossilized dinosaur skeletons? Look in the library or on the Internet for information about the evolutionary relationship between dinosaurs and birds. List the similarities and differences you find.

Scientists have long recognized similarities between birds and some dinosaurs, including an S-shaped neck, a unique ankle joint, and hollow bones.

Name ______________ Date ________ Class ________

CHAPTER 4 STUDENT WORKSHEET — DISCOVERY LAB

Why Birds of a Beak Eat Together

You are part of a group of hungry birds looking for a good place to eat. How do you know how to find such a place? Well, it depends on the type of food available in the area and how easily you can get to the food.

Luckily, there are many types of feeding habitats nearby. In this activity, you and your flock will fly to each one of the habitats and try to obtain food.

Happy flying and good eating!

MATERIALS

- One of the following tools: spoon with slots or holes, large tongs, short straw or eye-dropper, small tweezers, fork, or pliers
- plastic cup

Objective

To model the beak adaptations of birds and study how effective the adaptations are in obtaining various types of food

Let's Get Pecking, Birds!

1. Your teacher will provide your flock with a model of a beak and a plastic cup. Six different feeding "habitats" are arranged around the room. Your flock's job is to determine the habitat your beak is best suited for. First walk around the room and examine each habitat. Then predict in which habitat you think it will be easiest to obtain food. Record your prediction below.

____

____

____

SAFETY ALERT!

Exercise caution when working with sharp objects such as tweezers, forks, or pliers.

WARNING

Do not eat the food you collect!

2. Move to your first habitat, and designate one student to obtain the food.

3. When your teacher signals to begin, have this student use the "beak" to collect as much food as possible in the time allotted. The collected food should be transferred to the plastic cup.

4. When your teacher signals to stop, discuss with your flock how easy it was to get food in this habitat. Record your results in the Feeding Chart on page 232.

5. Return the collected food to the station, leaving the station for the next group in the same condition as you found it.

6. Move around the room to each habitat. At each habitat, repeat steps 3–4. Be sure that every student contributes to the discussions.

Name ______________ Date ________ Class ________

Feeding Chart

Habitat	Feeding results
1	Answers will vary, depending on circumstances. However, students should describe their feeding results with clear and precise details.
2	
3	
4	
5	
6	
7	

Beak-ause All Birds Are Different

7. In which habitat was it easiest for your flock to obtain food? Explain.

   Answers will vary, depending on specific materials and equipment, but students should provide clear and logical explanations for their answer.

Name ______________ Date ________ Class ________

8. How does your answer compare with your prediction at the beginning of this activity?

   Answers will vary, depending on students' original predictions. Students may find that their beak model works well in more than one habitat. However, encourage students to decide in which habitat their beak works best.

9. Based on the results of this activity, why do you think beaks have adapted the way they have?

   Birds have evolved specialized beaks in response to the unique conditions of their environment.

Critical Thinking

10. What would happen if the habitat to which your flock were best suited were destroyed? Are there any other habitats in which your flock could easily survive? Justify your answer.

    Sample answer: The hawk uses a forklike beak to spear its food. This beak could also be used to pick up small insects from bark.

Answer to Going Further:

In the class discussion, be sure that students relate what they learned in the video to what they learned in this activity.

Going Further

Watch a video about the eating habits of birds that live in different habitats. Then discuss with the rest of the class what you learned from the video.

Name ________ Date ________ Class ________

CHAPTER 4 **BIRDS AND MAMMALS**

Chapter 4 Test

USING VOCABULARY *(Recommended 3 pts. each)*

To complete the following sentences, choose the correct term from each pair of terms listed, and write the term in the blank.

1. ___Preening___ is a behavior among birds in which they spread oil on their feathers. (Preening or Brooding)
2. A mammal's ___diaphragm___ helps the mammal draw air into its lungs. (placenta or diaphragm)
3. ___Mammary glands___ distinguish mammals from all other animals. (Lungs or Mammary glands)
4. ___Therapsids___ are the reptilian ancestors of mammals. (Marsupials or Therapsids)
5. ___Precocial___ chicks quickly learn to feed themselves after they hatch. (Precocial or Altricial)

UNDERSTANDING CONCEPTS

Multiple Choice *(Recommended 5 pts. each)*
Circle the correct answer.

6. A bird's streamlined body surface is the result of
   a. down feathers.
   b. thick scales.
   (c.) contour feathers.
   d. a pointed beak.
7. What part of a bird's digestive tract grinds up food?
   a. crop
   b. teeth
   (c.) gizzard
   d. intestine
8. Which of the following is NOT characteristic of primates?
   a. forward-facing eyes
   b. flat fingernails instead of claws
   c. very intelligent
   (d.) development of embryos in pouches
9. Which of the following is NOT an adaptation for sustained flight in birds?
   (a.) excellent eyesight
   b. hollow bones
   c. rapid metabolic rate
   d. strong flight muscles
10. Which of the following birds is accurately described?
   a. parrot: is a songbird
   (b.) owl: is a bird of prey
   c. emu: has a large keel
   d. falcon: has webbed feet

Name ________ Date ________ Class ________

11. Both birds and reptiles
   (a.) lay eggs.
   b. brood their young.
   c. have crops.
   d. All of the above
12. Birds that primarily eat meat and have good vision are known as
   a. flightless birds.
   b. perching birds.
   c. waterfowl.
   (d.) birds of prey.

Short Answer *(Recommended 8 pts. each)*

13. Why do scientists think that birds evolved from dinosaurs?

Birds share some similar characteristics with reptiles, which are closely related to dinosaurs. Both are vertebrates that reproduce by internal fertilization and lay amniotic eggs. Birds' legs and feet are covered by thick, dry scales like a reptile's, and the skin around their beaks is also scaly. Paleontologists have also found fossil evidence linking birds to dinosaurs.

14. How does the shape of a bird's wing enable it to fly?

Air moving over the curved top of the wing moves faster than air moving underneath the wing. The faster-moving air creates a pocket of lower pressure, and that creates an upward lift on the wing. This is known as the Bernoulli effect.

15. List three ways that marsupials and monotremes are similar.

Sample answer: Marsupials and monotremes are mammals. Both marsupials and monotremes have mammary glands. Also, both have specialized teeth.

Name ______________ Date ________ Class ________

Chapter 4 Test, continued

CONCEPT MAPPING *(Recommended 1 pt. each)*

16. Use the following terms to complete the concept map below: placental mammal, egg, marsupial, uterus, monotreme, embryo.

After
- an incubation period, the **egg** of a **monotreme** hatches and an immature **embryo** emerges
- birth, a **marsupial** infant attaches itself to its mother's **nipple** and continues its **development**
- a period of **gestation** in the **uterus** of a **placental mammal** a **baby** is born

CRITICAL THINKING AND PROBLEM SOLVING *(Recommended 6 pts.)*

17. Suppose you find a baby bird in the schoolyard. Its eyes are closed, it has no feathers, and it is flopping around on the ground. How would you classify this chick? Explain your answer.

The chick is altricial. Altricial chicks hatch weak, naked, and helpless. They cannot fly or walk. It takes several days for the chicks to learn to fly after they have grown their first flight feathers.

Name ______________ Date ________ Class ________

Chapter 4 Test, continued

INTERPRETING GRAPHICS *(Recommended 8 pts.)*

The graph below shows the range of environmental temperatures over which various mammals can maintain a constant metabolic rate.

sloth
night monkey
human
marmoset
ground squirrel
polar bear cub
Eskimo dog
arctic fox

–30 –20 –10 0 10 20 30 40

Environmental Temperature in Degrees Celsius

18. Which mammal can tolerate a wider range of temperatures before altering its metabolism: a human, a night monkey, or a marmoset?

The marmoset can maintain a constant metabolic rate over a wider temperature range than either the human or the night monkey can.

MATH IN SCIENCE *(Recommended 6 pts.)*

19. One gram of fat yields about 9 kcal of energy. One gram of carbohydrate yields about 4 kcal. How many more calories are yielded by the breakdown of 50 g of fat than by the same amount of carbohydrate? (1 kcal = 1,000 cal) Show your work.

50 g of fat $\times$ 9,000 cal/g = 450,000 cal

50 g of carbohydrates $\times$ 4,000 cal/g = 200,000 cal

The complete breakdown of 50 grams of fat yields about 250,000 more calories than the same mass of carbohydrate.

Name ______ Date ______ Class ______

CHAPTER 4 BIRDS AND MAMMALS — SKILL BUILDER

Chapter 4 Performance-Based Assessment

MATERIALS
- graduated cylinder
- hot water
- 2 aluminum cans
- thermometer
- aluminum foil
- down pillow
- clock or watch

Objective

All birds have two types of feathers that have different functions. In this activity you will examine these two feather types and demonstrate their differences.

Know the Score!

As you work through the activity, keep in mind that you will be earning a grade for the following:
- how well you work with materials and equipment (10%)
- how well you make observations about different types of feathers (40%)
- how well you explain your observations (50%)

Procedure

1. Pour 250 mL of hot water into each aluminum can. Measure the temperature of the water in each can. Record the temperatures.

   Sample answer: The temperature of the water in each can is 76°C.

2. Cover the tops of the cans with aluminum foil. Put one can aside and cover the other one completely with the pillow, being careful not to spill the water. After 15 minutes, measure the temperature of the water in each can. What are the temperatures now?

   Answers will vary. Sample answer: The temperature of the water in the can surrounded by feathers is 63°C. The temperature of the water in the other can is 59°C.

Analysis

3. How did the down feathers affect the temperature of the water?

   Sample answer: The can under the pillow was warmer after 15 minutes. The down feathers insulated the can.

Name ______ Date ______ Class ______

4. Examine the illustrations below. Label the parts of the feathers with these terms: shaft, barb, barbule.

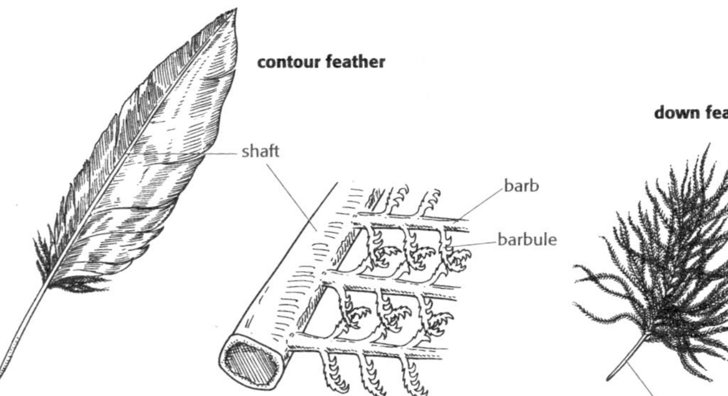

5. Describe how the structure of each feather part affects the feather's function.

   Down feathers are fuzzy and airy, which is perfect for trapping body heat and keeping the bird warm. The function of the rigid shaft is to maintain the structure of the feather. The function of the barbs on a contour feather is to form a smooth, aerodynamic surface. Barbs and barbules link together to give the feather strength and shape.